Congratulations

You have just purchased a book that was developed by hospitality industry experts.

Keep this book — you will use it throughout your career.

BASIC FINANCIAL ACCOUNTING
for the
HOSPITALITY INDUSTRY

Educational Institute Books

MAINTENANCE AND ENGINEERING FOR LODGING AND
FOODSERVICE FACILITIES
Frank D. Borsenik

CONVENTION MANAGEMENT & SERVICE
Frank W. Berkman/David C. Dorf/Leonard R. Oakes

HOSPITALITY FOR SALE
C. DeWitt Coffman

UNIFORM SYSTEM OF ACCOUNTS AND EXPENSE DICTIONARY
FOR SMALL HOTELS AND MOTELS
Revised Edition

RESORT DEVELOPMENT AND MANAGEMENT
Chuck Y. Gee

BASIC FINANCIAL ACCOUNTING FOR THE HOSPITALITY INDUSTRY
Clifford T. Fay, Jr./Raymond S. Schmidgall/Stanley B. Tarr

PLANNING AND CONTROL FOR FOOD AND BEVERAGE OPERATIONS
Jack D. Ninemeier

STRATEGIC MARKETING PLANNING IN THE HOSPITALITY INDUSTRY:
A BOOK OF READINGS
Edited by Robert L. Blomstrom

TRAINING FOR THE HOSPITALITY INDUSTRY
Lewis C. Forrest, Jr.

UNDERSTANDING HOTEL/MOTEL LAW
Jack P. Jefferies

SUPERVISION IN THE HOSPITALITY INDUSTRY
John P. Daschler/Jack D. Ninemeier

SANITATION MANAGEMENT: STRATEGIES FOR SUCCESS
Ronald F. Cichy

ENERGY MANAGEMENT
Robert E. Aulbach

PRINCIPLES OF FOOD AND BEVERAGE OPERATIONS
Jack D. Ninemeier

MANAGING FRONT OFFICE OPERATIONS
Charles E. Steadmon

STRATEGIC HOTEL/MOTEL MARKETING
David A. Troy

MANAGING SERVICE IN FOOD AND BEVERAGE OPERATIONS
Anthony M. Rey/Ferdinand Wieland

THE LODGING AND FOOD SERVICE INDUSTRY
Gerald W. Lattin

BASIC FINANCIAL
ACCOUNTING
for the
HOSPITALITY INDUSTRY

Clifford T. Fay, Jr., C.P.A.
Raymond S. Schmidgall, Ph.D., C.P.A.
Stanley B. Tarr, C.P.A.

the EDUCATIONAL INSTITUTE
OF THE AMERICAN HOTEL & MOTEL ASSOCIATION

Disclaimer

Clifford T. Fay, Jr., Raymond S. Schmidgall, and Stanley B. Tarr, the authors, are solely responsible for the contents of this publication. All views expressed herein are solely those of the authors and do not necessarily reflect the views of the Educational Institute of the American Hotel & Motel Association (the "Institute") or the American Hotel & Motel Association ("AH&MA"). Nothing contained in this publication shall constitute an endorsement by the Institute or AH&MA of any information, opinion, procedure, or product mentioned, and the Institute and AH&MA disclaim any liability with respect to the use of any such information, procedure, or product, or reliance thereon.

The information contained herein is in no way to be construed as a recommendation by the Institute or AH&MA of any industry standard, or as a recommendation of any kind to be adopted by or binding upon any member of the hospitality industry.

©Copyright 1982
By the EDUCATIONAL INSTITUTE of the
AMERICAN HOTEL & MOTEL ASSOCIATION
1407 South Harrison Road
East Lansing, Michigan 48823

The Educational Institute of the American
Hotel & Motel Association is a nonprofit
educational foundation.

Accredited by the Accrediting
Commission of the National
Home Study Council.

Printed in the United States of America
10 9 8 7 6 5 4

Library of Congress Cataloging in Publication Data

Fay, Clifford T.
  Basic Financial Accounting for the Hospitality Industry

  Includes index.
  1. Hotels, taverns, etc.—Accounting. 2. Motels—
Accounting. I. Schmidgall, Raymond S., 1945-   . II. Tarr, Stanley B.
III. Title.
HF5686.H75F39 1982   657'.837   82-13865
  ISBN 0-86612-010-6

Editor: Susan J. Berman

Contents

The Educational Institute
of the
American Hotel & Motel Association
awards this
Diploma
to

Chris Jones

Attesting that the required program of study
has been successfully completed.

May, 1984

This text, used in conjunction with the corresponding student manual, is one in a series of courses available through the Educational Institute of the American Hotel & Motel Association leading to completion of a certification program. To date, nearly 400,000 courses have been taken by 235,000 students interested in furthering their knowledge of the hospitality industry. For information regarding the available programs, please contact:

The Educational Institute of AH&MA
Stephen S. Nisbet Building
1407 South Harrison Road
East Lansing, Michigan 48823
(517) 353-5500

Preface

Basic Financial Accounting for the Hospitality Industry provides basic accounting knowledge specifically aimed at the hospitality industry. This introductory text offers much new material compared to the book it replaces, *Basic Bookkeeping for the Hospitality Industry,* as well as revises and reorganizes the approach to basic accounting.

Three chapters address the mechanics of accounting, compared to two in the older book. Further, *Basic Financial Accounting* contains a separate chapter on each of the three major financial statements while *Basic Bookkeeping* discussed them all in a single chapter. The new text combines front office procedures and the function of the night auditor into one chapter, recognizing their interdependency, rather than treating them separately as before. Finally, a chapter on equities has been added.

The format is a new one, designed to present the information clearly and make it easily accessible. Key phrases in the margin draw attention to main points on each page. Numerous illustrations and examples clarify concepts and procedures. For the student at home or in the classroom, Discussion Questions and Problems encourage further use of the material in each chapter.

Most important, the organization of the chapters takes the reader step-by-step through the mechanics of accounting. Chapter 1, an overview of the "why and how" of accounting, is followed by three chapters covering basic accounting techniques such as the debit/credit concept, double-entry bookkeeping, the fundamental accounting equation, adjusting entries, and closing entries. Chapters 5 through 7 explain the three major financial statements: balance sheet, income statement, and the statement of changes in financial position. The discussion of these financial statements is based on the *Uniform System of Accounts for Small Hotels and Motels,* another publication of the Educational Institute of the American Hotel & Motel Association. To bring "real life" into the picture, actual financial statements from Hilton Corporation show these statements in use.

Chapters 8 through 12 stand independent of each other. Chapter 8, Accounting for Expenses, Fixed Assets, and Inventory, discusses control procedures in addition to accounting for each area. Different methods of depreciation are presented as well as several ways to calculate the value of inventory and cost of sales. Chapter 9, Accounting for Equities, covers accounting for liabilities and owners' equity. Accounting differences based on the type of business organization are explained and illustrated.

Chapter 10, Accounting in the Front Office, outlines the different positions in the front office and explains front office accounting and the night audit. Chapter 11, Accounting for Sales, addresses accounting procedures for sales revenue in the various profit centers of a hospitality operation. Several controls are described in detail. Finally, Chapter 12, Payroll Accounting, recognizing that the largest single expense of a hospitality operation is labor, discusses control methods, accounting, and minimum/maximum wage legislation.

An extensive glossary defines major accounting terms at the end of the text. And last, an index helps readers find their way through the material. Both the glossary and index make the text an extremely useful reference in any accounting or administrative office.

The authors would like to acknowledge with gratitude the assistance of several people in the creation of this text. We thank Barbara Schmidgall for her excellent work in typing the original manuscript. Professor Michael Kasavana made helpful suggestions for the chapter on front office accounting. Heidi Kovanda reviewed the problems following each chapter for accuracy and workability. Susan J. Berman provided valuable editorial, design, and production assistance.

Several members of the American Hotel & Motel Association Financial Management Committee reviewed the text and we appreciate their useful ideas:

- John D. Lesure, CPA
- Ralph Norquest
- Fred Eydt
- George R. Conrade

Finally, we offer our thanks to those companies that responded to our request for samples of forms and financial statements, many of which appear in the text:

- Alameda Plaza
- Hilton Corporation
- Holiday Inns, Inc.
- Loews Hotels
- The Regency Hotel of New York
- Rockresorts
- The Sheraton Corporation
- Westin Hotels

Chapter
One

The Why and How of Accounting: An Overview

Perspective

Accounting—how do we define it? What does it accomplish? What are the purposes of accounting and how does it function? What activities make up the profession of accounting? How is accounting different from bookkeeping?

This first chapter answers these questions as well as introduces a business's major financial statements:

- balance sheet
- income statement
- statement of changes in financial position

These documents are examined intensely in later chapters.

Modern accounting reflects modern business practices, as a brief history of accounting makes clear.

Last is an explanation of the three possible structures for a business:

- sole proprietorship
- partnership
- corporation

The Why and How of Accounting: An Overview

For any business operation, the purpose of accounting is to provide financial information for making decisions. Managers employed in the hospitality industry have undoubtedly asked some of the following questions.

- How much cash is available to pay bills?
- What was the total payroll last pay period?
- What amount of property taxes were paid this year?
- What amount of interest was paid on long-term debt last year and how much must be paid during the current year?
- How much does a current guest owe the hotel?
- What were the total food sales for the dinner period last night?
- What amount of food inventory was on hand at the beginning of the month?
- When was the kitchen range purchased and how much did it cost?
- How much do we owe the bank on the mortgage?
- What are payroll costs as a percentage of room sales?
- What amount of dividends were paid stockholders this past year?
- What is the ratio of food and beverage sales to room sales this past month?
- How much is owed to the meat purveyor?
- When is the utility bill, received yesterday, due?
- How was this hotel corporation financed?

The list is endless. Hospitality operations, whether hotel, motel, resort, club, restaurant, airline or hospital, perform a multitude of activities each day. They sell assorted products as well as provide a variety of services. The need to keep track of these myriad activities has produced modern accounting systems. *Basic Financial Accounting for the*

Hospitality Industry offers the means of answering these and similar familiar questions that hotel managers have.

Along with the hospitality management's need for information to provide efficient service and quality products, many other concerns demand accurate, timely, and easily understandable financial information. Suppliers want financial information prior to extending credit. Bankers require financial statements prior to lending funds for building, remodeling, or major purchases. Various governmental agencies such as the Internal Revenue Service also require financial information. **Who needs accounting information?**

The Essence of Accounting

The essence of accounting is found in three basic activities required whenever an operation undertakes a financial transaction — recording, classifying, and summarizing. In accounting systems, transactions are recorded, classified, and summarized into meaningful reports, such as the firm's financial statements to stockholders or creditors, tax reports to federal, state, and local governments, or budget reports to management to help them control the firm's operations. **Recorded, classified, summarized**

The accounting process must be properly performed so that the information it provides accurately reflects the operation's financial situation. In general as a business becomes more complex, it needs more information which, in turn, results in a more complex accounting system. Managers who make decisions based on faulty financial information will most likely make wrong decisions and the firm will suffer financially.

Thus, the accounting department is a service department in that it provides financial information to users in a concise and understandable form. The financial reports are not ends in themselves but must communicate to the user.

Nature of Accounting

Financial record keeping began before the time of Christ. In fact, some accounting concepts can be traced back to the early Greek and Roman periods. For example, a Roman architect is quoted as stating that valuation of a wall should be determined not by the cost alone, but only after deducting from the cost one eightieth for each year the wall has been standing.

These very early records and concepts are interesting. However, alone they were insufficient to form our current theory of accounting. First, a system of bookkeeping, or recording financial transactions, had to be developed. The methods of recording transactions used today are based on a system of bookkeeping known as double entry. The oldest significant treatise on double entry bookkeeping known was published by a Franciscan monk, Luca Paciolo of Venice, in 1492. Although accounting has developed much greater sophistication in the United States during this century, it is still based on the fundamental concepts developed in the fifteenth century.

Of various definitions of accounting, probably the best known is that of the American Institute of Certified Public Accountants: accounting is "the art of recording, classifying, and summarizing in a significant manner and in terms of money, transactions, and events which are, in part at least, of a financial character and interpreting the results thereof." **Accounting defined**

Transactions

A business transaction is an exchange of property or services. A guest buys a meal in the hotel's restaurant. The hotel gives food in return for money from the guest. Hotel personnel record this activity as a sale and a receipt of cash. The physical process of writing down the transaction is recording. When recorded, the transaction is classified as "food sales." If the guest purchases a toy at the gift shop in the restaurant, the sale would be classified as "gift shop sales."

Summarizing

At the end of a specified period, chosen by the hotel management, the transactions are summarized. The hotel sales for each business day will be summarized by type, room sales, food sales, gift shop sales, and others. Accounts are used to summarize business transactions. The unit of exchange for transactions is money. In the United States, transactions, therefore, are recorded in dollars and cents. The amount of the food sale to the customer is based on the amount of money exchanged for the food.

Unit of exchange—dollars and cents

Financial statements

Lastly, summarized activity is accumulated in accounts and reported in financial statements which can then be interpreted. The financial statements are to communicate. If management and others cannot properly interpret them, they will serve little purpose.

Bookkeeping vs. accounting

There is a difference between bookkeeping and accounting, though many look upon them as one and the same. Bookkeeping is only a part of accounting — that of recording, classifying, and summarizing transactions. Accounting also includes interpretation, which is beyond the scope of bookkeeping.

A bookkeeper records and classifies transactions, usually a routine and clerical task, whereas an accountant supervises the work of the bookkeeper and interprets the financial statements. The accountant must also be able to survey a business's transactions, how its accounting data is to be used and so on, and then be able to design an accounting system to fit the business. After the designed system is installed, the accountant must be able to supervise the bookkeeper's work, review it for accuracy, and report to management and others in quantitative terms the firm's activity for the period and its financial position at a given time. Thus, the demands upon an accountant are much greater than upon the bookkeeper, and the required training is more extensive.

Accounting activities

Accounting activities may be classified into the following fields:

1. General accounting — the recording, classifying, and summarizing processes as previously defined.
2. Accounting system building — the design/revision and installation of the accounting system.
3. Cost accounting — determining costs, generally unit costs, of a product or service.
4. Auditing — the process of verifying accounting records and financial reports prepared from the accounting records. (This should not be confused with the night audit, which is, for the most part, a bookkeeping process.)
5. Tax accounting — determining the correct liabilities for taxes, such as income taxes and payroll taxes, and preparing the required tax forms.
6. Budgeting — the planning and control of business operations in financial terms.

Major Financial Statements

The major documents that communicate a firm's financial information are discussed briefly here.

Balance sheet

The balance sheet is also called the statement of financial position, as it reflects the financial position at a point in time. The balance sheet consists of things the business owns called assets and claims to those assets called equities. The claims to assets by parties external to the business are called liabilities, while claims by owners are referred to in general terms as proprietorship or stockholders' equity. Both assets and liabilities are subdivided into different classes. Assets may be classified as current, fixed, intangible, and other, while liabilities are classified as either current or long-term. A recent Caneel Bay, Inc.* balance sheet is reproduced in Exhibit 1. This example also compares the previous year's figures with the current year's. Chapter 5 discusses each classification of assets and liabilities as well as the balance sheet itself in detail.

Assets, equities, and liabilities

Income Statement

The income statement shows the results of operations for a period of time. The period of time covered by the income statement usually ends at the date of the balance sheet. The income statement is prepared monthly for management's purposes and generally less frequently for outside users. For example, the information in the income statement is provided annually to the Internal Revenue Service. This statement has various other names, such as the earnings statement, profit and loss statement, and statement of income and expenses. Chapter 6 discusses the income statement in depth. A Caneel Bay income statement appears in Exhibit 2. It includes both budgeted and actual amounts, as well as figures from the same period of the previous year.

Statement of Changes in Financial Position

The statement of changes in financial position measures the flow of funds for a period of time. Exhibit 3 presents a sample of this financial report for the end of a financial period. Chapter 7 addresses this statement more fully.

Additional financial reports to communicate financial information to management are prepared according to management's need for information. Usually, the general manager will want the daily report of operations, the operations budget report, and the cash flow statement, among others. Exhibit 4 lists twelve reports with their frequency, content, comparisons, personnel receiving the report, and purpose. Examples of the daily report of operations and departmental analysis included in this list are shown in Exhibits 5 and 6.

Additional reports

Accounting and Modern Business

The growth and sophistication of today's business have created the need for our present accounting methods for several reasons.

Size and complexity

Business corporations have grown to unprecedented size. The operations of many corporations are too extensive, complex, and diverse

---

*The Caneel Bay, Inc. financial statements are reproduced with permission.

Exhibit 1

CANEEL BAY, INC.
Balance Sheets

	May 31	
Assets	19XX	19X1
Current assets		
Cash	$ 156,152	$ 54,274
Time Deposits	847,377	1,230,091
Accounts Receivable, Net (note 3)	561,620	466,350
Inventories (notes 2 and 4)	887,447	719,859
Prepaid Federal Income Taxes	48,500	—
Prepaid Expenses	177,903	191,187
Total Current Assets	2,678,999	2,661,761
Property, Plant and Equipment, Less Accumulated Depreciation ($8,394,084 in 1981 and $8,006,801 in 1980) (notes 2, 5, 6, and 10)	7,361,987	6,788,638
Other Assets		
Deposits	72,050	72,050
Deferred Charges and Other Assets (notes 2 and 7)	26,698	30,631
	$10,139,734	$9,553,080

	May 31	
Liabilities and Stockholder's Equity	19XX	19X1
Current Liabilities		
Accounts Payable	$ 717,669	$ 457,748
Federal Income Tax	—	124,000
Payroll Taxes Payable and Accrued	116,153	102,787
Accrued Expenses	686,856	666,579
Guest Deposits	1,306,315	1,086,286
Current Portion of Long-Term Debt (note 6)	222,512	222,512
Total Current Liabilities	3,049,505	2,659,912
Deferred Federal Income Taxes (note 9)	18,300	—
Long-term Debt, Less Current Portion (note 6)	3,549,761	3,724,765
Deferred Income	27,032	60,000
Deferred Credit — Federal Grant (note 11)	54,747	62,047
Total Liabilities	6,699,345	6,506,724
Stockholder's Equity (notes 1 and 12) Preferred Stock — $100 par value, Authorized 2,000 Shares. Issued and Outstanding 1,500 Shares — Series A 6% Cumulative	150,000	150,000
Common Stock — No Par Value, Authorized 20,000 Shares; Issued and Outstanding 100 Shares	1,000	1,000
Additional Paid-in Capital	11,649,038	11,649,038
Accumulated (Deficit)	(8,359,649)	(8,753,682)
	3,440,389	3,046,356
	$10,139,734	$ 9,553,080

See notes to financial statements

Exhibit 2

CANEEL BAY, INC.
Statement of Income and Accumulated (Deficit)

	19XX (May 31)					19X1				
	Sales	Cost of Sales	Payroll and Related	Other Expenses	Profit	Sales	Cost of Sales	Payroll and Related	Other Expenses	Profit
Operated Departments										
Rooms	$ 6,490,246	$ —	$ 901,445	$ 715,041	$ 4,873,760	$ 5,459,040	$ —	$ 663,522	$ 619,634	$ 4,175,884
Food	3,496,407	1,720,713	1,305,094	401,899	68,701	2,995,731	1,482,955	1,036,076	299,506	177,194
Beverage	778,092	213,062	182,023	83,468	299,539	691,984	186,641	171,260	77,612	256,471
Gift shop	926,105	568,659	115,949	31,752	209,745	785,361	460,388	85,310	12,381	227,282
Boats	351,359	32,803	190,800	97,742	30,014	296,451	29,261	146,545	65,348	55,297
Guest Laundry	6,515	—	—	—	6,515	2,162	2,806	—	—	(644)
Other	148,870	—	—	—	148,870	151,935	—	—	—	151,935
House Totals	12,197,594	2,535,237	2,695,311	1,329,902	5,637,144	10,382,664	2,162,051	2,102,713	1,074,481	5,043,419
Cinnamon Bay	974,728	311,173	300,749	270,394	92,412	938,892	297,098	257,215	263,310	121,269
Trunk Bay	126,775	43,256	25,487	5,973	52,059	144,571	52,027	17,395	11,387	63,762
Concession Totals	1,101,503	354,429	326,236	276,367	144,471	1,083,463	349,125	274,610	274,697	185,031
Cruz Bay Housing	72,500	—	—	54,403	18,097	62,027	—	—	48,743	13,284
Gross Operating Income	13,371,597	2,889,666	3,021,547	1,660,672	5,799,712	11,528,154	2,511,176	2,377,323	1,397,921	5,241,734
Overhead Departments										
Administrative and General			469,456	936,901	1,406,357			467,863	901,405	1,369,268
Advertising and Business Promotion				362,868	362,868				266,273	266,273
Heat, Light and Power			39,095	787,141	826,236			26,659	543,765	570,424
Repair and Maintenance — General			395,437	280,020	675,457			314,923	227,068	541,991
Repair and Maintenance — Grounds			242,095	44,121	286,216			191,259	42,306	233,565
Security			155,210	11,666	166,876			111,917	15,005	126,922
Total Overhead			1,301,293	2,422,717	3,724,010			1,112,621	1,995,822	3,108,443
House Profit	$13,371,597	$2,889,666	$4,322,840	$4,083,389	2,075,702	$11,528,154	$2,511,176	$3,489,944	$3,393,743	2,133,291
Other Deductions										
Land Rent (note 10)					70,000					70,000
Gross Receipts and Real Estate Taxes					304,115					266,197
Interest					145,745					159,661
Insurance					160,575					106,589
Mortgage Expense					1,011					1,011
Depreciation (note 2)					898,194					805,469
					1,579,640					1,408,927
Income Before Federal Income Tax and Extraordinary Item					496,062					724,364
Provision for Federal Income Tax										
Current					74,729					162,800
Deferred					18,300					—
					93,029					162,800
Income before Extraordinary Item					403,033					561,564
Extraordinary Item (note 9) Reduction of Federal Income Tax Arising from Change in Method of Recording Guests Deposits for Tax Purposes										38,800
Net Income					403,033					600,364
Accumulated (Deficit) Beginning of Year					(8,753,682)					(9,349,546)
Less Dividends Paid (note 12)					9,000					4,500
Accumulated (Deficit) End of Year					$(8,359,649)					$(8,753,682)

See notes to financial statements

Exhibit 3

CANEEL BAY, INC.
Statements of Changes in Financial Position

	Years Ended May 31	
	19XX	19X1
Funds Provided		
Income before Extraordinary Items	$ 403,033	$ 561,564
Add Charges (credits) Not Requiring the Current Use of Working Capital		
Depreciation	898,194	805,469
Amortization of Deferred Charges	3,511	3,511
Increase in Deferred Federal Income Taxes	18,300	——
Amortization of Federal Grant	(7,300)	(7,299)
Working Capital Provided from Operations Before Extraordinary Items	1,315,738	1,363,245
Extraordinary Item		
Reduction of Federal Income Tax Arising from Change in Method of Recording Guest Deposits for Tax Purposes	——	38,800
Working Capital Provided from Operations	1,315,738	1,402,045
Decrease in Deferred Charges and Other Assets	422	29,776
Increase in Deferred Income	——	60,000
Preferred Stock Issued from Conversion of Capital Surplus	——	150,000
	1,316,160	1,641,821
Funds Applied		
Additions to Property, Plant and Equipment	1,471,543	662,384
Decrease in Deferred Income	32,968	——
Reduction in Long-Term Debt		
First and Second Mortgages	175,004	175,004
Dividends Paid	9,000	4,500
Decrease in Capital Surplus Due to Preferred Stock Conversion	——	150,000
	1,688,515	991,888
Increase (Decrease) in Working Capital	(372,355)	649,933
Changes in Components of Working Capital		
Increase (Decrease) in Current Assets		
Cash	101,878	(34,459)
Time Deposits	(382,714)	826,680
Accounts Receivable	95,270	96,128
Inventories	167,588	141,185
Prepaid Taxes	48,500	——
Prepaid Expenses	(13,284)	13,993
	17,238	1,043,527
Increase (decrease) in Current Liabilities		
Accounts Payable	259,921	(53,943)
Federal Income Tax	(124,000)	124,000
Payroll Taxes Payable and Accrued	13,366	(2,078)
Accrued Expenses	20,277	45,379
Guest Deposits	220,029	242,728
Current Portion of Long-term Debt	——	37,508
Increase (Decrease) in Working Capital	389,593	393,594
	$ (372,355)	$ 649,933

See notes to finiancial statements

Exhibit 4*

Report	Frequency	Content	Comparisons	Who Gets It	Purpose
Daily Report of Operations	Daily, on a cumulative basis for the month, the year to date.	Occupancy, average rate, revenue by outlet, and pertinent statistics.	To operating plan for current period and to prior year results.	Top management and supervisors responsible for day to day operation.	Basis for evaluating the current health of the enterprise.
Weekly Forecasts	Weekly.	Volume in covers, occupancy.	Previous periods.	Top management and supervisory personnel.	Staffing and scheduling; promotion.
Summary Report — Flash	Monthly at end of month (prior to monthly financial statement).	Known elements of revenue and direct costs; estimated departmental indirect costs.	To operating plan; to prior year results.	Top management and supervisory personnel responsible for function reported.	Provides immediate information on financial results for rooms, food and beverages, and other.
Cash Flow Analysis	Monthly (and on a revolving 12-month basis.)	Receipts and disbursements by time periods.	With cash flow plan for month and for year to date.	Top management.	Predicts availability of cash for operating needs. Provides information on interim financing requirements.
Labor Productivity Analysis	Daily Weekly Monthly	Dollar cost; man-power hours expended; hours as related to sales and services (covers, rooms occupied, etc.)	To committed hours in the operating plan (standards for amount of work to prior year statistics).	Top management and supervisory personnel.	Labor cost control through informed staffing and scheduling. Helps refine forecasting.
Departmental Analysis	Monthly (early in following month.)	Details on main categories of income; same on expense.	To operating plan (month and year to date) and to prior year.	Top management and supervisors by function (e.g., rooms, each food and beverage outlet, laundry, telephone, other profit centers.	Knowing where business stands, and immediate corrective actions.
Room Rate Analysis	Daily, monthly, year to date.	Actual rates compared to rack rates by rate category or type of room.	To operating plan and to prior year results.	Top management and supervisors of sales and front office operations.	If goal is not being achieved, analysis of strengths and weaknesses is prompted.
Return on Investment	Actual computation, at least twice a year. Computation based on forecast, immediately prior to plan for year ahead.	Earnings as a percentage rate of return on average investment or equity committed.	To plan for operation and to prior periods.	Top management.	If goal is not being achieved, prompt assessment of strengths and weaknesses.
Long-Range Planning	Annually.	5-year projections of revenue and expenses. Operating plan expressed in financial terms.	Prior years.	Top management.	Involves staff in success or failure of enterprise. Injects more realism into plans for property and service modifications.
Exception Reporting	Concurrent with monthly reports and financial statements.	Summary listing of line item variances from predetermined norm.	With operating budgets.	Top management and supervisors responsible for function reported.	Immediate focusing on problem before more detailed statement analysis can be made.
Guest History Analysis	At least semi-annually; quarterly or monthly is recommended.	Historical records of corporate business, travel agencies, group bookings.	With previous reports.	Top management and sales.	Give direction to marketing efforts.
Future Bookings Report	Monthly.	Analysis of reservations and bookings.	With several prior years.	Top management, sales and marketing, department management.	Provides information on changing guest profile. Exposes strong and weak points of facility. Guides (1) sales planning and (2) expansion plans.

*Reprinted from *Lodging*, July 1979, p 40-41.

Exhibit 5

DAILY REPORT — Holiday Inn

ACCT. PERIOD # _____ DAY OF PERIOD _____ DAY OF WEEK _____ DATE _____ WEATHER _____
LOCATION: _____ NAME _____ LOC # _____

SUMMARY OF REVENUE, CHARGES, AND ACCOUNTS RECEIVABLE

LINE NO.	Description	ACC. # FOR HOME OFFICE USE ONLY	COLUMN 1 TODAY	COLUMN 2 PERIOD TO DATE	COLUMN 3 LAST YEAR PERIOD TO DATE
1	ROOM	400.00			
2	TAX-(ROOM)	208.01			
3	PHONE-LOCAL	600.00			
4	PHONE-LONG DISTANCE	661.00			
5	DINING ROOM #1				
6	FOOD-BREAKFAST (Excluding Employee Meals)				
7	FOOD-LUNCH (Excluding Employee Meals)				
8	FOOD-DINNER (Excluding Employee Meals)				
9	TOTAL DINING ROOM #1	500.01			
10	TOTAL DINING ROOM #2	500.02			
11	FOOD-BANQUET	502.00			
12	TOTAL FOOD SALES (Excluding Employee Meals)				
13	SUNDRY-RESTAURANT	504.00			
14	BANQUET-ROOM RENTAL	506.00			
15	TOTAL RESTAURANT SALES (Excluding Employee Meals)				
16	SALES TAX-RESTAURANT	208.02			
17	TIPS-RESTAURANT	1188.03			
18	BAR #1 SALES	501.01			
19	BAR #2 SALES	501.02			
20	BAR-BANQUET	503.00			
21	TOTAL BAR SALES	208.03			
22	SALES TAX-BAR	1188.03			
23	TIPS-BAR	505.05			
24	COVER CHARGES	1188.02			
25	RETURNED CHECKS	1060.01			
26	GUEST LAUNDRY	418.01			
27	EMPLOYEE MEALS-SALES	1062.00			
28	MAGAZINE, NEWSPAPER, POST CARD SALES	1064.01			
29	CANDY SALES	208.04			
30	SALES TAX CANDY & MAG. & NEWS				
31	VENDING COMMISSIONS	1071.00			
32	VENDING MACHINE SALES	1065.01			
33	GUEST PAID-OUTS	1188.03			
34	PAY STATION COMMISSIONS	603.00			
35	MISCELLANEOUS				
36					
37					
38					
39					
40	TOTAL REVENUE	1186.00			
41	LESS-DISCOUNTS	423.00			
42	LESS-TRAVEL AGENTS' COMMISSIONS				
43	LESS-PAID (Net After Refunds But Before Paid Outs)				
44	PLUS-PREVIOUS TOTAL-OUTSTANDING				
45	TOTAL OUTSTANDING TO DATE				

ACCOUNTS REC.: TRAY | CREDIT CARDS | CITY LEDGER | ADVANCE PAY | TOTAL

PAID OUTS AND BANK DEPOSITS

			COLUMN 4 TODAY	COLUMN 5 PERIOD TO DATE
46	CASH RECEIVED (After Refunds But Before Paid Outs)			
47	LESS: TOTAL PAID OUTS			
48	DEPOSIT			
49	+ OVER − SHORT	1188.01		
50	ACTUAL DEPOSIT	6.01		

PAID OUTS: LIST TOTALS BY TYPE
51	CHARGED TIPS (REST. & BAR)	1188.03
52	FOOD PURCHASES	507.00
53	REST. SUNDRY PURCHASES	209.00
54	BAR PURCHASES	508.00
55	GUEST LAUNDRY	1060.02
56	RETURNED CHECKS	1188.02
57	OFFICIAL	418.02
58	GUEST PD. OUT	1188.03
59	VENDING MACHINE PUR.	1065.02
60	BANKAMERICARD	30.01
61	MASTERCHARGE	30.02
62	MAGAZINES, NEWSPAPER	1090.00
63		
64		
65–75	TOTAL PAID OUTS	

STATISTICS
NO. ROOMS OCC.—1 PERSON; NO. ROOMS OCC.—MORE THAN 1 PERSON; RE-RENTS; TOTAL OCCUPIED ROOMS; NO. ROOMS COMPLIMENTARY; NO. ROOMS VACANT; NO. ROOMS OUT OF ORDER; TOTAL NO. ROOMS AVAILABLE; NO. ROOM GUESTS; NO. OF TURNAWAYS; NO. OF "NO SHOW" ROOMS; NO. BREAKFAST GUESTS; NO. LUNCH GUESTS; NO. DINNER GUESTS; TL. DINING RM. #1 GUESTS; NO. BANQUET GUESTS; NO. DINING RM. #2 GSTS.; TOTAL GUESTS

COL. 6 TODAY | COL. 7 PERIOD TO DATE | COL. 8 THIS PER. LAST YR. TO SAME DATE

COMPLIMENTARY ROOMS
(1) NAME / COMPANY / REASON
(2) NAME / COMPANY / REASON
(3) NAME / COMPANY / REASON

DAILY AND PERIOD TO DATE COMPARATIVE PERCENTAGES AND AVERAGES

LINE NO.		COLUMN 9 TODAY	COLUMN 10 THIS PERIOD TO DATE	COLUMN 11 THIS PERIOD LAST YEAR TO SAME DATE
76	AVERAGE FOOD SALES			
77	AVERAGE BAR SALES			
78	FOOD COST			
79	FOOD COST (% FOOD SALES)			
80	BAR COST			
81	BAR COST (% BAR SALES)			
82	PERCENTAGE OF OCCUPANCY			
83	REVENUE PER OCCUPIED ROOM			

PAYROLL: NO. OF EMPLOYEES | COLUMN 13 TODAY (AMOUNT / % REVENUE) | COLUMN 14 THIS PERIOD TO DATE (AMOUNT / % REVENUE) | COLUMN 15 THIS PERIOD LAST YR. TO DATE (AMOUNT / % REVENUE)
ROOM PAYROLL (% ROOM SALES); RESTAURANT PAYROLL (% FOOD SALES); BAR PAYROLL (% BAR SALES); OTHER PAYROLL (% TOTAL REVENUE); TOTAL (% TOTAL REVENUE)

APPROVED AS CORRECT BY: _____ INNKEEPER

FORM 3-690 — HOLIDAY PRESS

Exhibit 6

ROOM STATISTICS REPORT
ACTUAL—LAST YEAR

	JAN	FEB	MAR	APR	MAY	JUNE	JULY	AUG	SEPT	OCT	NOV	DEC	TOTAL
TOTAL NO. OF ROOMS	10726-	9688-	10726-	10380-	10726-	10380-	10726-	10726-	10380-	10726-	10380-	10726-	126290-
LESS PERM. HOUSE USE	310-	280-	310-	300-	310-	300-	310-	310-	300-	310-	300-	310-	3650-
NO OF ROOMS PER PLAN	10416	9408	10416	10080	10416	10080	10416	10416	10080	10416	10080	10416	122640
NO ROOMS OCC. REG TR	3920	5169	5911	5264	5661	4444	4791	6641	5185	5345	5929	4450	62710
NO ROOMS OCC. GROUP	3585	2186	2803	2938	2623	3612	2562	1825	2153	3304	2078	1161	30830
TOTAL OCCUPIED	7505	7355	8714	8202	8284	8056	7353	8466	7338	8649	8007	5611	93540
NO OF ROOMS - COMP	71	105	117	139	122	207	122	89	111	101	91	66	1341
NO ROOMS OUT OF ORD	28	27	55	110	202	140	300	24	66	17	35	317	3597
NO ROOMS TEMP H.U.	311	292	531	108	202	100	310	200	100	175	350		107
TOTAL ROOMS VACANT	2781	1892	1527	1728	1988	1803	2916	1937	2555	1644	1927	4701	27229
TOTAL ROOMS PER PLAN	10416	9408	10416	10080	10416	10080	10416	10416	10080	10416	10080	10416	122640
% OCC-REG TRANSIENT	37.63	54.94	56.75	52.22	54.35	44.09	46.00	63.76	51.44	51.32	58.82	42.72	51.13
% OCC-GROUP OCC	34.42	23.24	26.91	29.15	25.18	35.83	24.60	17.52	21.36	31.72	20.63	11.15	25.14
TOTAL % OCC-PAID	72.05	78.18	83.66	81.37	79.53	79.92	70.59	81.28	72.80	83.04	79.43	53.87	76.27
TOTAL % OCCUPIED	73.03	79.60	84.81	82.75	80.72	81.97	71.76	82.13	74.80	84.05	80.54	54.57	77.45
AVG DAILY RATE/ROOM													
REG TRAN ROOM	36.78	36.11	36.93	37.07	36.37	37.35	36.32	37.30	38.67	39.19	40.31	37.89-	37.56-
GROUP ROOM	35.59	34.48	35.65	34.91	37.70	33.34	35.94	33.91	35.21	36.52	37.19	37.20-	35.54-
AVG DAILY RT OVERALL	36.21	35.63	36.52	36.29	36.79	35.55	36.20	36.57	37.65	38.17	39.50	37.74-	36.90-
NO GUESTS-REG	4851	6343	7545	6602	7056	5192	6630	8762	6736	6369	7806	5642	80532
NO GUESTS-GROUP	5421	3125	4531	4256	4011	6155	3970	2793	2879	5155	3152	1607	47056
TOTAL NO OF GUESTS	10272	9463	12076	10858	11067	12347	10600	11555	9615	11524	10958	7247	127588
NO GUESTS/OCC ROOMS	1.36	1.27	1.37	1.30	1.32	1.49	1.42	1.35	1.29	1.32	1.35	1.28	1.34
NO GUESTS DBL OCC	2707	2338	2976	2702	2755	3818	3149	3001	2333	2777	1583	1583	3273
% DBL OCCUPANCY	25.99	24.78	28.57	26.81	26.45	37.86	30.23	28.01	23.19	26.66	25.76	15.83	26.69
COST PER OCC ROOMS													
HOUSEKEEPING	2.46	2.46	2.39	2.32	2.24	2.20	3.15	2.38	2.51	2.19	2.72	2.43	2.43
FRONT OFFICE	1.21	1.40	2.88	2.02	2.00	2.05	3.45	2.85	2.14	2.09	2.09	2.07	1.80
BELLMAN	4.07	4.02	3.84	3.86	3.82	3.72	4.43	3.85	4.06	3.68	3.97	4.74	3.93
SALARIES & WAGES	5.03	4.85	3.61	4.05	3.52	3.49	4.88	4.79	5.07	4.41	4.65	4.92	4.34
GUEST SUPPLIES	.64	.36	.21	.27	.44	.72	.70	.71	.29	.29	.72	.72	.35
RESV. EXPENSE	.79	.85	.80	.55	.74	.75	.51	.41	.77	.59	.63	.52	.59
LINEN/LAUNDRY	2.09	3.03	1.60	3.04	2.24	2.23	2.65	2.53	2.91	2.51	2.54	2.75	2.95
TOTAL OTHER EXPENSE	7.12	7.88	6.15	8.14	2.76	2.72	2.65	7.37	2.61	2.91	2.54	2.85-	2.95
TOTAL ROOMS EXPENSE	28.60	27.11	29.87	27.55	29.49	27.94	27.16	28.87	29.04	30.79	31.87	28.51-	28.95-
DEPARTMENT PROFIT													
NO ROOMS CLEANED	7323	7480	8844	8245	8490	8383	7227	8586	7327	8342	8327	5731	94360
MAID HOURS	4033	3757	4536	3742	4093	4402	3651	4220	3754	3603	3583	2457	45784
MAID DAYS	504	470	567	463	512	550	451	528	469	450	448	307	5723
NO OF ROOMS PER MAID	14.54	15.93	15.60	17.63	16.59	15.23	16.50	16.28	15.61	18.52	18.59	18.82	16.49
MAID HOURS/OCC ROOMS	.55	.50	.51	.45	.48	.53	.50	.49	.51	.43	.43	.43	.49

for a manager to comprehend without summarized reports. A number of large hospitality corporations own several subsidiaries whose activities are indirectly related to lodging and food service. Further, a few large hospitality chains are owned by major airlines which have additional subsidiaries distinct from the hospitality service industries.

Separation of Management from Ownership and Increased Number of Investors

In the corporate form of business organization managers are often not owners, and owners are not directly involved in day to day operations of the business. Further, many persons may be investors in a corporation. This separation and increasing number of owners, in part, is evidenced by corporations whose stock is traded publicly, especially over the two largest United States stock exchanges, the New York and American exchanges. The hospitality industry reflects this continuing growth and separation. Approximately twenty years ago, six stocks listed on the two largest exchanges were classified as hotels and motels and twelve companies were listed in the restaurant and food serving group. Most of these achieved this growth in diverse ownership since World War II. This growth is continuing in the hospitality industries to the present day, with nearly fifty firms' stock listed on the two largest stock exchanges. With this separation, management must control the organization's operations, and the stockholders control management. Therefore, it is imperative that owners have reports that indicate how management is performing its stewardship.

Stockholders control management

Competition

The more intense the competition, the narrower the profit margins. Many businesses in the hospitality industry find their profit margins are currently as low as 1 to 3 %. When profit margins are this low, information obtained from accurate accounting records can be of prime importance to enable management to reduce costs and avoid selling services at an economically unsound price. When profit margins are so low, haphazard guessing may be disastrous, incurring operating losses and ultimately bankruptcy.

Low profit margins

Taxes and Government Control

The federal government and many state and local governments have enacted income tax laws that require the exact computation of income. Corporations whose stock is traded publicly must file periodic financial reports with the Securities and Exchange Commission. In 1977, the federal government passed the Foreign Corrupt Practices Act which requires large corporations to maintain adequate systems of internal accounting control. The necessity to comply with this law and others has forced businesspersons to maintain more records of their business activities than any previous time in United States history.

Uniform Records

A tendency to use accounting methods planned for the convenience of the individual business has given way to a trend toward greater uniformity in accounting systems, especially for firms within the same industry, for several reasons.

Statistics are valuable to individual managers in forming policies and comparable accounting records are an important source of statistics. Two national accounting firms serving the hospitality industry, Pannell Kerr Forster and Laventhol & Horwath, annually issue several

Exhibit 7

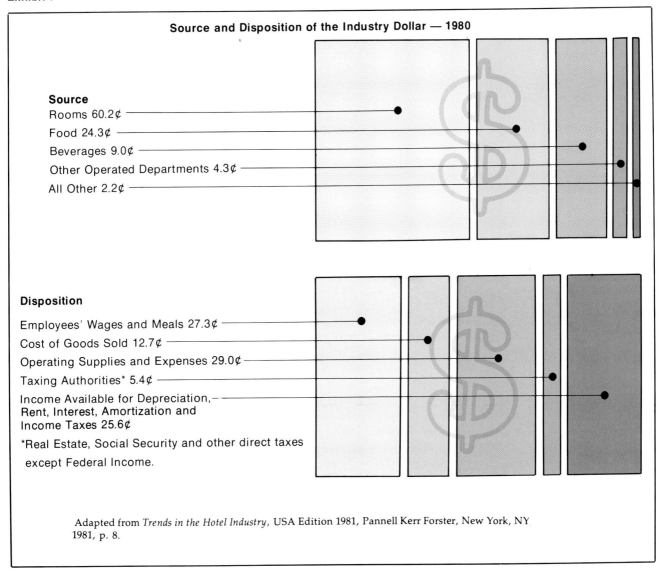

Source and Disposition of the Industry Dollar — 1980

Source
Rooms 60.2¢
Food 24.3¢
Beverages 9.0¢
Other Operated Departments 4.3¢
All Other 2.2¢

Disposition

Employees' Wages and Meals 27.3¢
Cost of Goods Sold 12.7¢
Operating Supplies and Expenses 29.0¢
Taxing Authorities* 5.4¢
Income Available for Depreciation,
Rent, Interest, Amortization and
Income Taxes 25.6¢

*Real Estate, Social Security and other direct taxes
 except Federal Income.

Adapted from *Trends in the Hotel Industry*, USA Edition 1981, Pannell Kerr Forster, New York, NY 1981, p. 8.

statistical reports. For example, Exhibit 7, taken from *Trends in the Hotel Industry – 1980*, graphically presents the source and disposition of the lodging industry dollar, based on a sample of 800 hotels and motels by Pannell Kerr Forster.

Credit reports are simplified when the financial reports on which they are based are comparable with similar reports.

Various accounting organizations and trade associations have been instrumental in the drive for more uniformity. The American Institute of Certified Public Accountants established the Accounting Principles Board (APB) in 1959. Its prime purpose was to review and refine generally acceptable accounting principles. In 1973 the Financial Accounting Standards Board (FASB) replaced the APB, but its reason for existence is basically the same. If generally acceptable accounting principles are refined, then firms' financial reports will be more comparable.

Within the lodging and food service industries, organizations such as the American Hotel & Motel Association, National Restaurant Association, and Club Managers Association have promulgated uniform systems of accounts for businesses within their respective industries.

Generally acceptable accounting principles

Types of Business Organizations

A hospitality business may be organized as a sole proprietorship, partnership, or corporation. Historically, most hospitality organizations were organized as sole proprietorships, whereas at present, the majority of hotel and motel firms are corporations.

Sole proprietorship

A sole proprietorship is owned by a single individual who has sole responsibility for all aspects of the business. This type of organization is not considered a separate legal entity apart from the owner — as is a corporation — and the income or loss from the business is included in the owner's personal tax return. Further, business debts are the owner's personal responsibility, even if they are in excess of the amount invested in the business.

Partnership

The partnership form of organization is similar to sole proprietorship in that there is unlimited liability on the part of the owners, so the hotel or motel organized as a partnership is not a separate legal entity. However, partnerships have two or more owners, and the income or loss from the partnership operations is distributed to the partners' accounts on the partnership books, and partners also recognize income or loss on their personal tax returns.

Corporation

The third possible organizational form is the corporation. Incorporated under state laws, corporations are recognized as separate legal entities apart from their owners. The owners are not responsible for the corporation's debts. Other advantages of the corporate form of organization include the ease of transferring ownership, continuous existence, and some tax advantages.

Most motels and hotels are organized as corporations. However, in the next three chapters, for ease of presentation, the concepts generally presented are for a hotel or motel organized as a sole proprietorship. When relevant, alternative accounting treatments for partnerships and corporations are also shown.

Organization of Text

Chapters 2 to 4 cover basic accounting concepts and techniques. The concepts in Chapter 2 are the foundation for the techniques in later chapters. The essentials of accounting techniques are reduced to recording, posting, and summarizing, which flow as follows:

Recording includes both recording business transactions and adjusting entries in the books. Transferring the recorded amounts to ledger accounts is called posting. Accounts are summarized by the three major financial statements discussed earlier.

Financial statements

Chapters 5 to 7 cover in detail the balance sheet, the income statement, and the statement of changes in financial position. The financial information contained in these statements is taken from financial information recorded in accounts as discussed in Chapters 2 to 4.

Chapter 8 pertains to accounting for expenses, fixed assets, and inventory. A business's fixed assets and inventory are included in the balance sheet. The "used" inventory and the "used" portion of the fixed assets are expenses which, along with other expenses, are included in the income statement. The different methods of depreciating fixed assets and of valuing inventory are discussed, as well as control procedures for each area.

Expenses, fixed assets, inventory

Chapter 9 deals with accounting for equities, broadly defined as the claims to assets held by outsiders (liabilities) and owners (proprietorship). The chapter discusses notes payable and illustrates the calculation of interest pertaining to notes. Further, the owner's section of the balance sheet is presented for the three types of organization, including a discussion of dividends.

Equities

Chapter 10 presents accounting in the front office, as well as front office organization and function. However, the emphasis is on accounting, including a detailed discussion of the vouchers, journals, and ledgers maintained in the front office. The steps and forms used to conduct the night audit are also presented.

Front office

The topic of Chapter 11 is accounting for sales. Sales occur in the rooms department, food and beverage department, telephone department, and laundry department, etc. The chapter discusses accounting for sales in these departments, including the control procedures necessary to insure all sales are recorded. Also, a daily report of operations is illustrated.

Sales

Finally, Chapter 12 covers payroll accounting. The largest single expense of a hotel or motel is labor. This chapter illustrates the mechanics of computing a payroll and contains a fairly complete discussion of payroll taxes, tips, tip credit, and minimum wages. Also included are copies of several forms relating to payroll. The federal payroll tax is emphasized since the multitude of variations makes a complete discussion of state and local taxes impractical.

Payroll

Discussion Questions

1. What is the difference among "recording," "classifying," and "summarizing?"
2. Distinguish between bookkeeping and accounting.
3. What interest do government agencies, bankers, and suppliers have in financial statements?
4. What are the various fields of accounting, and how do they differ?
5. In what ways has modern business created the need for sophisticated accounting methods?
6. What are the benefits of uniform records?
7. What are the three possible organizational forms for a hotel or motel?
8. What are the three largest sources of revenue for the "average" lodging firm?
9. What are the two largest expenses of the "average" lodging firm?
10. What are the three major financial statements, and what does each show?

Chapter Two

Basic Accounting Concepts

Perspective

The second chapter introduces more of the basics of accounting.

Accounting is the recording of all transactions. *When* transactions are recorded depends on whether a cash or accrual accounting method is in use. The more common accrual system is examined in detail.

A business has:

- assets—its properties
- liabilities—ownership rights to assets
- proprietorships—the accounting value of ownership rights

The fundamental accounting equation expresses the relationship of these elements:

$$ASSETS = LIABILITIES + PROPRIETORSHIP$$

Fundamental because, no matter how small or large a business, this equation expresses its financial condition.

Basic Accounting Concepts

The basic accounting concepts presented here include several principles of accounting, cash versus accrual accounting, and the fundamental accounting equation.

Generally accepted accounting principles

The foundations for accounting methods are called accounting principles. These principles have gained general acceptance over time and accountants often refer to them as "generally accepted accounting principles."

Accrual accounting is a more precise measurement of the results of a hotel or motel's operations than accounting on a cash basis, although many very small firms use cash basis accounting. This chapter distinguishes cash basis accounting from accrual basis accounting.

Accounting equation

Finally, the accounting equation, which many call the bookkeeping equation, is presented. Several business transactions illustrate the effect of business activity on the accounting equation.

Principles of Accounting

Accounting methods are based on accounting principles that have evolved over time partly from common usage by the accounting profession and partly from the work of such groups as the American Institute of Certified Public Accountants, the American Accounting Association, and the Financial Accounting Standards Board. Generally accepted accounting principles provide a uniform basis for preparing financial statements.

The Cost Principle

Transaction price establishes recorded value

The definition of accounting given in Chapter 1 stated that transactions are recorded in terms of money. The transaction price establishes the recorded value for the goods or services purchased. For example, if the hotel buys a dishwasher, the price agreed upon by the hotel and the supplier determines the amount to be recorded. If the agreed purchase price is $5,000, then the dishwasher is initially valued at $5,000 in the hotel's accounting records. The supplier may have bought the dishwasher from the manufacturer for $4,000; the hotel may receive an offer of $5,500 for it the day it is purchased. However, the cost to the hotel establishes the amount recorded. If other amounts, such as estimates or appraisals, were used in recording transactions, then accounting records would lose their usefulness. When cost is the basis for recording a transaction, the two parties, buyer and seller dealing in an arm's length transaction, determine the amount to be recorded. This amount is generally an objective and fair measure of the value of the goods or services purchased.

Business Entity

Accounting and financial statements are based on the concept that each business entity maintains its own set of accounts, and that these accounts are separate from the owner's other financial interests. For example, if a restaurant owner takes food home from the restaurant for personal use, it should be properly charged to the owner's account.

Business's accounts maintained separately

Going Concern Principle

In preparing accounting records and reports, it is assumed that the business will continue indefinitely and that liquidation is not in prospect. This assumption is based on the concept that the real value of the hotel or motel is its ability to earn a profit, rather than the amount its assets would bring in liquidation. Under this concept, the market value of the fixed assets need not appear on financial statements, and prepaid expenses are considered assets.

Business will continue indefinitely

Unit of Measurement

Financial statements are based on transactions expressed in monetary terms. The monetary unit is assumed to represent a stable unit of value, so that past and current transactions can be included on the same statement. However, price levels have changed significantly in recent years, and our monetary unit is not as stable as in the past.

Stable unit of value

During recent years, inflation, as measured by the Consumer Price Index, has exceeded 10% each year. To show the effect of inflation, many lodging firms are providing supplementary financial statements that contain the current values of their assets. For several lodging firms, the current values of their assets are more than twice that originally recorded on the books.

Effect of inflation

Objective Evidence

Accounting transactions and the resulting accounting records should be based on objectively determined evidence to the greatest possible extent. The transactions are to be based on dollar amounts determined in the marketplace and, therefore, subject to verification.

Transactions based on objective evidence

Estimates or judgments may be used only in the absence of objective evidence. For example, a restaurant owner contributes equipment purchased several years ago for personal use to a restaurant corporation in exchange for 100 shares of stock. There is no known market value for the stock. Therefore, an independent party should estimate the value of the equipment contributed in order to record the asset and the issuance of stock.

Full Disclosure

Financial statements must provide information on all the significant facts that have a bearing on their interpretation. The types of disclosures include the accounting methods used, changes in the account-

Significant facts disclosed

ing methods, contingent liabilities, events subsequent to the financial statement date, and unusual and nonrecurring items. For example:

Type of Disclosure	Example
Accounting methods used	Straight-line method of depreciation
Change in the accounting methods	A change from depreciating a fixed asset using the straight-line method to using the double declining balance method
Contingent liability	A lawsuit against the company for alleged failure to provide adequate security for guest who suffered personal injury
Events occurring subsequent to the financial statement date	A fire destroys significant uninsured assets of the hotel company one week after the end of the year
Unusual and nonrecurring items	A hotel firm in Michigan suffers significant losses due to a tornado

Full disclosure is accomplished either by reporting the information in the body of the financial statements or in the footnotes. Footnotes to financial statements are discussed in more detail in chapter 5.

Consistency

Follow one accounting method consistently

Frequently, several accounting methods are available for reporting a specific kind of accounting transaction, but there is usually one best method. The consistency principle requires that once an accounting method has been adopted, it should be followed consistently. When it becomes necessary to change to another method, the change must be disclosed and the dollar effect on earnings and/or the balance sheet reported.

Matching

Relate expenses to revenue

The matching principle pertains to relating expenses to revenues. For example, a front office posting machine will benefit the hotel for several years. Therefore, the machine's cost is recorded as a fixed asset and written-off over its life. The result is a partial write-off of the fixed asset each year against the revenue generated in part by using the machine. This process is referred to as matching and is the basis for most adjusting entries prepared by accountants at the end of each accounting period.

Cash Versus Accrual Accounting

There are two alternative methods of determining when to record a transaction. The *cash basis* recognizes an accounting transaction at the point of cash inflow or outflow. Although this is the simpler of the two methods, its use is generally limited to the small motel where the owner is also the manager.

Accrual matches expenses with revenues

The more common method is the *accrual basis* which recognizes all revenues earned during the accounting period, and, similarly, records all expenses incurred to earn the revenues in that same period. Since revenues earned, whether or not they have been received, and expenses incurred, whether or not they have been paid for, are all recognized within the accounting period, revenues are matched with expenses. At the close of any accounting period, the accrual method allows a more meaningful evaluation of the business's operation because it matches expenses with revenue.

Under the accrual method, procedures must be set up to record all transactions relating to a particular time period during that same period. For instance, a telephone bill for one month may arrive late in the following month, yet the expense must be recognized in the earlier month when it actually occurred. Another problem is that some expenses, such as payroll, do not exactly match the accounting period. Payrolls are paid periodically on a certain day of the week. Only rarely would that date correspond to the end of the accounting period. It is necessary, therefore, to adjust payroll costs to the accounting period.

Accrual allows depreciation

Other kinds of transactions receive special treatment under the accrual method of accounting. Purchases of long-lived furniture and equipment are not considered an expense only of the period in which they are purchased. Instead, a pro rata share of the cost, in the form of depreciation expense is charged to each accounting period during the useful life of long-lived purchases. Inventory purchase transactions are another example. Only when the inventory is sold does it become a cost in determining operating performance. Calculation of the cost of goods sold involves beginning and ending inventories plus purchases.

Accrual requires adjusting entries

Obviously the accrual method requires a number of *adjusting entries* at the end of each accounting period. (These will be discussed in detail in Chapter 4.) Once the adjusting entries have been recorded, the income and expense for the period will provide a reasonable basis for measuring the business's financial and operating progress.

The Fundamental Accounting Equation

In accounting, a business's properties are called its assets, and ownership rights in these assets are called equities. Therefore, assets must equal equities. For example, if James Rail establishes a lodging business separate from his personal effects and invests $10,000 in it, the business, Rail Motel, will show assets of $10,000 and equities of $10,000. In this case, the assets of $10,000 are cash, and the equities of $10,000 are the ownership rights to assets. The accounting value of the ownership rights of the proprietor, James Rail, in the assets of the business enterprise, is commonly shown under the name of the proprietor followed by the word capital, as below.

ASSETS	=	EQUITIES
Cash, $10,000		James Rail, Capital, $10,000

Assets must equal equities

James Rail may find, as he acquires assets such as a building and equipment, that he is unable to finance all the assets acquired from his personal assets. He will finance these additional assets by borrowing money from others and then purchasing the assets, or by buying the assets on account, that is buying with a promise to pay at a later date. These business people from whom James Rail buys assets on account are known as creditors. The creditors of a business also have a claim to the assets of the Rail Motel.

Assume that James Rail purchases furniture for $40,000 for a 50 room motel (which he will rent) and obtains complete financing from First National Bank. He signs a promissory note that indicates, among other things, the amount, due date, and the interest rate. The accounting equation is now expanded.

ASSETS		=	LIABILITIES		+	PROPRIETORSHIP
Cash	$10,000	=		$ —	+	James Rail, Capital $10,000
Furniture	40,000	=	Loan	40,000	+	——
	$50,000			$40,000	+	$10,000

Claims of owner and creditor on assets

The accounting equation now shows that there are two types of claims on assets: the claims of the owner, James Rail, and the claims of the creditor, First National Bank. If James Rail does not pay First National Bank the amount due when required per the loan agreement, then the First National Bank has the right to force sale of the furniture to secure its money.

The equation, Assets = Liabilities + Proprietorship, is the fundamental equation upon which all double entry bookkeeping is based. The equation may be rearranged as:

ASSETS − LIABILITIES = PROPRIETORSHIP
or
ASSETS − PROPRIETORSHIP = LIABILITIES

The balance sheet, a basic financial statement that expresses the business's financial position at a point in time, is an expression of the accounting equation, Assets = Liabilities + Proprietorship. The balance sheet for the Rail Motel after the first two transactions would be:

Balance Sheet Rail Motel			
Assets		**Liabilities**	
Cash	$10,000	Proprietorship	
Furniture	40,000	James Rail, Capital	$10,000
		Notes Payable	40,000
Total Assets	$50,000	Total Liabilities and Proprietorship	$50,000

Before introducing more transactions and their effects on the accounting equation, let us define what we have so far. *Assets* may be defined as anything of value owned by a business. They include cash, investments, accounts receivable, food inventory, beverage inventory, buildings, equipment, prepaid insurance, and so forth.

Liabilities are obligations to pay money or other assets, or to render services, to another party (person or business enterprise) either now or in the future. Liabilities represent claims of nonowners on assets of the firm. Liabilities include accounts payable, loans payable, wages payable, rent payable, unearned revenue, bonds payable, notes payable, and so on.

Proprietorship is the excess of assets over liabilities. The claims of the firm's owners to the firm's assets are represented by proprietorship. Proprietorship is also called net worth at times. If the firm is a corporation, it will probably be called stockholders' equity.

Equities then are all claims to assets. This term includes both liabilities — the claims of creditors, and proprietorship — the claims of owners.

Effect of Transactions on the Accounting Equation

The previous discussion of the accounting equation included two transactions:

1. James Rail, proprietor, invested $10,000 in the business.
2. He purchased furniture for $40,000, borrowed from the First National Bank.

Each transaction affects the elements of the accounting equation. As previously shown, assets were increased from $-0- to $10,000 when the proprietor made his investment in the business. Further, assets were increased by $40,000 when the furniture was purchased. The effects of these two transactions on the accounting equation are shown again below. Note that the equation remains in balance after each transaction.

Elements of accounting equation changed by transactions

ASSETS		LIABILITIES		PROPRIETORSHIP
		Notes Payable		
Cash	+ Furniture =	(First National Bank)	+	James Rail, Capital
(1) $10,000	$ ——	$ ——		$10,000
(2) ——	40,000	40,000		——
$10,000 +	$40,000 =	$40,000	+	$10,000

Then three more transactions followed.

3. James Rail purchased with cash a front office posting machine for $5,000.
4. He purchased on account $1,000 worth of office supplies from Henning Office Supply.
5. He paid one month's rent of $3,000 on the fifty room motel.

The effects of these transactions are shown below.

								PROPRI-
		ASSETS			=	LIABILITIES +		ETORSHIP
						Accounts Payable (Henning Office	Notes Payable (First National	James Rail,
Cash	+ Office Supplies +	Prepaid Rent +	Equipment +	Furniture	= Supply) +		Bank) +	Capital
(1) $10,000	$ ——	$ ——	$ ——	$ ——	$ ——		$ ——	$10,000
(2) ——	——	——	——	40,000	——		40,000	——
10,000				40,000			40,000	10,000
(3) -5,000	——	——	5,000	——	——		——	——
5,000			5,000	40,000			40,000	10,000
(4) ——	1,000	——	——	——	1,000		——	——
5,000	1,000		5,000	40,000	1,000		40,000	10,000
(5) -3,000	——	3,000	——	——	——		——	——
$ 2,000 +	$1,000 +	$3,000 +	$5,000 +	$40,000 =	$1,000 +		$40,000 +	$10,000

Transaction 3 results in the exchange of one asset, cash, for another asset, equipment. Liabilities and proprietorship remain unchanged.

Transaction 4 increases an asset, office supplies, and liabilities. Again, proprietorship is not affected, as the creditor, Henning Office Supply, has claim to the increased assets.

Transaction 5 results in an increase of an asset, prepaid rent, and the decrease of an asset, cash. The effect on the elements of the accounting equation is similar to transaction 3.

James Rail's primary objective in investing his resources in the lodging business is to increase his proprietorship by earning profits. He will accomplish this objective by renting space (rooms) to guests. Profits will be earned only if revenue from renting rooms is greater than expenses incurred. To illustrate the effect of revenues and expenses on proprietorship, consider three additional transactions:

Profits when revenue is greater than expenses

6. Sally Smith rented one room for $10 for one night. She paid cash the following morning.

7. Jim Williams rented one room for $15 for one night. He promised to pay the $15 within thirty days.

8. The maid hired to clean the rooms rented was paid $5 for her work.

The effects of these transactions on the accounting equation are:

		ASSETS					=	LIABILITIES		+	PROPRI-ETORSHIP
Cash	Accounts Receivable (Jim Williams)	Office Supplies	Prepaid Rent	Equipment	Furniture	=	Accounts Payable (Henning Office Supply)	Notes Payable (First National Bank)			James Rail, Capital
(1) $10,000	$ —	$ —	$ —	$ —	$ —		$ —	$ —			$10,000
(2) —	—	—	—	—	40,000		—	40,000			—
10,000					40,000			40,000			10,000
(3) −5,000	—	—	—	5,000	—		—	—			—
5,000				5,000	40,000			40,000			10,000
(4) —	—	1,000	—		—		1,000	—			—
5,000		1,000		5,000	40,000		1,000	40,000			10,000
(5) −3,000	—	—	3,000	—				—			—
2,000		1,000	3,000	5,000	40,000		1,000	40,000			10,000
(6) 10	—	—	—	—				—			10
2,010		1,000	3,000	5,000	40,000		1,000	40,000			10,010
(7) —	15	—	—	—				—			15
2,010	15	1,000	3,000	5,000	40,000		1,000	40,000			10,025
(8) −5	—							—			−5
$ 2,005 +	$ 15 +	$1,000 +	$3,000 +	$5,000 +	$40,000 =		$1,000 +	$40,000 +			$10,020

Revenues received for services

Transaction 6 results in an increase in cash, an asset, of $10, and an increase in proprietorship of $10. The claim to the $10 received is by James Rail, proprietor, as the $10 was paid for services rendered to the guest, Sally Smith. The $10 collected from the guest is known in accounting as a revenue. A revenue is an inflow of cash, accounts receivable, or other asset in exchange for services in this illustration.

Transaction 7 also results in an equal increase of assets and proprietorship by $15. The $15 receivable is an asset as it represents a claim by the Rail Motel on the assets of Jim Williams. Jim Williams has promised to pay $15 in the future for services received, therefore, the claim is reported as an accounts receivable. The $15 is another example of a revenue.

Both transactions 6 and 7 demonstrate the effects of revenue on assets and proprietorship of the business. Revenue increases assets and also increases proprietorship.

Transaction 8 is an example of an expense. An expense is a voluntary use of assets to derive revenues. In this illustration $5 was paid to the maid for cleaning the rooms. The result is a decrease in cash and a similar decrease in proprietorship. All expenses decrease proprietorship and either decrease assets or increase liabilities.

Expense uses assets to yield revenue

After transaction 8, the assets of $51,020 equal the liabilities of $41,000 plus the proprietorship of $10,020. Thus, the accounting equation remains in balance after the eight transactions.

Discussion Questions

1. What is the relationship between principles and methods of accounting?
2. How does cash basis accounting differ from accrual basis accounting?
3. What is the going concern principle?
4. Which principle of accounting has inflation most affected, and how have some hospitality firms reacted?
5. When are estimates of a fixed asset's value acceptable for accounting purposes?
6. What are five types of disclosure? Give an example of each.
7. Explain the cost principle.
8. What is the fundamental accounting equation, and which financial statement reflects this equation?
9. When a business borrows $10,000 from a financial institution, how does this affect elements of the accounting equation?
10. How do room sales transactions on account affect elements of the accounting equation? If the room sales were for cash, how would this affect elements of the accounting equation?

Problems

Problem 1

Duane Schmidt opened a small cafe which he called Schmidt's Cafe. During the first week he completed the following transactions:

a) Sold a personal investment in Fork Motor Co. stock and deposited $100,000 of the proceeds in a bank account opened in the name of Schmidt's Cafe.

b) Purchased an old building converted into the cafe for $85,000. The appraisal value is $88,000.

c) Purchased food and beverages for $3,000 on account from Jerry's Wholesale Food Co.

d) Sold fifteen meals for $70 cash to Randall Construction Co. The entire amount was paid by Jim Randall. The cost of the food and beverage sold was $20.

e) Paid the cook $30 for one day's work.

Required:

1. Arrange the following asset, liability, and proprietorship titles in an expanded accounting equation like that shown in the chapter: Cash, Food and Beverage Inventory, Building, Accounts Payable (Jerry's Wholesale Food Co.), Duane Schmidt, Capital.

2. Show by additions and subtractions the effects of each transaction on the assets, liabilities, and proprietorship of Schmidt's Cafe. Show net totals for all items after each transaction.

Problem 2

The following equation shows the effects of five transactions on the assets and equities of the Spartan Inn. Each transaction is identified by a letter.

	ASSETS				LIABILITIES		PROPRI-ETORSHIP
Cash	+ Office Supplies	+ Office Equipment	+ Building	=	Accounts Payable (Kern Office Supply)	+	Lee Spartan, Capital
1,000	$100	$2,000	$10,000		$100		$13,000
a) −100	——	——	——		−100		——
900	100	2,000	10,000		0		13,000
b) ——	−50	——	——		——		−50
900	50	2,000	10,000		0		12,950
c) −500	——	1,000	——		500		——
400	50	3,000	10,000		500		12,950
d) 100	——	——	——		——		100
500	50	3,000	10,000		500		13,050
e) −25	——	——	——		——		−25
$ 475	$ 50	$3,000	$10,000		$500		$13,025

Required:

Briefly discuss the probable nature of each transaction.

Problem 3

Melvin Dwight owns a small catering business called M.D.'s Catering. At the beginning of the current month, the business had the following assets: cash, $2,500; food inventory, $500; beverage inventory, $2,500; office supplies, $200; delivery truck, $2,000. M.D.'s owed Lawrence Supply Co. $500 and First Auto Bank $1,500. On the first day of the month, M.D.'s Catering completed the following transactions:

a) The proprietor invested $500 more in M.D.'s.

b) Food costing $250 was purchased on account from Lawrence Supply Co.

c) Twenty dinners were served to L&M Trucking Co. Board of Directors, and L&M was charged $5.50 for each dinner. Cash was received from L&M. The cost of food and beverage served was $40 and $15 respectively.

d) Paid $20 for repair work to the delivery truck. (Note: This expenditure should be considered an expense.)

e) Paid J. D. Hill $15 for labor services received.

f) Paid First Auto Bank $50 on account.

g) Melvin Dwight withdrew $300 from the firm for personal use.

Required:

1. Arrange the asset, liability, and proprietorship titles in an expanded accounting equation like that shown in the chapter.

2. Enter the assets and liabilities of M.D.'s under the titles of the equation. Determine Melvin Dwight's equity and enter it under the title of Melvin Dwight, Capital.

3. Show by additions and subtractions the effects of each transaction on the elements of the equation. Show new totals after each transaction.

Chapter Three

The Accounting
Process Through Posting

Perspective

Transactions are recorded, posted—that is classified—and summarized in accounts. Accounts can be either asset, liability, or proprietorship accounts.

For example, Cash, Notes Receivable, and Accounts Receivable are all asset accounts.

Notes Payable, Accounts Payable, and Taxes Payable are all liability accounts.

Capital Accounts, Revenue, and Expense Accounts are proprietorship accounts.

Every account has a debit side and a credit side, which leads to a discussion of the mechanics of double entry bookkeeping. Eleven transactions illustrate the rules of debit and credit.

A trial balance—what and why—is followed by a five-step approach for preparing one.

Transactions are not first recorded in accounts but in journals, then transferred—posted—to accounts in a process explained in this chapter.

The Accounting Process Through Posting

In the first chapter, accounting was defined as "the art of recording, classifying, and summarizing in a significant manner and in terms of money, transactions, and events which are, in part at least, of a financial character and interpreting the results thereof." This chapter discusses and illustrates the processes of recording and classifying.

The Rail Motel, used to illustrate concepts presented in Chapter 2, will be used extensively to illustrate the concepts in this chapter.

Accounts

Balancing an account

An account is a device to record the increases and decreases in a single asset, liability, or proprietorship item. In its simplest form, an account looks like the letter "T" and is called a "T-account."

(Name of Account)	
(left side)	(right side)

On a T-account for assets, increases are recorded on the left side and decreases on the right. For liability and proprietorship accounts increases are recorded on the right side and decreases on the left side. Subtracting the decreases from the increases determines the aggregate effect of all the transactions for a period of time on the account. This process is called obtaining the balance of an account.

The increases and decreases of cash of the Rail Motel discussed in Chapter 2 recorded in a T-account are:

Cash			
Investment	10,000	Purchase of equipment	5,000
Receipt from Sally Smith	10	Payment of rent	3,000
		Payment of wages	5
Balance	2,005		

The total of the increases of $10,010 (10,000 + 10) less the total of the decreases of $8,005 (5,000 + 3,000 + 5) equals $2,005 — the balance of the cash account of the Rail Motel.

Each asset, liability, and proprietorship item for which an individual record is desired requires a separate account. Thus, even a small business enterprise uses a large number of accounts.

The group of accounts a business uses is called a ledger. The group of general accounts discussed below is called the general ledger.

Accounts make up ledger

The specific accounts used in the hospitality service industries vary from one business to another but the following are most common.

Asset Accounts

Cash — Cash includes cash on hand in the custody of cashiers and other employees plus the cash on deposit with banks. Accountants maintain a separate cash account for each cash fund and each account with the bank.

Notes Receivable — A formal written promise to pay a sum of money at a fixed future date is called a promissory note. These notes are referred to as notes receivable. Generally this account contains only notes receivable from debtors on open account. Notes receivable from officers, employees and affiliated companies are shown in separate accounts.

Accounts Receivable — Goods or services are often sold to guests on the basis of an oral or implied promise of future payment. Such sales are known as sales on account and the promises to pay are known as accounts receivable. Accounts receivable are segregated by type of debtor. Accounts receivable from guests would be shown in one account, while amounts due from officers, employees, and companies affiliated or associated with the business would be shown in separate accounts.

Accrued Interest Receivable — This account consists of interest earned on interest-bearing assets at the date of the balance sheet that the business has not yet received.

Marketable Securities — Securities (stocks and bonds) purchased as short-term investments and thus readily convertible to cash are classified as marketable securities.

Inventories of Merchandise — Several accounts will be maintained for the inventory of goods for sale, including but not limited to Beverage Inventory, Food Inventory, and Gift Merchandise Inventory. The amount of inventory on hand at the end of the accounting period is usually determined by a physical count.

Office Supplies — Stamps, stationery, paper, pencils, and similar items are known as office supplies. They are assets when purchased. As they are used in the business, they become expenses.

Other Prepaid Expenses — Prepaid expenses are items that are assets when purchased but become expenses as they are used. Prepaid items are prepaid rent, unexpired insurance, prepaid taxes, and laundry supplies. Each type of prepaid expense is accounted for in a separate account.

Investments — Investments in securities of affiliated or associated companies and other securities purchased as nontemporary investments are included under an investment account.

Fixed Assets — This class of assets includes land, buildings, furniture, carpets, linen, china, glassware, and uniforms. A separate account is maintained for each type of fixed asset.

Liability Accounts

Notes Payable — This account includes promissory notes given to creditors. Promissory notes given to banks may be shown separately from other creditors.

Accounts Payable — An account payable is an amount owed to a creditor resulting from an oral, written, or implied promise to pay at some future date.

Taxes Payable — All taxes collected from guests or withheld from employees are generally recorded in separate accounts such as Sales Taxes Payable, FICA Payable, Federal Income Taxes Withheld, State Income Taxes Withheld, and City Income Taxes Withheld.

Income Taxes Payable — The amount of federal, state, and city income taxes due for prior fiscal years will be recorded in separate accounts. The estimated liability for income taxes on the current year's net income to date will also be recorded in these accounts.

Accrued Expenses — Expenses for a period not yet billed nor paid at the date of the balance sheet, such as wages, salaries, interest, and utilities, are recorded as well as the liability. A separate account is maintained for each item.

Unearned Income — This is the unearned portion of revenue received from a guest for a period subsequent to the date of the balance sheet. Also deposits on banquets and room reservations may be shown as unearned income.

Mortgage Payable — A mortgage payable is a long-term debt for which the creditor has a secured prior claim against one or more assets of the firm.

Proprietorship Accounts

Many transactions affect the proprietorship of a business enterprise, including the investment of the proprietor, withdrawal of assets by the proprietor, and revenues earned and expenses incurred by the organization. In Chapter 2, where the effects of transactions on the elements of the accounting equation were shown, all increases and decreases in proprietorship, including revenues and expenses, were placed in a single account under the proprietor's name. The single account simplified the material covered in this chapter, but does not lend itself to segregating the kind of increases and decreases. Therefore, in order to readily obtain information on the various kinds of increases and decreases in proprietorship, a different account is used for each type of increase or decrease.

Capital Account — When an individual invests in a business, organized as a sole proprietorship, the investment is recorded in an account bearing the investor's name. All other capital accounts will be "closed" into this account periodically. (This will be discussed in more detail in the next chapter.) If the firm is incorporated, the capital account is replaced by two types of accounts. First, Capital Stock, in which different accounts are maintained for different types of stock, and second, Retained Earnings, in which the results of operations less dividends declared are recorded.

Revenue and Expense Accounts — Revenues increase proprietorship, whereas expenses decrease proprietorship. Earning profit is the prime objective of a business enterprise, and if it is to be successful, detailed information as to kinds of revenues and expenses must be supplied to

Different proprietorship account for each type of increase or decrease

management on a timely basis. This information is obtained by including in the ledger a separate account for each revenue and expense item in which the activity of the firm will be recorded. Several common revenue and expense accounts are:

Revenues	Expenses
Room Sales	Cost of Beverages Sold
Food Sales	Cost of Food Sold
Beverage Sales	Wages
Gift Shop Sales	Payroll Taxes
Green Fees	Office Supplies
Pro Shop Sales	Rent
Banquet Sales	Cleaning Supplies
Interest Income	Electricity
Dividend Income	Fuel
	Insurance
	Interest
	Advertising
	Travel Expenses
	Property Taxes
	Income Taxes

The kind of revenue and expense recorded in each of the above accounts is evident from its title, as is true of most revenue and expense accounts.

Debit and Credit

The left side of any account is called the "debit" side and the right side is called the "credit" side, as arbitrarily established by accountants. Debit and credit are abbreviated as "dr" and "cr" respectively. To debit an account means to record an amount on the left side of the account, whereas to credit an account means to record an amount on the right side of the account. The difference between the total debits and credits of an account is called the "balance." Thus, an account may either have a debit or credit balance.

Debits minus credits equals balance

When James Rail invests $10,000 in his lodging business, cash is debited for $10,000, as the $10,000 is recorded on the left side of the Cash T-account below. The account, James Rail, Capital, is credited for the $10,000, as this is recorded on the right side:

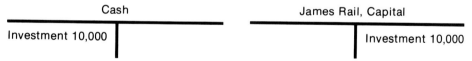

When James Rail invested $10,000 in his business, both cash and Rail's proprietorship increased. Observe, however, that one increase, that of cash, is recorded on the left side of the Cash account, while the other increase, that of proprietorship, is recorded on the right side of the James Rail, Capital, account. This results from the mechanics of double-entry bookkeeping.

Mechanics of Double-Entry Bookkeeping

In double-entry bookkeeping every transaction affects and is recorded in at least two accounts, and the debits of the entry must equal the credits of the entry. Equal debits and credits for each transaction offer a proof of the recording accuracy. If every transaction is recorded with equal debits and credits, then the sum of the debits recorded must equal the sum of the credits recorded. The equality of debits and credits in the ledger is tested by preparing a trial balance, discussed in detail later in this chapter.

Equal debits and credits in recording transactions result under a double-entry system because the system is based on the accounting equation, assets = liabilities + proprietorship. Increases in assets are recorded by debits while decreases in assets are recorded by credits. Increases in liabilities and proprietorship are recorded by credits while decreases are recorded by debits. These rules are shown as follows:

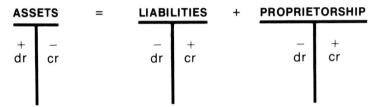

Increases in revenues are recorded by credits to the revenue account, whereas decreases are recorded by debits. The opposite is true for expenses, as increases and decreases are recorded as debits and credits, respectively. Therefore, the expanded accounting equation can be shown:

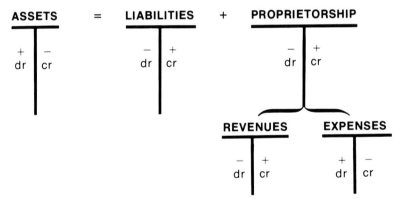

Normal Balance

The normal balance of an account is the kind of balance, either debit or credit, which an account generally shows. This balance results from increases in the account, and only on occasion does the balance of an account result from an excess of decreases over increases. The major classes of accounts have normal balances as follows:

Type of Account	Normal Balance
Asset	Debit
Liability	Credit
Proprietorship:	
Capital	Credit
Revenue	Credit
Expense	Debit

The accountant and bookkeeper know the normal balance of every account of the accounting system for their firm and are skeptical of an account with a balance opposite from normal. Their investigation will show either an error or an unusual transaction. For example, if the food inventory account has a credit balance, an error has most certainly been made. On the other hand, a guest's account will have a credit balance if the guest made a deposit with his reservation.

Transactions Illustrating Debit and Credit Rules

The following transactions of the Rail Motel illustrate the rules of debit and credit and show how transactions are recorded in the accounts. The number preceding each transaction is used throughout the illustration to identify the transaction as it appears in the accounts. (The first eight transactions are the same as those used in Chapter 2 to illustrate the effect of transactions on the elements of the accounting equation.)

James Rail:

1. Invested $10,000 in a lodging business.
2. Purchased furniture for $40,000 with a loan from the First National Bank.
3. Purchased a front office posting machine for cash, $5,000.
4. Purchased office supplies from Henning Office Supply on account, $1,000.
5. Paid one month's rent, $3,000.
6. Received for renting a room to Sally Smith, $10.
7. Rented a room on account to Jim Williams, $15.
8. Paid the maid wages, $5.
9. Paid electric bill, $5.
10. Received on account from Jim Williams, $10.
11. Paid newspaper advertising, $3.

Before a transaction is recorded, it must be analyzed into its debit and credit elements. This analysis consists of two parts as follows:

Separate debits and credits before recording

1. Determine what asset, liability, or proprietorship accounts are affected — increased or decreased.
2. Apply the rules of debit and credit to determine the debit and credit effect of the increases or decreases.

An analysis of each of the above transactions of the Rail Motel demonstrates this process. T-accounts are used to show the debit and credit effects.

1. Invested $10,000 in a lodging business.
    The transaction increased cash of the Rail Motel and also increased equity of James Rail in the assets of the business. Asset accounts are debited for increases and the proprietorship account is credited. Therefore, Cash is debited and James Rail, Capital is credited for $10,000.

Cash	James Rail, Capital
(1) 10,000	(1) 10,000

2. Purchased furniture for $40,000 with a loan from the First National Bank.
    The asset, furniture, is increased and a liability is increased by the same amount, as the Rail Motel financed the purchase of fixed assets by borrowing money from the bank. The First National Bank has claims to assets of the Rail Motel of $40,000. Increases in asset accounts are recorded by debits and increases in liability accounts are recorded by credits. Therefore, debit Furniture and credit Notes Payable (First National Bank) for $40,000.

Furniture	Notes Payable (First National Bank)
(2) 40,000	(2) 40,000

3. Purchased a front office posting machine for cash, $5,000.

   The asset, equipment, is increased and the asset, cash, is decreased. Increases in asset accounts are recorded by debits, whereas decreases in asset accounts are recorded by credits. Therefore, debit Equipment and credit Cash for $5,000. The balance of the cash account after transactions 1 and 3 is $5,000.

Cash		Equipment	
(1) 10,000	(3) 5,000	(3) 5,000	

4. Purchased office supplies from Henning Office Supply on account, $1,000.

   The asset, office supplies, is increased and the liability, accounts payable (Henning Office Supply) is increased. Henning Office Supply has claims to assets of Rail Motel of $1,000. Therefore, Office Supplies is debited and Accounts Payable (Henning Office Supply) is credited.

Office Supplies		Accounts Payable (Henning Office Supply)	
(4) 1,000			(4) 1,000

5. Paid one month's rent, $3,000.

   The asset, prepaid rent, is increased while the asset, cash, is decreased. This is an exchange of one asset for another asset. Therefore, Prepaid Rent is debited and Cash is credited for $3,000.

Cash		Prepaid Rent	
(1) 10,000	(3) 5,000	(5) 3,000	
	(5) 3,000		

6. Received for renting a room to Sally Smith, $10.

   Assets and proprietorship are increased by this transaction. The asset, cash, is received from Sally Smith, so Cash is debited. The proprietorship account, Room Sales, is increased. An increase in proprietorship and, in particular, revenue accounts, is recorded with a credit entry. Thus, Room Sales is credited for $10.

Cash		Room Sales	
(1) 10,000	(3) 5,000		(6) 10
(6) 10	(5) 3,000		

7. Rented a room on account to Jim Williams, $15.

   Assets and proprietorship are increased by $15. The promise to pay by Jim Williams is recorded as an asset, accounts receivable. Increases in assets are recorded by debits, so that Accounts Receivable (Jim Williams) is debited and Room Sales is credited for $15.

Accounts Receivable (Jim Williams)		Room Sales	
(7) 15			(6) 10
			(7) 15

8. Paid the maid wages, $5.

   Assets and proprietorship are decreased by $5. Decreases in assets are recorded by credits while decreases in proprietorship are recorded by debits. The proprietorship account to be used is Wages Expense which properly reflects the activity, that of the maid providing services to the Rail Motel. Cash is credited and Wages Expense is debited for $5.

Cash		Wages Expense	
(1) 10,000	(3) 5,000	(8) 5	
(6) 10	(5) 3,000		
	(8) 5		

9. Paid electric bill, $5.

   This transaction is similar to transaction 8, in that assets and proprietorship are both decreased. Therefore, the asset account, Cash, is credited for $5, and the proprietorship account, Electric Expense, is debited for $5.

Cash		Electric Expense	
(1) 10,000	(3) 5,000	(9) 5	
(6) 10	(5) 3,000		
	(8) 5		
	(9) 5		

10. Received on account from Jim Williams, $10.

This transaction increased an asset account, cash, by $10, and also resulted in a decrease of an asset account, accounts receivable (Jim Williams) by $10. Thus, Cash is debited and Accounts Receivable (Jim Williams) is credited for $10. Note that the account of Jim Williams now shows that he owes the Rail Motel $5.

Cash		Accounts Receivable (Jim Williams)	
(1) 10,000	(3) 5,000	(7) 15	(10) 10
(6) 10	(5) 3,000	5	
	(8) 5		
(10) 10	(9) 5		

11. Paid newspaper advertising, $3.

This transaction is similar to transactions 8 and 9 in that an asset and proprietorship account are both decreased. Therefore, the asset account, Cash, is credited, and the proprietorship account, Advertising Expense, is debited for $3.

Cash		Advertising Expense	
(1) 10,000	(3) 5,000	(11) 3	
(6) 10	(5) 3,000		
(10) 10	(8) 5		
	(9) 5		
	(11) 3		

Preparing a Trial Balance

The trial balance is a listing of the accounts and their debit and credit balances. It is prepared to test the equality of debits and credits as follows:

List debit and credit account balances for trial balance

1. Determine the balance of each account in the ledger.

2. List the accounts and show debit balances in one column and credit balances in a separate column.

3. Add the debit balances.

4. Add the credit balances.

5. Compare the total of the debit and credit balances.

When the total of debit balance accounts equals the total of the credit balance accounts, the trial balance is in balance. If the trial balance does not balance, the bookkeeper has made errors in recording the transactions, in determining the balances of each account, or in preparing the trial balance. However, a balanced trial balance is not proof that all transactions have been recorded properly. For example, if transaction 11 was recorded by debiting Wages rather than Advertising, the trial balance would be in balance, yet the amount of wages and advertising would be incorrectly recorded. The trial balance, if correct, only indicates that debits equal credits.

Balance no proof of recording accuracy

In Exhibit 1, the balance of each account of the Rail Motel is determined after the recording of transactions 1 through 11.

Exhibit 1

Accounts of Rail Motel			
ASSETS	= **LIABILITIES**	+	**PROPRIETORSHIP**

ASSETS

Cash

(1) 10,000	(3) 5,000
(6) 10	(5) 3,000
(10) 10	(8) 5
	(9) 5
	(11) 3
10,020	8,013
−8,013	
2,007	

Accounts Receivable
(Jim Williams)

(7) 15	(10) 10
15	10
−10	
5	

Office Supplies

(4) 1,000	
1,000	

Prepaid Rent

(5) 3,000	
3,000	

Furniture

(2) 40,000	
40,000	

Equipment

(3) 5,000	
5,000	

LIABILITIES

Notes Payable
(First National Bank)

	(2) 40,000
	40,000

Accounts Payable
(Henning Office Supply)

	(4) 1,000
	1,000

PROPRIETORSHIP

James Rail, Capital

	(1) 10,000
	10,000

Room Sales

	(6) 10
	(7) 15
	25

Advertising

(11) 3	
3	

Electric Expense

(9) 5	
5	

Wages Expense

(8) 5	
5	

Exhibit 2

Rail Motel Trial Balance		
Cash	$ 2,007	
Accounts Receivable (Jim Williams)	5	
Office Supplies	1,000	
Prepaid Rent	3,000	
Furniture	40,000	
Equipment	5,000	
Notes Payable (First National Bank)		40,000
Accounts Payable (Henning Office Supply)		1,000
James Rail, Capital		10,000
Room Sales		25
Advertising	3	
Electric Expense	5	
Wage Expense	5	
	$51,025	$51,025

Exhibit 2 shows the trial balance for the Rail Motel. Since the total of debit balance accounts of $51,025 equals the total of credit balance accounts of $51,025, the trial balance is in balance.

The Need for Journalizing

The discussion thus far concerning accounts has centered on recording transactions directly in the T-accounts. However, in actual practice, transactions are seldom recorded directly in the ledger accounts for three reasons:

1. Too little information can be recorded in an account. Accounts are mainly for classifying and summarizing financial information. If an account includes all the details, it does not serve as well as a device for classifying and summarizing.

2. Account entries fail to record in any one place a complete record of each transaction, as a ledger has many accounts, each located on a separate page. As discussed previously, each transaction affects at least two accounts.

3. If transactions are recorded directly in the accounts, errors are easily made and are difficult for the bookkeeper to locate.

Therefore, the bookkeeper, rather than recording directly in the accounts, records the transaction first in a journal. This process is called journalizing. The information recorded in the journal is then "transferred" to the ledger accounts.

A journal is commonly called the book of original entry, as the transaction is first recorded there, while the ledger is referred to as a book of final entry.

Transactions first recorded in journal

The General Journal

Firms in the hospitality service industry maintain several kinds of journals as discussed throughout this book. However, the simplest and most flexible is the general journal. A general journal provides for recording:

1. Date of the transaction

2. Titles of the accounts used

3. Explanation of the transaction

4. Page numbers of ledger accounts to which the debit and credit amounts of the transaction are "transferred"

5. Debit and credit effect of the transaction on the accounts listed.

Exhibit 3 is a standard form of a general journal page with two journal entries.

Exhibit 3

Date		Accounts/Explanation	Folio	Debit	Credit
1982					
Jan	31	Depreciation Expense		10000	
		Accumulated Depreciation, Building			10000
		To record depreciation expense for building			
		for the month of January			
Jan	31	Payroll Expense		6040	
		Accrued Payroll			6040
		To record the accrued payroll at January 31, 1982			

The folio column is not completed until the amounts are transferred to the ledger accounts. Then the account numbers of ledger accounts to which the debits and credits are transferred are entered in the folio column. This is discussed in more detail later in this chapter.

Standard Account Forms

Folio column left blank when journalizing

T-accounts are commonly used in teaching, since details are eliminated and the student can concentrate on ideas. Firms, however, do not use T-accounts to record transactions. Exhibit 4 illustrates the account form most commonly used by firms today.

Exhibit 4

Account Title ___*Cash*___   Account No. ___*101*___

Date		Explanation	Folio	Debit	Credit	Balance
Jan	*1*	*Initial investment*	*GJ-1*	3 0 0 0		3 0 0 0
	2	*Purchase of equipment*	*GJ-2*		1 0 0 0	2 0 0 0
	3	*Purchase of supplies*	*GJ-3*		5 0	1 9 5 0

Balance column

The cash account (Exhibit 4) is not divided into two sides as is the T-account but has debit and credit columns next to each other. Further, this account has a balance column so the bookkeeper can maintain the balance of the account at all times. After the three transactions recorded in the cash account, the balance is $1,950.

The balance column in Exhibit 4 does not indicate whether the cash account has a debit or credit balance since the balance of an account is always assumed to be the normal type unless otherwise indicated. Therefore, the cash account will have a debit balance. If a transaction causes an opposite balance, such as a credit balance in the cash account, this is indicated by entering the balance in red, by circling the amount, or placing the amount in brackets.

Abnormal balance is in red, circled or bracketed

Account numbers identify accounts

Account numbers are assigned to identify accounts. For example, accounts 101-199 may be asset accounts, and further, 101-149 may be current asset accounts while 150-199 are non-current asset accounts. Account numbers are also used to simplify the posting process. For example, when $3,000 of depreciation expense is posted to the depreciation expense account, the account number rather than the account title is written in the general journal. Each firm has a different system of numbering its accounts, depending on its needs. The Rail Motel uses a three digit numbering system:

Type of Account	Account Numbers
Asset	101-199
Liability	201-249
Proprletorship:	
Capital	251
Revenue	301-399
Expense	401-499

The account numbers used by the Rail Motel for the accounts discussed in this chapter are:

Cash	101
Accounts Receivable (Jim Williams)	111
Office Supplies	131
Prepaid Rent	135
Furniture	151
Equipment	155
Notes Payable (First National Bank)	201
Accounts Payable (Henning Office Supply)	211
James Rail, Capital	251
Room Sales	301
Wage Expense	401
Electric Expense	441
Advertising	451

Posting

The process of transferring amounts recorded in the general journal to ledger accounts is called posting. Posting is done periodically, even daily. When the amount is posted to the ledger account, the folio column in the general journal is completed by indicating the account number to which the amount is posted, as well as the general journal page where the posted amount was journalized. Journal debits are posted as ledger account debits and journal credits as ledger account credits.

Journal amounts posted to ledger

Discussion Questions

1. Explain the difference between the terms "debit" and "credit."
2. What is the normal balance of each major class of account?
3. Explain the different effects sales and expense have on the proprietorship account, L. B. Smith, Capital.
4. What is the purpose of preparing a trial balance?
5. Does a trial balance "in balance" insure that the bookkeeper has performed flawlessly? Why or why not?
6. Explain the term "journalizing."
7. What is the difference between a journal and a ledger?
8. What is the posting process?
9. Explain the difference between an account receivable and a note receivable.
10. What is the normal balance for each of the following accounts?

Cash	Advertising Expense
Equipment	Accounts Receivable
Rent Expense	Food Sales
Interest Income	Cost of Food Sold
L. J. Smith, Capital	Wages Payable

Problems

Problem 1

Paul Olivia opened a pizza business under the name of Olivia's Pizza Parlor and during the first week completed the following transactions:

a) Invested cash of $2,000 and the following assets at their fair market values: furniture — $2,000; equipment — $3,000; and building — $8,000.
b) Purchased food and beverages on account costing $500 and $100 respectively from Kris Food Supply.
c) Purchased a typewriter with cash, $200.
d) Paid for newspaper advertising, $30.
e) Paid utility bills, $50.
f) Paid wages for the week, $250.
g) Paid for cooking supplies used during the week, $10.
h) Paid $100 on account to Kris Food Supply.
i) Received $900 from customers for pizza and beverages sold. Pizza sales amounted to $750, the remainder was beverage sales. The cost of food sold totaled $300 while the cost of beverages sold totaled $50.

Required:

1. Set up the following T-accounts: Cash; Furniture; Equipment; Building; Food Inventory; Beverage Inventory; Accounts Payable (Kris Food Supply); Paul Olivia, Capital; Food Sales; Beverage Sales; Advertising Expense; Utilities Expense; Wages Expense; Cooking Supplies Expense; Cost of Food Sales; Cost of Beverage Sales.

2. Record the transactions in the accounts with each amount identified by its transaction letter.

3. Prepare a trial balance.

Problem 2

The trial balance of Stephanie's Steakhouse at the beginning of the day, July 1, 1981, was:

Cash	$ 1,500	
Marketable Securities	5,000	
Accounts Receivable (Erica Lee)	20	
Accounts Receivable (Monica Ray)	15	
Food Inventory	2,250	
Beverage Inventory	500	
Furniture	1,000	
Equipment	2,000	
Accounts Payable (Stacie Supply Inc.)		$ 400
Notes Payable (Mineral State Bank)		1,500
Stephanie Smith, Capital		2,085
Food Sales		25,000
Beverage Sales		7,000
Cost of Food Sold	10,000	
Cost of Beverages Sold	2,000	
Wages Expense	8,000	
Utilities	1,000	
Rent Expense	2,000	
Insurance	500	
Office Supplies	100	
Advertising	100	
	$35,985	$35,985

Transactions for July 1, 1981, were as follows:

a) Received cash on account from Erica Lee, $10.

b) Paid rent for the month of June, $200.

c) Purchased food on account from Stacie Supply Inc., $250.

d) Paid utilities bill for June, $100.

e) Paid advertising bill for newspaper advertisement for July 1, $5.

f) Paid temporary help for their labor for the day, $20.

g) Sales on account to Monica Ray, $5, $4 for food and $1 for beverage.

h) Cash sales for the day were $750 — food, $150 — beverage.

i) The cost of food and beverage sales for the day, $250 and $60 respectively.

Required:

1. Set up T-accounts for each account listed in the trial balance of Stephanie's Steakhouse.

2. Record the amount in each account per the trial balance. (Be sure to record the amounts on the proper side of the account.) For example, the $1,500 should be recorded as follows:

Cash

Beg. Bal 1,500

3. Record the transactions for July 1, 1981.

4. Prepare a trial balance for July 1, 1981 (end of the day).

Problem 3

The following alphabetically arranged accounts and their balances were taken from the ledger of Art's Supply Company on December 31 of the current year.

Accounts Payable	$ 2,400	Office Equipment	$ 1,600
Accounts Receivable	4,500	Office Supplies	85
Building	25,500	Prepaid Insurance	160
Cash	2,000	Prepaid Interest	15
Delivery Equipment	2,500	Revenue	35,950
Interest Expense	200	Store Equipment	5,450
Interest Payable	150	Store Supplies	155
Jerry Dukes, Capital	18,300	Taxes Payable	250
Land	8,200	Telephone Expense	110
Merchandise Inventory	9,500	Truck Repairs	130
Mortgage Payable	6,500	Wages Expense	4,420
Notes Payable	1,200	Wages Payable	75
Notes Receivable	300		

Required:

Without changing the alphabetical arrangement of the accounts, prepare a trial balance for the company.

Problem 4

			Debit	Credit
Feb	3	Cash	12000	
		Equipment	10000	
		Adam Ackerson, Capital		22000
	3	Pre Paid Rent	1000	
		Cash		1000
	3	Food Inventory	2000	
		Beverage Inventory	500	
		Accounts Payable (Bixby Food Co.)		2500
	3	Supplies	200	
		Cash		200
	4	Cash	2000	
		Equipment		1500
		Gain on Sale of Equipment		500
	4	Cash	500	
		Accounts Receivable	200	
		Food Sales		600
		Beverage Sales		100
	4	Cost of food sales	200	
		Cost of Beverage sales	35	
		Food Inventory		200
		Beverage Inventory		35
	5	Equipment	2000	
		Accounts Payable (Bixby Food Co.)		1000
		Cash		1000

	5	Cash							1	0	0									
		Accounts Receivable													1	0	0			
	5	Cash							8	0	0									
		Accounts Receivable							2	0	0									
		Food Sales													8	5	0			
		Beverage Sales													1	5	0			
Feb	5	Cost of Food Sales							2	5	0									
		Cost of Beverage Sales								5	0									
		Food Inventory													2	5	0			
		Beverage Inventory														5	0			
	5	Food Inventory							3	0	0									
		Cash													3	0	0			
	5	Beverage Inventory							1	0	0									
		Accounts Payable (Bixby Food Co.)													1	0	0			
	5	Accounts Payable (Bixby Food Co.)							5	0	0									
		Cash													5	0	0			
	5	Marketable Securities							5	0	0	0								
		Cash													5	0	0	0		

Required:

1. Write a general journal explanation for each of the foregoing entries.

2. Open the following balance column accounts (the type discussed in the section titled "Standard Account Forms"): Cash; Equipment; Adam Ackerson, Capital; Prepaid Rent; Food Inventory; Beverage Inventory; Accounts Payable (Bixby Food Co.); Supplies; Gain on Sale of Equipment; Accounts Receivable; Food Sales; Beverage Sales; Cost of Food Sales; Cost of Beverage Sales; and Marketable Securities.

3. Post the journal entries and prepare a trial balance of the accounts as of February 5.

Chapter
Four

Adjusting Entries
and Closing Entries

Perspective

Each financial period some accounts need adjusting entries to give a more accurate picture of a business's financial condition. Accounts for prepaid expenses, depreciation, and accrual expenses generally need adjusting.

After adjusting entries, an adjusted trial balance can be found from which to prepare the income statement and balance sheet.

At the end of each accounting period, closing entries transfer all revenue and expenses to the proprietorship account.

The accounting cycle that started with journalizing ends with preparation of the post-closing trial balance.

Work sheets can reduce the chance of errors in adjusting accounts, help to prepare balance sheets and income statements and determine net income.

Last, the chapter details how to handle withdrawals by the proprietors and capital accounts in corporations.

Adjusting Entries and Closing Entries

Adjusting and closing journal entries are not based on a single transaction, such as entries discussed heretofore. Adjusting entries are generally prepared at the end of each month to enable financial information to be more accurately presented on financial statements. Closing entries are generally prepared at the end of the year to close all revenue and expense accounts. New revenue and expense accounts are opened at the beginning of the next year. The balance sheet and income statement are briefly discussed in this chapter to illustrate the completion of the accounting process from recording to preparing financial statements.

Throughout this chapter, the Manson Motel's financial records are used to illustrate the concepts presented. The Manson Motel is a 50 room budget motel without facilities for serving food, thus the only activity is renting rooms. The Manson Motel, owned by Melvin Manson, has been in operation for several years. Melvin Manson does not play an active role in the operation but has hired Warren Willets to manage the motel.

The Income Statement and Balance Sheet

To determine a business's exact net income for any period of time all assets must be converted to cash. Yet, some of the items that enter into the determination of income are based on estimates, such as depreciation. Because firms want to continue operations, they are unwilling to convert assets to cash periodically for an exact determination of net income. Further, it is impractical to wait until the end of the organization's life to learn of its exact earnings because:

- Successful businesses continue for many years.

- Income tax regulations require payment of taxes on earnings annually.

- Management requires financial information periodically in order to properly manage the business.

So instead of converting assets to cash, it is universal practice for a firm to determine the value of its assets periodically, using estimated values for assets where necessary. Generally, one year is used to measure taxable income and thus income taxes to satisfy the government. However, financial statements are produced more frequently, at least monthly, to assist management in making decisions.

Determine total value of assets — estimating where necessary

The two main financial statements prepared from information contained in the ledger accounts are the income statement and the balance sheet. The income statement is prepared for a period of time and thus is referred to as a flow statement. The income statement reports the activity — revenues and expenses — for a period of time. Many consider the income statement more important than the balance sheet, as it reflects performance, that is, whether or not the business has accomplished its primary objective of generating earnings. Exhibit 1 shows the income statement of the Manson Motel for the year 1980. This chapter will illustrate the accounting process from the trial balance to the income statement for 1980.

Income statement and balance sheet introduced

The balance sheet in Exhibit 2 shows the financial position of the Manson Motel at a single date: December 31, 1980. The balance sheet shows that assets equal liabilities plus proprietorship. It is a nonclassified balance sheet, that is, the categories of assets and liabilities are not segregated into current and noncurrent categories.

Nonclassified balance sheet

Financial statements are introduced at this point only because they result from the accounting process. The next chapter extensively discusses the various categories of assets and liabilities.

Exhibit 1

Manson Motel
Income Statement
For the year ended December 31, 1980

Room Sales		$140,000
Expenses:		
Manager's Salary	$ 14,500	
Assistant Manager's Salary	7,000	
Maids' Wages	14,500	
Payroll Taxes	2,500	
Cleaning Supplies Expense	2,500	
Office Supplies	1,000	
Utilities	4,500	
Advertising	600	
Repairs and Maintenance	8,500	
Insurance Expense	1,400	
Depreciation Expense, Furniture	4,000	
Depreciation Expense, Equipment	1,000	
Depreciation Expense, Building	10,000	
Property Taxes	21,000	
Interest Expense	8,500	101,500
Net Income		$ 38,500

Exhibit 2

Manson Motel **Balance Sheet** December 31, 1980		

Assets:
Cash		$ 2,500
Accounts Receivable		5,000
Cleaning Supplies		2,500
Furniture	$ 40,000	
Less: Accumulated Depreciation	20,000	20,000
Equipment	10,000	
Less: Accumulated Depreciation	5,000	5,000
Building	300,000	
Less: Accumulated Depreciation	100,000	200,000
Land		20,000
Total Assets		$255,000
Liabilities:		
Accounts Payable		$ 8,000
Notes Payable		23,700
Wages Payable		300
Mortgage Payable		120,000
Total Liabilities		152,000
Proprietorship:		
Melvin Manson, Capital at January 1, 1980	$64,500	
Net Income for 1980	38,500	
Melvin Manson, Capital at December 31, 1980		103,000
Total Liabilities and Proprietorship		$255,000

The Need for Adjustments

An income statement prepared at the end of the accounting period cannot be one hundred percent exact due to required estimates but should reflect as nearly as can be measured revenue and expense for the period. The balance sheet, prepared for the last day of the accounting period, should reflect as fairly as possible the amounts of assets, liabilities, and proprietorship.

Adjusting entries correct inaccurate account balances

Normally, at the end of the accounting period, several account balances in the trial balance do not show the proper amounts for the financial statements. In part this is because the balances of some accounts become inaccurate simply as costs expire over time. An example of this is prepaid insurance of the Manson Motel. The insurance premium of $4,500 was paid for three years from January 1, 1980 to December 31, 1982. Therefore, one third of the premium of $4,500 should be expensed for 1980. This is accomplished by preparing an adjusting entry. Several other accounts must be adjusted before the financial statements can be prepared.

Exhibit 3 shows the trial balance of the Manson Motel, prepared from the ledger accounts as of December 31, 1980. The trial balance does not include adjusting journal entries. Notice that the total of the debit column equals the total of the credit column.

Exhibit 3

Manson Motel Trial Balance December 31, 1980		
Cash	$ 5,000	
Marketable Securities	10,000	
Accounts Receivable	8,000	
Cleaning Supplies	2,500	
Prepaid Insurance	4,500	
Furniture	40,000	
Accumulated Depreciation, Furniture		$ 20,000
Equipment	10,000	
Accumulated Depreciation, Equipment		5,000
Building	300,000	
Accumulated Depreciation, Building		100,000
Land	20,000	
Accounts Payable		5,000
Notes Payable		5,000
Mortgage Payable		100,000
Melvin Manson, Capital		103,000
Room Revenue		150,000
Manager's Salary	15,000	
Assistant Manager's Salary	7,500	
Maids' Wages	15,000	
Payroll Taxes	3,000	
Cleaning Supplies Expense	2,000	
Office Supplies	1,000	
Utilities	5,000	
Advertising	500	
Repairs and Maintenance	9,000	
Property Taxes	22,000	
Interest Expense	8,000	
Total	$488,000	$488,000

Adjustment of Accounts Illustrated

The number of adjusting journal entries required at the end of an accounting period depends partly upon the sophistication of the accounting system. However, no matter how sophisticated, all accounting systems require some adjusting journal entries. The adjustments here for the Manson Motel do not attempt to illustrate every conceivable adjustment but only several commonly required. Elementary accounting texts usually more thoroughly discuss a larger number of adjusting entries.

All accounting systems require adjustments

Prepaid Expenses

As the name indicates, a prepaid expense has been paid for in advance of its use. An asset is acquired when the payment is made, and as it is used or consumed, it is expensed. For example, on January 1, 1980, the Manson Motel paid a three year insurance premium of $4,500. This payment provides insurance coverage for the firm for three years. As each day passes, the firm should theoretically recognize in-

Prepaid assets expensed as consumed

surance expense for 1/1096 of the $4,500. However, Manson Motel personnel make no entry until the end of the year. Then, to properly recognize insurance expense for the period for the asset, prepaid insurance, adjusting entry #1 is written as:

Dec	31	Insurance Expense		1500	
		Prepaid Insurance			1500
		To record insurance expense for the year (⅓ of 4,500)			
		= 1,500			

The adjusting journal entry (AJE) is recorded in the general journal and posted to ledger accounts as follows:

Insurance Expense		Prepaid Insurance	
AJE #1 1,500		Bal. 4,500	AJE #1 1,500

After the entry is posted, both the Prepaid Insurance and the Insurance Expense accounts reflect the proper financial statement amounts.

Adjusting supplies based on inventory

Another prepaid expense that requires adjusting is Cleaning Supplies, $2,500. At the end of each year, the assistant general manager, together with the housekeeping supervisor, takes a physical inventory of cleaning supplies. The assistant general manager determines the cost of each item on hand at year-end — the December 31, 1980, inventory of cleaning supplies totals $1,800. Cleaning supplies bought during the year, $700 worth, are expensed as purchased.

However, the ledger account lists Cleaning Supplies, Asset, on hand of $2,500 and Cleaning Supplies, Expense of $2,000. An adjusting journal entry is required to reflect the dollar amount of cleaning supplies used during the year in excess of the amount purchased. AJE #2 is recorded as follows:

Dec	31	Cleaning Supplies Expense		700	
		Cleaning Supplies			700
		To record additional cleaning supplies used.			

The effect of the foregoing Adjusting Journal Entry on the accounts is as follows:

Cleaning Supplies		Cleaning Supplies Expense	
Bal. 2,500	AJE #2 700	Bal. 2,000	
		AJE #2 700	

So this adjustment, posted properly, adjusts the asset and expense accounts for financial statements.

The Manson Motel purchases a minor amount of office supplies and generally uses most supplies purchased in one year in that year. Therefore, the office supplies are expensed when purchased. Warren Willets, the general manager, considers the cost of labor to take a physical inventory, to determine the cost of the inventory, and to record the inventory greater than the benefit derived. This decision not to inventory office supplies was made by a responsible, knowledgeable employee of Manson Motel, as appropriate for these types of decisions.

Depreciation

When a firm purchases a fixed asset, it in effect purchases an item that will benefit the firm for several years. Day by day, as the fixed asset is used in the operations of the firm, a portion of it is consumed. This is known as depreciation.

Fixed assets depreciate through use

The depreciation of a fixed asset is an expense, just like prepaid insurance which decreases through expiration. However, over a short period of time, depreciation is more difficult to measure — it can only be estimated.

The Manson Motel purchased its building ten years prior to January 1, 1980, and its equipment and furniture five years prior to January 1, 1980. The estimated lives and salvage values of the three classes of items are as follows:

	Cost	Estimated Life	Salvage Value
Furniture	$ 40,000	10 years	$ -0-
Equipment	10,000	8 years	2,000
Building	300,000	25 years	50,000

The straight-line method (three methods of depreciation are discussed in Chapter 8) is used to determine depreciation expense for the year. Depreciation is not recorded until the end of the year.

The formula calculating annual depreciation expense is:

$$\frac{\text{Cost} - \text{Salvage Value}}{\text{Estimated Life in Years}} = \text{Depreciation Expense for Year}$$

Cost is the amount paid for the fixed asset at date of purchase. Salvage value is the estimated value at the end of the fixed asset's useful life. Estimated life is the number of years the fixed asset should be useful to the owner.

The depreciation expense for 1980 is calculated as follows:

Furniture $\quad \dfrac{\$40,000}{10} = \$4,000$

Equipment $\quad \dfrac{\$10,000 - \$2,000}{8} = \$1,000$

Building $\quad \dfrac{\$300,000 - \$50,000}{25} = \$10,000$

Adjusting journal entries #3 to #5 are required to record the depreciation expense for the year and to reduce the book value — the cost of the fixed assets less accumulated depreciation of the fixed assets:

		AJE #3		
Dec	31	Depreciation Expense, Furniture	4000	
		Accumulated Depreciation, Furniture		4000
		To record depreciation of furniture for the year		

		AJE #4		
Dec	31	Depreciation Expense, Equipment	1000	
		Accumulated Depreciation, Equipment		1000
		To record depreciation of equipment for the year		

		AJE #5		
Dec	31	Depreciation Expense, Building	10000	
		Accumulated Depreciation, Building		10000
		To record depreciation of building for the year		

The effect of the adjustments on the ledger accounts is as follows:

Furniture	Depreciation Expense, Furniture	Accumulated Depreciation, Furniture
Bal. 40,000	AJE #3 4,000	Bal. 20,000 AJE #3 4,000

Equipment	Depreciation Expense, Equipment	Accumulated Depreciation, Equipment
Bal. 10,000	AJE #4 1,000	Bal. 5,000 AJE #4 1,000

Building	Depreciation Expense, Building	Accumulated Depreciation, Building
Bal. 300,000	AJE #5 10,000	Bal. 100,000 AJE #5 10,000

The depreciation expense is not credited directly to the fixed asset accounts but is recorded in a contra account. A contra account's balance is subtracted from the balance of a second account to show a net amount for the item recorded in the second account. Depreciation is recorded in a contra account because, first, depreciation is only an estimate, and second, the contra account better preserves the record of the life of the fixed asset. In the financial statement (see Exhibit 2) the amount of Accumulated Depreciation, Furniture per the ledger account will be subtracted from the amount recorded in the furniture account.

Contra-account for fixed assets depreciation

Accrued Expenses

Most expenses are recorded during the accounting period when they are paid. However, at the end of a period, some expenses generally have been incurred but not paid since they are not yet due, and thus are not recorded. These are accrued expenses. Unpaid wages is an example of an accrued expense. The Manson Motel paid the manager and assistant manager on December 31, 1980, for their services through that date. The maids were paid for their services through December 27, 1980. The $150 they earned for December 28-31, 1980, should be recorded as expense for 1980. The adjusting entry, AJE #6, accomplishes this plus properly states the amount of accrued wages, a liability, as of December 31, 1980.

Accrued expenses not paid, due, or recorded

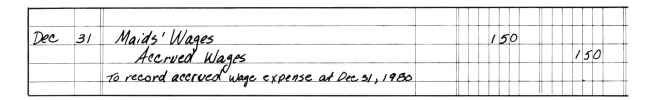

The effect of the adjustments on the ledger accounts is as follows:

Maids' Wages		Accrued Wages	
Bal. 15,000			AJE #6 150
AJE #6 150			

After AJE #6 has been posted, the two accounts, Maids' Wages and Accrued Wages, are correctly stated for financial statement purposes. No adjustment is made for payroll taxes on the accrued wages of $150 since the amount is insignificant — less than $10.

Adjusted Trial Balance and Financial Statements

A trial balance prepared after the adjusting journal entries are recorded and posted to the ledger accounts is called an adjusted trial balance. The adjusted trial balance is used in preparing the income statement and balance sheet. The adjusted trial balance of the Manson Motel is in Exhibit 4.

Adjusted trial balance for financial statements

It is relatively easy to prepare the balance sheet and income statement from the adjusted trial balance. The revenue and expense items must be rearranged into the income statement, and the accounts repre-

Rearrangements for balance sheets

Exhibit 4

Manson Motel Adjusted Trial Balance December 31, 1980		
Cash	$ 5,000	
Marketable Securities	10,000	
Accounts Receivable	8,000	
Cleaning Supplies	1,800	
Prepaid Insurance	3,000	
Furniture	40,000	
Accumulated Depreciation, Furniture		$ 24,000
Equipment	10,000	
Accumulated Depreciation, Equipment		6,000
Building	300,000	
Accumulated Depreciation, Building		110,000
Land	20,000	
Accounts Payable		5,000
Notes Payable		5,000
Accrued Wages		150
Mortgage Payable		100,000
Melvin Manson, Capital		103,000
Room Revenue		150,000
Manager's Salary	15,000	
Assistant Manager's Salary	7,500	
Maids' Wages	15,150	
Payroll Taxes	3,000	
Cleaning Supplies Expense	2,700	
Office Supplies	1,000	
Utilities	5,000	
Advertising	500	
Repairs and Maintenance	9,000	
Insurance Expense	1,500	
Depreciation Expense, Furniture	4,000	
Depreciation Expense, Equipment	1,000	
Depreciation Expense, Building	10,000	
Property Taxes	22,000	
Interest Expense	8,000	
Total	$503,150	$503,150

senting assets, liabilities, and proprietorship must be rearranged into the balance sheet, as shown in Exhibits 5 and 6. Again, the balance sheet categories of assets and liabilities have not been divided into current and noncurrent categories for reasons discussed heretofore.

The Need for Closing Entries

In the presentation of the accounting equation in Chapter 2, all increases and decreases in proprietorship, including revenues and expenses, were placed in a single column under the name of the proprietor, James Rail. But in reality revenues and expenses are not recorded directly in the proprietor's capital account, but in separate accounts for each revenue and expense item. This is so that detailed information as to the kind of revenues and expenses can more easily be provided. These separate accounts must be closed and cleared at the end of each accounting period, and the balance of each account transferred to the proprietor's capital account. This is done through journal entries called closing entries. They are recorded in the general journal and posted to the ledger accounts.

Closing entries clear separate account balances into capital account

Exhibit 5

Manson Motel Adjusted Trial Balance December 31, 1980			Manson Motel Balance Sheet December 31, 1980		
			Assets:		
Cash	$ 5,000		Cash		$ 5,000
Marketable Securities	10,000		Marketable Securities		10,000
Accounts Receivable	8,000		Accounts Receivable		8,000
Cleaning Supplies	1,800		Cleaning Supplies		1,800
Prepaid Insurance	3,000		Prepaid Insurance		3,000
Furniture	40,000		Furniture	$ 40,000	
Accumulated Depreciation, Furniture		$ 24,000	Less: Accumulated Depreciation	24,000	16,000
Equipment	10,000		Equipment	10,000	
Accumulated Depreciation, Equipment		6,000	Less: Accumulated Depreciation	6,000	4,000
Building	300,000		Building	300,000	
Accumulated Depreciation, Building		110,000	Less: Accumulated Depreciation	110,000	190,000
Land	20,000		Land		20,000
			Total Assets		$257,800
			Liabilities:		
Accounts Payable		5,000	Accounts Payable		$ 5,000
Notes Payable		5,000	Notes Payable		5,000
Accrued Wages		150	Accrued Wages		150
Mortgage Payable		100,000	Mortgage Payable		100,000
Melvin Manson, Capital		103,000	Total Liabilities		110,150
Room Revenue		150,000			
Manager's Salary	15,000		**Proprietorship:**		
Assistant Manager's Salary	7,500		Melvin Manson, Capital at January 1, 1980	$103,000	
Maids' Wages	15,150		Net Income for 1980	44,650	
Payroll Taxes	3,000				
Cleaning Supplies Expense	2,700		Melvin Manson, Capital at December 31, 1980		147,650
Office Supplies	1,000				
Utilities	5,000		Total Liabilities and Proprietorship		$257,800
Advertising	500				
Repairs and Maintenance	9,000				
Insurance Expense	1,500				
Depreciation Expense, Furniture	4,000				
Depreciation Expense, Equipment	1,000		Net Income for 1980 (See Exhibit 6)		
Depreciation Expense, Building	10,000				
Property Taxes	22,000				
Interest Expense	8,000				
Total	$503,150	$503,150			

Exhibit 6

<table>
<tr><td colspan="3">Manson Motel
Adjusted Trial Balance
December 31, 1980</td></tr>
<tr><td>Cash</td><td>$ 5,000</td><td></td></tr>
<tr><td>Marketable Securities</td><td>10,000</td><td></td></tr>
<tr><td>Accounts Receivable</td><td>8,000</td><td></td></tr>
<tr><td>Cleaning Supplies</td><td>1,800</td><td></td></tr>
<tr><td>Prepaid Insurance</td><td>3,000</td><td></td></tr>
<tr><td>Furniture</td><td>40,000</td><td></td></tr>
<tr><td>Accumulated Depreciation,
Furniture</td><td></td><td>$ 24,000</td></tr>
<tr><td>Equipment</td><td>10,000</td><td></td></tr>
<tr><td>Accumulated Depreciation,
Equipment</td><td></td><td>6,000</td></tr>
<tr><td>Building</td><td>300,000</td><td></td></tr>
<tr><td>Accumulated Depreciation,
Building</td><td></td><td>110,000</td></tr>
<tr><td>Land</td><td>20,000</td><td></td></tr>
<tr><td>Accounts Payable</td><td></td><td>5,000</td></tr>
<tr><td>Notes Payable</td><td></td><td>5,000</td></tr>
<tr><td>Accrued Wages</td><td></td><td>150</td></tr>
<tr><td>Mortgage Payable</td><td></td><td>100,000</td></tr>
<tr><td>Melvin Manson, Capital</td><td></td><td>103,000</td></tr>
<tr><td>Room Revenue</td><td></td><td>150,000</td></tr>
<tr><td>Manager's Salary</td><td>15,000</td><td></td></tr>
<tr><td>Assistant Manager's Salary</td><td>7,500</td><td></td></tr>
<tr><td>Maids' Wages</td><td>15,150</td><td></td></tr>
<tr><td>Payroll Taxes</td><td>3,000</td><td></td></tr>
<tr><td>Cleaning Supplies Expense</td><td>2,700</td><td></td></tr>
<tr><td>Office Supplies</td><td>1,000</td><td></td></tr>
<tr><td>Utilities</td><td>5,000</td><td></td></tr>
<tr><td>Advertising</td><td>500</td><td></td></tr>
<tr><td>Repairs and Maintenance</td><td>9,000</td><td></td></tr>
<tr><td>Insurance Expense</td><td>1,500</td><td></td></tr>
<tr><td>Depreciation Expense,
Furniture</td><td>4,000</td><td></td></tr>
<tr><td>Depreciation Expense,
Equipment</td><td>1,000</td><td></td></tr>
<tr><td>Depreciation Expense,
Building</td><td>10,000</td><td></td></tr>
<tr><td>Property Taxes</td><td>22,000</td><td></td></tr>
<tr><td>Interest Expense</td><td>8,000</td><td></td></tr>
<tr><td align="right">Total</td><td>$503,150</td><td>$503,150</td></tr>
</table>

<table>
<tr><td colspan="2">Manson Motel
Income Statement
For the Year Ended December 31, 1980</td></tr>
<tr><td>Room Sales</td><td>$150,000</td></tr>
<tr><td>Expenses:</td><td></td></tr>
<tr><td>Manager's Salary</td><td>$ 15,000</td></tr>
<tr><td>Assistant Manager's Salary</td><td>7,500</td></tr>
<tr><td>Maids' Wages</td><td>15,150</td></tr>
<tr><td>Payroll Taxes</td><td>3,000</td></tr>
<tr><td>Cleaning Supplies Expense</td><td>2,700</td></tr>
<tr><td>Office Supplies</td><td>1,000</td></tr>
<tr><td>Utilities</td><td>5,000</td></tr>
<tr><td>Advertising</td><td>500</td></tr>
<tr><td>Repairs and Maintenance</td><td>9,000</td></tr>
<tr><td>Insurance Expense</td><td>1,500</td></tr>
<tr><td>Depreciation Expense,
Furniture</td><td>4,000</td></tr>
<tr><td>Depreciation Expense,
Equipment</td><td>1,000</td></tr>
<tr><td>Depreciation Expense,
Building</td><td>10,000</td></tr>
<tr><td>Property Taxes</td><td>22,000</td></tr>
<tr><td>Interest Expense</td><td>8,000</td></tr>
<tr><td align="right">Total</td><td>105,350</td></tr>
<tr><td align="right">Net Income</td><td>$ 44,650</td></tr>
</table>

Closing of Accounts Illustrated

Exhibit 4 shows the balances of the Manson Motel's revenue and expense accounts after the adjusting entries are posted. Note that the Melvin Manson, Capital, account shows only its January 1, 1980, balance of $103,000. After closing entries are recorded this account will show the December 31, 1980, proprietorship amount of $147,650 per the balance sheet in Exhibit 5.

First, the amounts recorded in the revenue and expense accounts are transferred into the Income Summary, a proprietorship account used only at the end of the accounting period. The amount recorded in the Income Summary account is then transferred into the Capital account. Exhibit 7 shows the flow of the amounts from revenue and expense accounts through the Income Summary account to the Capital account.

Exhibit 7

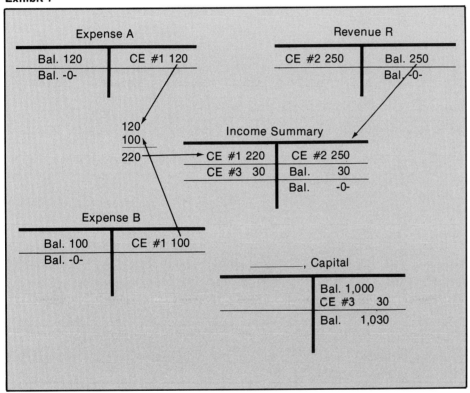

In closing entry (CE) #1 the amount in the expense accounts is transferred into the Income Summary account. Each expense account is credited for the amount of its prior debit balance, and the total of the credits to the expense accounts, $220, is debited to the Income Summary account.

CE #2 transfers the amount recorded in the revenue account into the Income Summary account. The revenue account is debited for the amount of its prior credit balance, and the debit to the revenue account of $250 is credited to the Income Summary account.

CE #3 transfers the balance of the Income Summary account of $30 to the Capital account by debiting the Income Summary account and crediting the Capital account.

The Manson Motel closing entries follow. The expense accounts per Exhibit 6 have debit balances, so to close and clear the expense

Closing entries

accounts, a compound closing entry debits the Income Summary and credits each expense account:

Dec.	31	Income Summary		105350	
		Manager's Salary			15000
		Assistant Manager's Salary			7500
		Maids' Wages			15150
		Payroll taxes			3000
		Cleaning Supplies Expense			2700
		Office Supplies			1000
		Utilities			5000
		Advertising			500
		Repairs & Maintenance			9000
		Insurance Expense			1500
		Depreciation Expense, Furniture			4000
		Depreciation Expense, Equipment			1000
		Depreciation Expense, Building			10000
		Property Taxes			22000
		Interest Expense			8000
		To close the expense accounts at year-end			

Closing entries transfer and clear

This closing entry has a two-fold effect. It transfers the balance of the expense accounts to the debit side of the Income Summary, and second, it clears each expense account of its balance.

The Room Revenue account per Exhibit 6 has a credit balance. Therefore, to close and clear a revenue account, the account must be debited for the balance and the Income Summary must be credited for the same.

Dec.	31	Room Revenue		150000	
		Income Summary			150000
		To close the Room Revenue account at year-end			

This closing entry also has the dual effect of first transferring the balance of the revenue account to the credit side of the Income Summary account, and second, clearing the Room Revenue account of its balance.

When a firm's revenue and expense accounts are closed into the Income Summary, the balance reflects the result of the year's operations, either net income or loss. After the two closing entries above, the Manson Motel's Income Summary T-account has a credit balance of $44,650, the amount of net income earned for 1980.

Income Summary

CE #1 105,350	CE #2 150,000
	Bal. 44,650

To close and clear the Income Summary account for the Manson Motel, it must be debited for $44,650 and Melvin Manson, Capital, account credited for $44,650:

Dec. 31	Income Summary	44650	
	Melvin Manson, Capital		44650
	To close Income Summary account at year-end		

Income Summary			Melvin Manson, Capital	
CE #1 105,350	CE #2 150,000		Bal. 103,000	
CE #3 44,650	Bal. 44,650		CE #3 44,650	
	Bal. -0-		Bal. 147,650	

Note again the dual purpose served by this closing entry: first it closes and clears the Income Summary account of its balance, and second, it transfers the amount of the net income to the Capital account. The balance of the Capital account of $147,650 equals the total of proprietorship interests in the assets of the Manson Motel as shown in Exhibit 5.

Post-Closing Trial Balance

The recording and posting of adjusting and closing entries is tedious, and the bookkeeper may make an error. Therefore, after the adjusting and closing processes are completed, a new trial balance, called a post-closing trial balance, is prepared to test the equality of the open accounts. Exhibit 8 is the post-closing trial balance for the Manson Motel as of December 31, 1980.

Testing equality of open accounts

Exhibit 8

Manson Motel Post-Closing Trial Balance December 31, 1980		
Cash	$ 5,000	
Marketable Securities	10,000	
Accounts Receivable	8,000	
Cleaning Supplies	1,800	
Prepaid Insurance	3,000	
Furniture	40,000	
Accumulated Depreciation, Furniture		$ 24,000
Equipment	10,000	
Accumulated Depreciation, Equipment		6,000
Building	300,000	
Accumulated Depreciation, Building		110,000
Land	20,000	
Accounts Payable		5,000
Notes Payable		5,000
Accrued Wages		150
Mortgage Payable		100,000
Melvin Manson, Capital		147,650
Total	$397,800	$397,800

The total of accounts with debit balances equals the total of accounts with credit balances. Further, revenue or expense accounts are not included, as they have been closed and cleared to the Capital account through the closing entries.

Accounting Cycle

In each accounting period of generally one year, an accounting cycle recurs, starting with journalizing and ending with the post-closing trial balance. All the steps in the accounting cycle have now been demonstrated, and they occur as follows:

1. Journalizing — analyzing, classifying, and recording transactions in a journal.
2. Posting — copying the debits and credits of journal entries in the ledger accounts.
3. Preparing a trial balance — summarizing the ledger accounts to prove the equality of debits and credits.
4. Preparing adjusting entries — determining the adjustments and recording them in the general journal.
5. Posting adjusting entries — posting the adjusting entries in the ledger accounts so that the final statements may be prepared.
6. Preparing an adjusted trial balance — summarizing the ledger accounts to prove the equality of debits and credits after the posting of the adjusting entries.
7. Preparing the financial statements — rearranging the adjusted trial balance into an income statement and balance sheet.
8. Closing the revenue and expense accounts — journalizing and posting the entries that close the revenue and expense accounts and transfer the net income or loss for the period to the Capital account.
9. Preparing a post-closing trial balance — summarizing the open ledger accounts to prove the equality of debits and credits.

The Work Sheet

An accountant may use a work sheet to reduce the chance of errors in adjusting the accounts and constructing the financial statements. The work sheet:

1. Adjusts the accounts without the need to post immediately to the ledger accounts (the posting process is done after the work sheet is completed).
2. Segregates the adjusted account balances into columns for preparing the income statement and the balance sheet.
3. Determines the net income or loss for the period.

The work sheet is only an accountant's tool, not for publication or the use of management. The decision to use or not to use a work sheet is the accountant's. He or she must weigh the benefit — reducing the chance for errors — against the additional time to prepare the work sheet. Yet this additional time may be less than the time required to find errors made because the accountant did not use a work sheet.

The work sheet for the Manson Motel for 1980 is shown in Exhibit 9. All amounts in the work sheet have been previously discussed in detail in this chapter.

Observe the following concerning the work sheet:

1. Column 1 contains the list of accounts of the Manson Motel. These were all taken from the ledger accounts except for the last five which result from the adjustments.

2. Columns 2 and 3 contain the trial balance prior to the adjusting entries as previously shown in Exhibit 3. The total of the debit column equals the total of the credit column.

3. Columns 4 and 5 contain the six adjusting entries discussed in the section, "Adjustment of Accounts Illustrated."

   Adjustment (a): To record insurance expense for the year.
   Adjustment (b): To record additional cleaning supplies used.
   Adjustment (c): To record depreciation of furniture for the year.
   Adjustment (d): To record depreciation of equipment for the year.
   Adjustment (e): To record depreciation of building for the year.
   Adjustment (f): To record accrued wages expense at December 31, 1980.

   The total of the debits of $17,350 equals the total of the credits of $17,350.

4. Columns 6 and 7 contain the adjusted trial balance. Again, the total of the debit balance accounts equals the total of the credit balance accounts. This adjusted trial balance on the work sheet duplicates the adjusted trial balance in Exhibit 4.

5. Columns 8 and 9 include the revenue and expense accounts that will be shown in the Income Statement. The total of the credit column exceeds the total of the debit column by $44,650, the net income the Manson Motel earned for 1980.

6. The last two columns include the remaining accounts, those that will be shown in the balance sheet. The total of the debit column exceeds the total of the credit column by $44,650, the net income for 1980. This difference agrees with the difference between the credit and debit columns for the income statement.

The steps in the accounting cycle are slightly rearranged if the work sheet is used:

1. Journalizing
2. Posting
3. Preparing a trial balance
4. Constructing a work sheet
5. Preparing the financial statements
6. Recording and posting the adjusting entries
7. Closing the revenue and expense accounts
8. Preparing a post-closing trial balance

Withdrawals by the Proprietor

The proprietor may withdraw cash or other assets from the firm for personal reasons. Such withdrawals are generally recorded in an account with a title such as Melvin Manson, Drawing. If Melvin Manson

Exhibit 9

Manson Motel
Work Sheet
For the year ended December 31, 1980

Account Title	Trial Balance Debit	Trial Balance Credit	Adjustments Debit	Adjustments Credit
Cash	5000			
Marketable Securities	10000			
Accounts Receivable	8000			
Cleaning Supplies	2500			(b) 700
Prepaid Insurance	4500			(a) 1500
Furniture	40000			
Accumulated Depreciation, Furniture		20000		(c) 4000
Equipment	10000			
Accumulated Depreciation, Equipment		5000		(d) 1000
Building	300000			
Accumulated Depreciation, Building		100000		(e) 10000
Land	20000			
Accounts Payable		5000		
Notes Payable		5000		
Mortgage Payable		100000		
Melvin Manson, Capital		103000		
Room Revenue		150000		
Managers Salary	15000			
Assistant Managers Salary	7500			
Maids' Wages	15000		(f) 150	
Payroll Taxes	3000			
Cleaning Supplies Expense	2000		(b) 700	
Office Supplies	1000			
Utilities	5000			
Advertising	500			
Repairs & Maintenance	9000			
Property Taxes	22000			
Intrest Expense	8000			
	488000	488000		
Insurance Expense			(a) 1500	
Depreciation Expense, Furniture			(c) 4000	
Depreciation Expense, Equipment			(d) 1000	
Depreciation Expense, Building			(e) 10000	
Accrued Wages				(f) 150
			17350	17350

Adjusted Trial Balance		Income Statement		Balance Sheet	
Debit	Credit	Debit	Credit	Debit	Credit
5000				5000	
0000				10000	
8000				8000	
1800				1800	
3000				3000	
0000				40000	
	24000				24000
0000				10000	
	6000				6000
0000				300000	
	110000				110000
0000				20000	
	5000				5000
	5000				5000
	100000				100000
	103000				103000
	150000		150000		
5000		15000			
7500		7500			
5150		15150			
3000		3000			
2700		2700			
1000		1000			
5000		5000			
500		500			
9000		9000			
2000		22000			
8000		8000			
1500		1500			
4000		4000			
1000		1000			
1000		10000			
	150				150
3150	503150	105350	150000	397800	353150
		44650			44650
		150000	150000	397800	397800

Close proprietor's drawing into capital account

withdraws $100 for personal use, Melvin Manson, Drawing, is debited and the cash account is credited. As a proprietorship account, it is closed into the Capital account at the end of the accounting period. It reduces the Capital account's balance and thus, the equity of the proprietor in the assets of the firm.

Capital Accounts Used By Corporations

Throughout the first four chapters, the discussion and illustrations have centered on unincorporated businesses owned by a single person. However, many hospitality businesses are either partnerships or corporations and their equity accounts differ from those used by a sole proprietor.

In a partnership, each partner has a capital account and a drawing account. For example, the K & C Inn is owned by M. L. Kasawana and R. E. Chicken. The equity accounts are:

M. L. Kasawana, Capital
M. L. Kasawana, Drawing
R. E. Chicken, Capital
R. E. Chicken, Drawing

Stock sales debit cash and credit capital

A corporation is a separate legal entity apart from its owners. The owners of the corporation purchase capital stock and are issued stock certificates as evidence of their ownership. See Chapter 9, Exhibit 2, for a sample stock certificate. When the corporation sells its stock, the Cash account is debited and the Capital Stock account is credited. For example, Holly Little buys 100 shares of stock in the Little Hotel Corporation for $1,000. The sale is recorded by Little Hotel Corporation as follows:

Cash		1000	
Capital Stock			1000
To record sale of stock to Holly Little.			

Any additional sales of stock would be recorded in a similar fashion.

The Little Hotel Corporation has a successful first year of operations and shows a profit of $15,000. The Income Summary account is closed into an account called Retained Earnings. All earnings and losses from operations in subsequent years will be recorded in this Retained Earnings account. After a few years of successful operations, the Little Hotel Corporation pays part of its past earnings to its stockholders, called cash dividends. These dividends reduce retained earnings. If $5,000 is paid to stockholders as dividends, the Little Hotel Corporation would record the payments as follows:

Cash dividends reduce retained earnings

Retained Earnings		5000	
Cash			5000
To record payment of dividends to stockholders			

Discussion Questions

1. What is the purpose of adjusting entries?

2. The office supplies inventory per the general ledger at December 31 is $1,000 and the physical inventory at December 31 is $500. What adjusting entry should be prepared?

3. The last payroll of the year for the Casa Nova Inn is on December 27, 1981. If the end of the year is December 31, 1981, and the Casa Nova Inn was open on December 28-31, 1981, what adjusting entry should be made to record accrued payroll? (Assume the next pay period ends on January 3, 1982.)

4. Explain the differences among a trial balance, an adjusted trial balance, and a post-closing trial balance.

5. What is the purpose of a work sheet?

6. What are closing entries and when are they prepared?

7. What is the account Income Summary and when is it used?

8. List the nine steps in the accounting cycle.

9. Keith Wills withdraws $500 from his business, Wills Cafe, for personal use. How should this entry be recorded?

10. Check which financial statement would contain the following accounts:

	Balance Sheet	Income Statement
Room Sales	_____	_____
Cash	_____	_____
Depreciation Expense	_____	_____
Accumulated Depreciation	_____	_____
Rent Expense	_____	_____
M. C. Woods, Drawing	_____	_____
Accounts Payable	_____	_____
Cost of Food Sold	_____	_____
Wages Payable	_____	_____
Salary Expense	_____	_____

Problems

Problem 1

Don Donuts, owned by Donald Week, has annual accounting periods ending each December 31. On December 31, 1981, after all transactions were recorded, the bookkeeper prepared the trial balance of accounts:

Don Donuts Trial Balance December 31,1981		
Cash	$ 2,500	
Supplies	1,250	
Unexpired Insurance	1,000	
Food and Beverage Inventory	2,000	
Equipment	10,000	
Accumulated Depreciation, Equipment		$ 4,000
Building	40,000	
Accumulated Depreciation, Building		6,000
Land	3,000	
Accounts Payable		600
Mortgage Payable		20,000
Donald Week, Capital		12,750
Donald Week, Drawing	4,000	
Food and Beverage Sales		85,000
Cost of Food and Beverage Sales	26,600	
Salaries Expense	30,000	
Advertising Expense	1,000	
Utilities Expense	3,000	
Supplies Expense	2,000	
Interest Expense	2,000	
	$128,350	$128,350

Required:

1. Open the accounts included in the trial balance plus these additional ones: Insurance Expense; Depreciation Expense, Equipment; Depreciation Expense, Building. (Note: Use accounts as shown in Chapter 3.) Enter the trial balance amounts in the balance column of each account.

2. Prepare and post adjusting journal entries based on the following information:

   a) The physical count of the food and beverage inventory at December 31, 1981, is $1,650.

   b) Insurance expired during the year, $500.

   c) Estimated depreciation of equipment for the year, $1,500.

   d) Estimated depreciation of the building for the year, $2,500.

3. Prepare an adjusted trial balance and income statement.

Problem 2

For this problem use the trial balance of Problem 1.

Required:

1. Enter the trial balance amounts in a work sheet and complete the work sheet using the following information:

   a) Unexpired insurance at December 31, 1981, $700.

   b) The physical inventory at December 31, 1981, of supplies, $1,450.

   c) Estimated depreciation expense of the equipment and building, $1,000 and $2,000, respectively.

2. From the work sheet, prepare a balance sheet and income statement.

3. From the work sheet, prepare adjusting and closing entries in general journal form.

4. Prepare a post-closing trial balance.

Problem 3 (Comprehensive)

On June 1 of the current year, Robert Trout opened Trout Ten Star Club. During the month, the following transactions were completed:

June 1 — Robert Trout invested $15,000 in the business from the sale of personal stocks and bonds.

1 — Signed a three year lease with Five Star Enterprises and paid the first six months' rent of $6,000.

1 — Purchased $15,000 worth of furniture for the club by paying $5,000 cash and signing a promissory note of $10,000 with Lowery's Deluxe Furniture Co.

2 — Purchased $4,000 of equipment on account from J. K. Dennison Co.

3 — Purchased food and beverage supplies from Wells Food & Beverage for $8,000, of which 50% was on account.

4 — Paid a one-year insurance premium of $1,200, covering the period of June 1 of the current year to May 31 of the following year.

4 — Paid $500 for supplies.

15 — Food and beverage sales for the first half of the month were $20,000. The cost of sales was 25% of total sales.

16 — Paid wages of $6,000 for the first half of June.

17 — Paid J. K. Dennison $2,000 on account.

18 — Purchased food and beverage on account from Wells Food & Beverage, $7,000.

19 — Paid Wells Food & Beverage $3,000 on account.

30 — Sales for the second half of June were $25,000. The cost of sales was 26% of total sales.

30 — Paid wages of $7,500 for the second half of June.

30 — Made the first payment of $200 to Lowery's on the note, of which $100 was interest.

30 — Paid utility bills for June, $400.

30 — Paid payroll taxes of 10% of the wages paid in June.

Required:

1. Open the following accounts: Cash; Food and Beverage Inventory; Supplies Inventory; Prepaid Rent; Prepaid Insurance; Furniture; Accumulated Depreciation, Furniture; Equipment; Accumulated Depreciation, Equipment; Accounts Payable (J. K. Dennison Co.); Accounts Payable (Wells Food & Beverage); Notes Payable (Lowery's Deluxe Furniture Co.); Robert Trout, Capital; Income Summary; Food and Beverage Sales; Cost of Sales; Wages Expense; Payroll Taxes; Supplies Expense; Utilities Expense; Rent Expense; Depreciation Expense, Furniture; Depreciation Expense, Equipment; Insurance Expense; and Interest Expense. (Note: Either type of account as illustrated may be used.)

2. Record the June transactions in general journal form.

3. Post the amounts to the ledger accounts.

4. Prepare a trial balance after completing the posting of transactions for June.

5. Record adjusting entries in general journal form based on the following:

   a) One month's insurance has expired.

   b) One month's rent has been "used."

   c) Estimated depreciation of furniture for the month is $150.

   d) Estimated depreciation of equipment for the month is $50.

   e) A physical inventory of supplies showed $245 worth on hand at the end of June.

6. Post the adjusting entries to the ledger accounts.

7. Prepare an adjusted trial balance.

8. Prepare an income statement for the month of June.

9. Prepare closing entries in general journal form.

10. Post the closing entries to the ledger accounts.

11. Prepare a post-closing trial balance as of June 30.

Chapter
Five

The Balance Sheet

Perspective

The balance sheet reveals a business's financial condition at the end of the accounting period. Managers, investors, and creditors all use balance sheet information but for different purposes.

The balance sheet is the culmination of the accounting cycle. All balance sheets follow the fundamental accounting equation, no matter the type of business:

ASSETS = LIABILITIES + PROPRIETORSHIP

There are two arrangements for the balance sheet—account or report form. In either case both assets and liabilities are divided into current and noncurrent.

The form of the proprietorship portion of the balance sheet depends on whether the business is a sole proprietorship, partnership, or corporation.

Finally, footnotes to the balance sheet add whatever information the user needs to evaluate correctly the business's financial position.

The Balance Sheet

Three types of financial statements

Owners and managers of hospitality firms need to know how profitable operations are and have information on the financial health of the business. The financial statements prepared at the end of each accounting period provide this information. The balance sheet reveals the financial condition of the business at the end of the accounting period. Income statements report on the results of operations. The statement of changes in financial position measures the factors that have affected the working capital.

The subject of Chapters 5 to 7 is financial statements. This chapter presents the organization and preparation of the balance sheet. Chapter 6 discusses the income statement, including the many departmental income statements. Chapter 7 follows with the presentation of the statement of changes in financial position. Footnotes to the financial statements, a very important element, are also presented in this chapter. Hilton Corporation's various financial statements from its 1981 annual report are used to illustrate how these three financial statements, including the footnotes, are presented to stockholders.

Purpose of the Balance Sheet

The balance sheet, also called the statement of financial position, reports the financial position of the hospitality firm as of the date on which the accounting period ends. It lists the ending balance in each asset, liability, and proprietorship account.

Net effect of all financial activities

These account balances are in effect the net accumulation of all the accounting transactions that have occurred since the inception of the business. All financial activities have been recorded in the accounts and their net effect reported in the balance sheet.

The principal users of the balance sheet are the firm's management, investors, and creditors. Management uses the balance sheet to find inventory balances, accounts receivable, accounts payable, cash, and maturing debt. Control of these items is necessary to make sure that funds are available to meet current obligations and to assure the liquidity of the business.

Investors look to the balance sheet to judge the firm's financial health. They analyze balance sheet data through the use of ratios and other relationships calculated from account balances. This evaluation is an important part of the information used in investment decisions.

Creditors are interested in the information on balance sheets because it reports the firm's level of debt and the resources available for repayment. So information found in the balance sheet influences credit decisions.

Preparing the Balance Sheet

The accounting period can be either monthly, quarterly, semi-annually, or annually. The shorter the time period, the more expensive the accounting system. However, the advantage of timely accounting reports can offset the higher cost.

The accounting data used in the balance sheet can come from either the general ledger or the work sheet described in the last chapter. The account balances used must reflect all end-of-the-period adjustments and closing entries. The proper proprietorship account balances will include the income or loss from the accounting period just ending.

Adjusting and closing entries reflected

Balance sheets from different companies are similar regardless of the nature of the business in that the account names are similar. However, the amounts and proportions will differ depending on the nature of the business. Income statements, on the other hand, are uniquely determined by the nature of the business. The income statement for a hospitality service firm will differ substantially from that of a manufacturer.

The balance sheet is an expression of the accounting equation — assets equal the total of the liabilities and proprietorship. Assets have debit balances, and liabilities and proprietorship accounts have credit balances, with rare exceptions.

Balance sheet expresses accounting equation

Balance Sheet Format

The balance sheet can be arranged in either the account or report format. The account format lists the asset accounts on the left side of the page and the liability and proprietorship accounts on the right. The balance sheet for the Manson Motel in the account format is shown in Exhibit 1.

Account versus report format

When using the report format, assets are listed first, followed by liabilities and proprietorship, rather than showing the accounts on both sides of the page. The group totals on the report form can show that either assets equal liabilities and proprietorship or that assets minus liabilities equal proprietorship. The balance sheet for the Manson Motel shown in Chapter 4, Exhibit 2, uses the report format.

Content of the Balance Sheet

Both the account and report formats group assets and liabilities into categories of accounts with common characteristics. An asset can be either current or noncurrent. Current assets are either cash, assets to be converted to cash in one year, or assets used in generating revenues

Current versus noncurrent assets

Exhibit 1

Manson Motel
Balance Sheet
December 31, 1980

ASSETS			LIABILITIES AND PROPRIETORSHIP		
Current Assets:			Current Liabilities:		
Cash	$ 2,500		Accounts Payable	$ 8,000	
Accounts Receivable	5,000		Notes Payable	23,700	
Cleaning Supplies	2,500		Wages Payable	300	
Total		10,000	Total		32,000
Fixed Assets:			Long-term Liabilities:		
Land	20,000		Mortgage Payable		120,000
Building	300,000		Proprietorship:		
Equipment	10,000		Melvin Manson,		
Furniture	40,000		Capital		103,000
	370,000		Total Liabilities and		
Less Accumulated Depreciation	125,000		Proprietorship		$255,000
		245,000			
Total Assets		$255,000			

within a year. Noncurrent assets are organizational resources that benefit the business for a period longer than a year.

Liabilities can also be categorized as either current or noncurrent. Current liabilities are obligations due to be paid within a year from the balance sheet date, while noncurrent liabilities are due to be paid in a future period beyond a year.

Current Assets

Current versus noncurrent

Current assets for hospitality firms typically consist of cash, marketable securities, receivables, inventory, and prepaid expenses. They are listed in order of liquidity. Receivables, for example, will generate cash earlier than inventory, which has yet to be used or sold, so are listed before inventory on the balance sheet.

Cash — Cash, of course, is the most liquid of current assets.

Marketable securities — Marketable securities are held as temporary investments and can decline in market price. Any loss in market value at the balance sheet date is recognized as a loss. The value of marketable securities is stated at the lower of cost or market while gains in value are not recognized until the marketable security is sold.

Accounts receivable — Accounts receivable are promises from guests to pay the lodging firm in the future for goods and services received. Unfortunately, not all receivables are collected; thus, losses occur. Under the accrual method, it is desirable, based on the matching principle, to estimate the losses on credit transactions in the period of the related credit sales. The amount of uncollectible accounts is usually estimated based on experience. For example, if in the past, 2% of credit sales have been uncollectible, a reasonable estimate is that 2% of the current period's credit sales will also be uncollectible. An adjusting entry records (debits) the estimated loss as bad debt expense. The credit is to a balance sheet account called allowance for doubtful accounts. The balance sheet reports accounts receivable at their full amount. Allowance for doubtful accounts is a contra-account and is shown as a reduction of accounts receivable on the balance sheet.

Contra-account for doubtful accounts

When it is eventually determined that an accounts receivable is uncollectible, an entry is made debiting allowance for doubtful accounts and crediting accounts receivable. This entry removes the uncollectible account. The related expense was previously recognized in the period of the sale.

Inventories — Inventories are also subject to valuations different than cost. When the market price is lower than the amount paid for any of the items in inventory, it is appropriate to price them at the current market price. So the rule of lower cost or market applies to inventories as well as marketable securities. This method of valuing inventories is disclosed on the balance sheet or as footnotes to the financial statements.

Prepaid expenses — Prepaid expenses, discussed in Chapter 4, include assets such as insurance premiums or cleaning supplies paid for in advance of being used.

Noncurrent Assets

Investments and Advances — Noncurrent assets include investments in affiliated companies and amounts due from them later than one year's time. Other securities purchased for long-term investment are also included in noncurrent assets. The basis of valuing these assets should be shown.

Fixed Assets — Fixed assets — property and equipment — are shown at cost on the balance sheet. For hospitality firms, fixed assets are usually land, land improvements, buildings, furniture, fixtures and equipment, china, glassware, silver, linen, and uniforms. They appear in this order on the balance sheet.

The accounting system provides a separate accumulated depreciation account for each type of fixed asset. Land is not depreciable; however, land improvements such as a parking lot are depreciable. China, glassware, silver, linen, and uniforms receive special treatment that is covered in Chapter 8.

Depreciation account for fixed assets

Accumulated depreciation is another example of a contra-account. It offsets the cost of the fixed asset to arrive at the net book value. This section of a typical balance sheet is given in Exhibit 2.

Exhibit 2

Fixed Assets	Cost	Accumulated Depreciation	Book Value
Land	$ 40,000	$ —	$ 40,000
Land Improvements	22,000	9,500	12,500
Buildings	400,000	104,200	295,800
Furniture, Fixtures, and Equipment	175,000	86,300	88,700
Total	$637,000	$200,000	$437,000

Future benefits from other noncurrent assets

Other Assets — The noncurrent assets called other assets are items such as deferred expenses, security deposits, and cash surrender value of life insurance. Charges for services that have been received but which are expected to benefit future periods are classified as deferred expense. Examples include pre-opening expenses, maintenance, advertising, and financing costs. Funds deposited with telephone, water, electric, or similar public utility companies are recorded as security deposits. Cash surrender value of life insurance represents the accrued cash surrender value as shown by the policy. Any loans against the policy should be netted against the cash surrender value.

Current Liabilities

Liabilities paid within 12 months

Current liabilities for hospitality firms are obligations due to be paid within the coming twelve months. The major types of current liabilities are short-term debt and the current portion of long-term debt, trade accounts payable, employee related liabilities, income tax liabilities, and other miscellaneous liabilities.

Obligations are incurred in the normal course of operating a business. Funds are borrowed to meet both short- and long-term needs. Established business practices allow a short delay in paying for goods and services, and a trade accounts payable ensues. Firms have obligations arising from amounts withheld from wages and other related items. Income tax is usually paid after the income is earned, and until it is paid, it is an obligation. The accrual method requires that all expenses be related to the time period incurred. If they are unpaid, they become an accrued expense included in current liabilities.

Income received prior to being earned is also an obligation of the firm. For example, a deposit a hotel receives today for a banquet to be held in thirty days is recorded as a liability. All of these events result in current liabilities and appear under this category on the balance sheet.

Noncurrent Liabilities

Noncurrent liabilities for hospitality firms include mortgages payable and other forms of long-term borrowing. Repayment is made over an extended period, and the amounts shown as noncurrent liabilities are due beyond a year from the balance sheet date.

Mortgages, etc.

Long-Term Debt — Long-term debt of lodging firms includes mortgages payable and other forms of long-term borrowing. Repayment is made over an extended period, and the amounts shown as noncurrent liabilities are due beyond a year from the balance sheet date.

Deferred Income Taxes — Deferred income taxes represent the tax effects of items reported in different periods for financial and income tax reporting purposes. Most significantly, depreciation causes these differences. Chapter 9 discusses deferred income taxes in more detail and includes an example of how to determine the amount of income taxes recognized as deferred.

Proprietorship

The content of the proprietorship section of the balance sheet depends on the structure of the organization: sole proprietorship, partnership, or corporation.

In the sole proprietorship form there is a single owner and the business is relatively small. The owner has complete responsibility for all debts and obligations and is entitled to all income. This organizational form is not considered a legal entity, and the income or loss from the business is included in the owner's personal tax return.

Sole proprietorship

The owner's investment in the business is recorded in an account bearing his or her name. Periodically the owner may need to withdraw funds from the business to meet personal needs. A drawing account is used to record withdrawals, as discussed in Chapter 4. Drawing accounts have debit balances and are contra-accounts to the owner's investment account on the balance sheet. At the end of the accounting period, the drawing account is normally closed out to the ownership account.

The partnership is similar to the sole proprietorship. However, partnerships have two or more owners and there is a drawing account for each partner. Transactions affecting the partners' drawing accounts are handled in the same manner as for sole proprietorships, except that income and losses are distributed to the individual partners on the basis of their partnership agreement. Like a sole proprietorship, a partnership is not a legal entity. Creditors can look to the personal assets of the partners in the fulfillment of business obligations. Profits or losses are included in the individual tax returns of the partners.

Partnership

The third possible organizational form is the corporation, incorporated under state laws. A corporation is a legal entity, and ownership is obtained through purchase of capital stock. There can be two classes of capital stock, preferred and common. Preferred stock has an established dividend rate and has preference in receiving dividend payments and return of capital invested in the event the corporation is dissolved. Common stock does not have an established dividend rate. In dividends and other distributions, it is subservient to the interest of the preferred stockholders. However, common stockholders generally have voting rights while preferred stockholders do not. Thus, control of the corporation is vested in the common stockholders.

Corporation

Common and preferred stock

The shareholders' equity section of a corporation balance sheet provides information on each class of stock including the par value, the number of shares authorized, and the number of shares issued. When a share of stock is sold for more than par value, an account called Additional Paid-In Capital is used to reflect the amount paid above par value. When stock is purchased back from a shareholder and held for possible resale, it is called treasury stock and is shown as a reduction of the shareholders' equity section of the balance sheet.

A separate proprietorship account entitled Retained Earnings shows the accumulated income and/or loss of corporations. Withdrawals of earnings from corporate entities are called dividends and are declared out of retained earnings. Owner/managers can also withdraw funds by being paid a salary.

Retained earnings and dividends

An example of the shareholders' equity section of the balance sheet is shown in Exhibit 3.

Footnotes to the Financial Statements

The readers of the balance sheet must have sufficient information to correctly evaluate the firm's financial position. The footnotes to the balance sheet provide information to aid in this process. Footnotes explain the nature and basis for valuing the various asset, liability, and equity accounts, and disclose any commitments and contingencies that might affect the firm's financial standing.

Footnotes for further explanation

Exhibit 3

Shareholders' Equity		
Preferred Stock, par value $100		
Authorized	10,000 shares	
Issued	8,000 shares	$ 800,000
Common Stock, par value $50		
Authorized	100,000 shares	
Issued	70,000 shares	3,500,000
Additional Paid-In Capital		400,000
Retained Earnings		1,025,000
		5,725,000
Less Common Stock in Treasury,		
at cost 1,000 shares		60,000
	Total Stockholders' Equity	$5,665,000

Balance Sheet and Footnotes of Hilton Corporation

Hilton Corporation's Balance Sheet for the years ended December 31, 1980 and 1981, and footnotes to the financial statements are shown in Exhibits 4 and 5 to illustrate how a large lodging firm reports its financial position to users. The lengthy footnotes provided to supplement the financial statements, including the income statement and the statement of changes in financial position, satisfy the full disclosure principle discussed in Chapter 2.

No amounts are provided by Hilton Corporation for "Commitments and Contingent Liabilities," but the reader is referred to "Note 8." Note 8, as shown in Exhibit 5, contains an extensive discussion of commitments and contingent liabilities.

Exhibit 4*

Hilton Hotels Corporation and Subsidiaries	Consolidated Balance Sheets *(In thousands of dollars)*		
	Assets December 31,	1981	1980
Current Assets	Cash	$ 11,647	17,950
	Temporary investments (at lower of cost		
	or market value)	133,981	127,625
	Accounts and notes receivable		
	Hotel and other (less allowance		
	for doubtful accounts of		
	$1,713 and $2,056)	40,942	36,224
	Casino (less allowance for		
	doubtful accounts of $4,736		
	and $5,308)	13,040	13,420
	Inventories — at cost (first-in, first-out)	8,910	8,748
	Other current assets	4,689	3,250
	Total current assets	213,209	207,217
Investments	Investments in and notes from 22%		
	to 50% owned companies	122,505	115,321
	Other investments	19,752	6,521
	Total investments	142,257	121,842

Exhibit 4 (continued)

Property and Equipment	Land		59,652	56,152
	Buildings and leasehold improvements		355,298	303,611
	Furniture and equipment		166,701	128,434
			581,651	488,197
	Less accumulated depreciation		186,411	164,517
			395,240	323,680
	Property held for future development or sale		34,733	31,609
	Construction in progress		25,390	6,709
	Net property and equipment		455,363	361,998
Other Assets			5,641	5,767
Total Assets			$816,470	696,824

See notes to financial statements

	Liabilities and Stockholders' Equity	December 31, 1981	1980
Current Liabilities	Accounts and notes payable	$ 85,765	61,351
	Current maturities of long-term debt	6,203	3,489
	Federal and state income taxes	12,169	10,314
	Total current liabilities	104,137	75,154
Long-term Debt	Mortgage bonds and notes, due 1982 to 2002	58,224	56,506
	8% collateral trust bonds, due 1993	13,258	14,050
	9% bank loan	50,000	50,000
	Other	4,245	3,535
		125,727	124,091
	Less current maturities	6,203	3,489
	Total long-term debt	119,524	120,602
Other Liabilities	Deferred income taxes	38,721	20,811
	Insurance reserves and other	21,533	21,379
	Total other liabilities	60,254	42,190
Commitments and Contingent Liabilities	(Note 8)		
Total Liabilities		283,915	237,946
Stockholders' Equity	Common stock, par value $2.50 per share, authorized 30,000,000 shares; issued 26,738,785 and 26,451,194 shares including shares in treasury	66,847	66,128
	Additional paid-in capital	7,224	—
	Retained earnings	460,023	394,289
		534,094	460,417
	Less 83,934 shares held in treasury (at cost)	1,539	1,539
	Total stockholders' equity	532,555	458,878
Total Liabilities and Stockholders' Equity		$816,470	696,824

*Exhibit 4 is reproduced from the Hilton Corporation's *1981 Annual Report* with permission.

Exhibit 5*

[8] Commitments and Contingent Liabilities

Commitments to various entertainers for appearances at the Company's hotel-casinos aggregated approximately $8,699,000 at December 31, 1981, substantially all of which is expected to be paid within one year.

At December 31, 1981, the Company had commitments at its wholly-owned and leased properties for major expansion and rehabilitation projects of approximately $82,163,000 of which $39,476,000 has been expended. These projects are being funded by internal cash flow.

In connection with the completion of the 1,056 room tower addition at the 50% owned Hilton Hawaiian Village, the Company has committed to make partnership contributions totalling approximately $11,500,000 in 1982.

The Company is party to an agreement with MGM Grand Hotels, Inc. for the development of property in Atlantic City, New Jersey, with each party to own a portion of the land for the construction of its own hotel-casino facilities. The agreement also provides for the sharing of the costs of developing and maintaining common areas, including a parking structure. The Company had expended approximately $29,344,000 for the Atlantic City land and development costs as of December 31, 1981. The Company has announced its intention to postpone construction of its Atlantic City hotel-casino. The project will require the approval of Nevada gaming authorities, the New Jersey Casino Control Commission and other regulatory agencies. There is no assurance that all requisite approvals will be obtained or that the hotel-casino will be constructed.

As a partner, the Company, with its partners, is jointly and severally liable for all liabilities (except non-recourse mortgage debt) of its 22% to 50% owned partnership joint ventures, other than one 27% owned company where the Company is proportionately liable. However, in each partnership, assets available to satisfy its recourse liabilities were in excess of such liabilities.

On February 10, 1981, a fire occurred at the Las Vegas Hilton which resulted in numerous claims and suits for personal injuries, wrongful deaths, property damage and punitive damages. The Company believes it will prevail or has adequate insurance coverage with respect to these claims.

The Company's property insurance covered the cost of the repairs to the hotel and the repair or replacement of damaged furniture and fixtures, as well as loss of profits and continuing expenses from business interruption. Business interruption recoveries totalling approximately $14,083,000 are included as "Other" under revenue in the accompanying Consolidated Statement of Income for the year ended December 31, 1981.

Several other lawsuits are pending against the Company. In the opinion of management, disposition of these lawsuits is expected to have no material effect on the accompanying financial statements.

*Exhibit 5 is reproduced from the Hilton Corporation's *1981 Annual Report* with permission.

Discussion Questions

1. What is the importance of the balance sheet to management, investors, and creditors?

2. Why are generally accepted accounting principles important as to how information is presented in the balance sheet?

3. How does the generally accepted accounting principle dealing with continuity of the business unit affect the bases of balance sheet assets?

4. What is the difference between short-term and long-term debt?

5. Does the account format or the report format for the balance sheet most closely represent a visual expression of the accounting equation?

6. What is the difference between a current and noncurrent asset? a current and noncurrent liability?

7. Why are marketable securities shown before accounts receivable on the balance sheet?

8. Why are deferred expenses shown after current assets on the balance sheet?

9. In what way does the liability associated with ownership of common stock differ from the liability of sole proprietors and partners?

10. When would a corporation have an additional paid-in capital account?

Problems

Problem 1

Part A. The Village Inn had $78,500 in charge sales during the month of June. In the past, 2% of charge sales on the average have proved to be uncollectible. (a) Prepare a general journal entry that establishes the bad debt expense for June and the addition to the allowance for doubtful accounts. (b) During July it was determined that a $350 accounts receivable account could not be collected. Prepare a journal entry to remove it from accounts receivable.

Part B. At the end of June when the financial statements were being prepared for the Village Inn, it was determined that items in the inventory costing $4,500 could now be purchased for $3,500. (a) Under the concept of the lower of cost or market, what should be done? (b) Marketable securities owned by the company and costing $50,000 now were worth $60,000. At what value should they be shown on the balance sheet?

Problem 2

From the list of the major balance sheet categories given below, identify the category in which the following accounts would be found:

    a. Current assets

    b. Fixed assets

    c. Deferred expenses

    d. Current liabilities

    e. Long-term liabilities

    f. Ownership equity

1. _____ Notes payable

2. _____ Building

3. _____ Accounts receivable

4. _____ Allowance for doubtful account

5. _____ Taxes payable and accrued

6. _____ Capital stock

7. _____ Prepaid supplies

8. _____ Organization expense

9. _____ Linen, china, and glassware

10. _____ Bonds payable

Problem 3

Using the account format, prepare the December 31, 1982, balance sheet for the Village Inn using the following account balances:

Assets	Debits	Credits
Accounts Receivable	$ 96,900	
Accumulated Depreciation		$338.400
Allowance for Doubtful Accounts		10,600
Building	786,400	
Land	115,500	
Cash	47,800	
Furniture & Fixtures	275,400	
Inventories	19,900	
Other Assets	172,200	
Prepaid Expense	2,400	
Liabilities & Proprietorship		
Accounts Payable		77,000
Accrued Liabilities		91,000
Additional Paid-in Capital		25,000
Common Stock		300,000
Current Portion — Long-term Debt		14,000
Long-term Debt		527,000
Other Current Liabilities		40,800
Retained Earnings		92,700

Chapter Six

The Income Statement

Perspective

In contrast to the balance sheet, which presents a business's financial condition at a given time, the income statement reports revenues and expenses, and thus income or loss, over a period of time. It is a flow statement. Information is grouped into revenues followed by expenses with net income on the bottom line.

The names and classifications of revenue and expense accounts are standardized throughout business, as well as specifically for the hospitality industry.

Creditors, investors, and governments all need the information on income statements. Since management needs more data than these external users to help in managing and controlling the business, more detailed income statements are prepared for internal use.

In addition to a company-wide income statement, management may want individual income statements by operating department and cost centers—called supporting schedules. They are brought forward and summarized in the income statement.

The Income Statement

The income statement reports on the results of operations by summarizing the revenues earned and the expenses incurred during a time period. When revenues exceed expenses, operations have been profitable. If the reverse is true, operations have lost money.

Balance sheet — moment in time

Income statement — period of time

The balance sheet is a static statement since it reports the financial position of the business at a moment in time. The income statement, on the other hand, is a flow statement because it reports revenues and expenses and the resulting income or loss for a period of time. Thus, the income statement reports the operations of a firm between two balance sheet dates, as shown below:

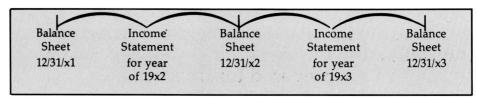

| Balance Sheet 12/31/x1 | Income Statement for year of 19x2 | Balance Sheet 12/31/x2 | Income Statement for year of 19x3 | Balance Sheet 12/31/x3 |

There is a logical relationship between the accounts of the balance sheet and the income statement. When revenues are earned, they result in an increase in an asset account. As expenses are incurred, they result in either a reduction in an asset account or an increase in a liability account. When operations are profitable and income is left in the business, the proprietorship account increases. A loss has the opposite effect on proprietorship. This relationship is illustrated below:

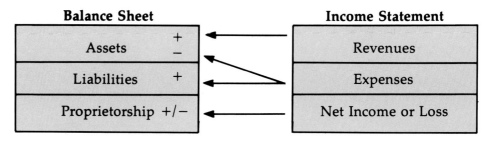

Balance Sheet		Income Statement
Assets	+ / −	Revenues
Liabilities	+	Expenses
Proprietorship	+/−	Net Income or Loss

The format of the income statement reveals net income by first stating the revenues followed by expenses. Subtracting expenses from revenues gives the income or loss for the period.

Revenues, increases in proprietorship, are principally generated from the sale of goods or from providing services. Revenues are also earned from investments and from gains on the sale of investments and assets the business no longer needs. The accounting entry for a revenue is a debit to an asset account (cash or accounts receivable) and a credit to a revenue account.

Revenues

Expenses, decreases in proprietorship, represent using organizational resources in conducting operations. The accounting entry is a debit to the expense account and a credit to either cash or a liability account such as accounts payable.

Expenses

When the income statement is prepared at the end of the accounting period, the revenue and expense accounts are closed out and the income or loss transferred to the proprietorship accounts, as discussed in Chapter 4.

External Users of Income Statements

For some external users, the income statement is the most important financial statement. Creditors look to this statement to determine the enterprise's profitability. A creditor will grant credit more readily if the information on the income statement indicates a profitable operation. The income statement reveals information on the cost structure and how the business might react to downward turns in the economy.

Creditors and investors look for profits on income statements

An investor uses the information on the income statement in making investment decisions. Increases in the value of a company are closely tied to its ability to earn a profit. The revenue and expense relationships shown on the income statement are helpful in making that determination.

Governments base taxes on income, and therefore, use the income statement. Large hospitality companies whose capital stock is listed on a securities exchange, such as the New York Stock Exchange, must provide financial statements to the Securities & Exchange Commission annually.

Government taxes and SEC reports

The format of the income statement for external users is usually less detailed than that for internal users. The external report will give revenues by major sources and expenses by revenue source as well as the expenses common to all activities. An example of this type of income statement is shown in Exhibit 1.

Income Statements for Internal Users

The income statement is an important source of management information and should contain revenue and expense data in sufficient detail to aid in managing and controlling the business. A small hospitality firm only offering basic services does not need a great amount of detail on the income statement. Larger organizations with many revenue generating activities, each directed by a different employee, require more detailed information.

Large organizations use the concept of responsibility accounting. Under this concept, revenues and/or expense data are reported sepa-

Responsibility accounting fosters control

Exhibit 1

Vacation Inn Income Statement For the year ended December 31, 1981	
Revenues	
Rooms	$1,041,200
Food and Beverage	626,165
Telephone	52,028
Total	1,719,393
Cost and Expenses	
Rooms	264,414
Food and Beverage	506,439
Telephone	67,638
Administrative and General	206,323
Property Operation, Maintenance, and Energy Costs	169,716
Rent, Property Taxes, and Insurance	200,861
Interest Expense	52,148
Depreciation and Amortization	115,860
Total	1,583,399
Income Before Income Taxes	135,994
Income Taxes	48,707
Net Income	$ 87,287

Cost vs. profit centers

rately for each area directed by an individual held responsible for its operation. The organization is divided into cost or profit centers. A cost center is a nonrevenue generating activity or function for which separately reported expense data is desired, such as the accounting department, the personnel department, and the sales department. Generally, the larger the hotel, the more cost centers.

A profit center is a revenue-generating activity where both revenue and expense data is maintained. The rooms department and food department are examples of profit centers.

In responsibility accounting the manner in which revenues and expenses are reported fosters accountability and control over expenditures. The revenues the center earns and the direct expenses the center manager can control are identified and reported. Having information available by organizational segment aids management. Information developed for the cost and profit centers is reported in supplemental schedules to the income statement. Revenues and expenses are shown in detail by center and in total on the income statement.

Uniform Systems

The *Uniform System of Accounts for Hotels** lists a comprehensive array of revenue and expense accounts and explains the nature of each.

The *Uniform System of Accounts and Expense Dictionary for Small Hotels and Motels (USASH)*** provides a standardized accounting system for small hotels and motels, both with and without restaurant op-

---

Uniform System of Accounts for Hotels, Hotel Association of New York City, New York, NY, 1977.

**Uniform System of Accounts and Expense Dictionary for Small Hotels and Motels,* Educational Institute of the American Hotel & Motel Association, East Lansing, MI, 1981.

Exhibit 2

Items	No Restaurant Operation	Restaurant Operation
Polish—Furniture	Rooms—Operating Supplies	Rooms; F&B—Operating Supplies
Polish—Metal	Rooms—Operating Supplies	Rooms; F&B—Operating Supplies
Portieres	POM&E—R&M	POM&E—Furniture, Fixtures, Equip. & Decor
Post Office Box Rental	General—Misc.	A&G—Misc.
Postage	General—Prtg., Stat. & Post.	A&G—Postage & Telegrams
Postage Due for Guest Mail	Rooms—Misc.	Rooms—Other Operating Expenses
Postage Meter Rentals	General—Prtg., Stat. & Post.	A&G—Postage & Telegrams
Postage—for Promotional Mailings	General—Mktg.	Mktg.—Other Selling & Promotion Expenses
Postcards (Guests)	Rooms—Operating Supplies	Rooms—Operating Supplies
Postcards—for Resale	Cost of Other Mdse. Purchased for Resale	Rentals & Other Income
Posters—Safety	General—Misc.	A&G—Misc.
Pots		F&B—Other Operating Expenses
Pouches—Key	Rooms—Uniforms	Rooms; F&B—Uniforms
Powder—Talcum (Guest)	Rooms—Operating Supplies	Rooms—Operating Supplies
Power, Cost of	POM&E—Electricity	POM&E—Electric Current
Preopening Expenses	Fixed Charges—Amort.	Depr. & Amort.—Amort.—Preopening Expenses
Preparation of Copy	General—Mktg.	Mktg.—Adv.—Other Adv. Expenses
Pressing Machine Covers	Rooms—Laundry & Dry Cleaning	House Laundry—Laundry Supplies
Printed Forms	Rooms—Operating Supplies; General—Prtg. Stat. & Post.	Rooms; F&B; etc.—Operating Supplies; A&G—Prtg. & Stat.
Printed Matter—Advertising	General—Mktg.	Mktg.—Adv.—Other Adv. Expenses
Printing & Stationery	Rooms—Misc.; General—Prtg., Stat. & Post.	Rooms; F&B; etc.—Operating Supplies; A&G—Prtg. & Stat.
Prizes—Bridge (Guest)	Rooms—Operating Supplies	Rooms; F&B—Operating Supplies
Prizes—Employee Awards for Suggestions	Employee Benefits	Employee Benefits—Misc.
Professional Entertainers		F&B—Music & Entertainment
Programs—Entertainment	General—Misc.	F&B—Music & Entertainment
Protective Service	General—Misc.	A&G—Misc.
Protectors—Mattresses	Rooms—China, Glassware & Linen	Rooms—China, Glassware & Linen
Protectors—Table		F&B—China, Glass, Silver & Linen
Protest Fees	General—Misc.	A&G—Misc.
Provision for Doubtful Accounts	General—Misc.	A&G—Provision for Doubtful Accounts
Public Address System Repairs	POM&E—R&M	POM&E—Elec. & Mech. Equip.
Public Liability Insurance	General—Insurance—General	A&G—Insurance—General
Public Rooms Cleaning (on Contract)—		
Banquet		F&B—Contract Cleaning
Non-Banquet	Rooms—Contract Cleaning	Rooms—Contract Cleaning

erations. In addition to the standardized accounting system, this publication includes an extensive expense dictionary with over 1,000 expense items and appropriate expense accounts. Exhibit 2 is one page of the expense dictionary from the USASH.

Uniform systems of accounts have also been developed for clubs* and restaurants.** A uniform system of accounts allows income statements of similar hospitality organizations to be compared. Also, industry accounting experts have developed and tested these systems over several years and view them as the best approach to presenting financial information for internal purposes. Finally, for the new hospitality business, the uniform system is a turnkey system that can be quickly adapted to the business.

Contents of the Income Statement

USASH

Revenues appear first

The contents of the income statement for internal use presented here are based on the USASH. Information on the income statement is arranged to help readers understand the nature of the business's revenue producing activities as well as the expenses. Revenues are reported first by source, so that a separate account must be maintained for each type of revenue. Only revenues minor in amount are combined in a single account. Revenues earned from nonoperating activities, such as investment income, are also recorded in separate accounts. When they are significant in size, they may be shown as a separate item on the income statement.

The amount of detail on an income statement for internal use is much greater than that for external purposes. To facilitate internal management and control, revenues can be reported by market source. Food and beverage revenues can be reported by restaurant location, if desired.

Next, direct expenses for revenue activities

After revenues, direct expenses for each revenue producing activity (profit center) appear. For example, salaries and wages of employees exclusively engaged in activities related to generating room revenues are direct expenses of the rooms department. All similar expenses, such as cleaning supplies and guest supplies, are considered direct expenses of the rooms department and are shown on the income statement accordingly. Related revenue minus direct expenses shows how much that activity contributes to covering expenses common to all activities (overhead) as well as to net income.

Undistributed operating expenses

The next items reported on the income statement are undistributed operating expenses — expenses not readily identifiable by revenue source. For example, the manager's salary, an expense of general benefit to all activities, is an undistributed operating expense. The major categories of this expense are administrative and general, marketing, and property operation, maintenance, and energy costs. Undistributed operating expenses subtracted from the total profit centers contribution results in total income before fixed expenses.

Fixed expenses

Fixed expenses follow the undistributed operating expenses on the income statement. Fixed expenses are largely a function of the passage of time. They include facility expenses such as rent, property taxes, insurance, depreciation, and amortization. Interest expense is also a fixed charge.

Sale of significant assets

Occasionally the business sells an asset, such as a piece of equipment no longer needed. If significant in size, the gain or loss from the

---

*Uniform System of Accounts for Clubs, Club Managers Association of America, Washington, DC, 1982.

**Uniform System of Accounts for Restaurants, National Restaurant Association, Chicago, IL, 1968.

sale is shown as a separate item near the bottom of the income statement.

The final item on the income statement prior to net income is income taxes. Income is subject to federal, state, and even municipal income taxes. The amount of income tax applicable to the current period is subtracted to arrive at the net income for the period.

Finally, income taxes

Departmental Income Statements

Departmental income statements are developed for internal use to provide management with detailed information on operations for each accounting period. The departmental income statement format provides for a summary income statement and supporting schedules that give detailed information by operating department and cost center. An operating department supporting schedule reports both revenue and expense data. A cost center supporting schedule reports expense information. Accumulated and less detailed revenue and expense data is brought forward to the summary income statement. The number and nature of the supporting schedules depend on the size and organizational structure of the hospitality firm.

The relation of departmental income statements to the basic income statement structure, based on the USASH, is illustrated in Exhibit 3.

Exhibit 3

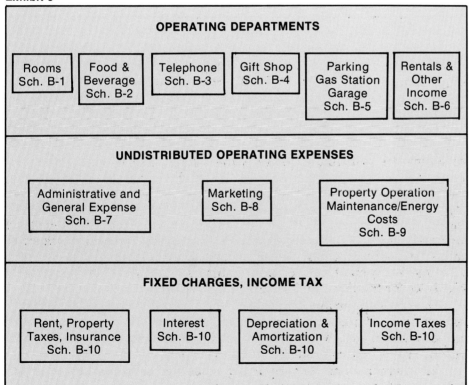

Income Statement and Supporting Schedules

A motel containing 175 rooms and a restaurant will be used to explain how the income statement and supporting schedules are inter-

Exhibit 4

	Schedule B-1
Vacation Inn	
Rooms	
For the year ended December 31, 1981	
Revenue	
Room Sales	$1,043,900
Allowances	2,700
Net Revenue	1,041,200
Expenses	
Salaries and Wages	159,304
Employee Benefits	26,030
Total Payroll and Related Expenses	185,334
Other Expenses	
China, Glassware, and Linen	12,494
Commissions	3,124
Laundry and Dry Cleaning	22,906
Operating Supplies	18,742
Other Operating Expenses	12,494
Reservation Expense	7,288
Uniforms	2,032
Total Other Expenses	79,080
Total Expenses	264,414
Departmental Income	$ 776,786

Operating department schedules

related. The motel has three operating departments: food and beverage, rooms, and telephone. Each operating department has a schedule showing the revenues earned and expenses incurred during the accounting period, as in Exhibits 4 to 6.

The motel has three cost centers for undistributed operating expenses. The first is the administrative and general expense cost center, for which the principal expense is the salaries and wages of management and other support personnel. All of the expenses included here are general in nature and would be difficult, if not impossible, to identify with a specific operating department. The second cost center is marketing. All expenses relating to sales promotion and advertising are included here. The third cost center is property operation, maintenance, and energy costs. These expenses are related to the use of a building, equipment, and energy. Exhibits 7 to 9 show the supporting schedules for the three undistributed operating expense cost centers.

The last supporting schedule to the income statement reports details of fixed charges and income taxes. Fixed charges include rent, property taxes, insurance, interest expense, depreciation, and amortization. This schedule is shown in Exhibit 10.

Schedules summarized on income statement

Information from the supporting schedules is brought forward and summarized on the income statement. For operating departments, summary totals of revenues, cost of sales, payroll and benefits, other expenses, and the department income or loss are brought forward. The cost centers report their payroll and other expenses on the income statement. With all the revenues and expenses summarized, the income or loss is determined. Exhibit 11 shows the summary income statement.

Exhibit 5

	Schedule B-2
Vacation Inn	
Food and Beverage	
For the year ended December 31, 1981	

Revenue	
Food	$442,471
Beverage	183,929
Total	626,400
Allowances	663
Net Revenue	625,737
Other Income	428
Total	626,165
Cost of Sales	
Cost of Food Consumed	177,873
Less Cost of Employee Meals	12,832
Net Cost of Food Sales	165,041
Cost of Beverage Sales	43,407
Net Cost of Sales	208,448
Gross Profit	417,717
Expenses	
Salaries and Wages	182,214
Employee Benefits	36,318
Total Payroll and Related Expenses	218,532
Other Expenses	
China, Glassware, Silver, and Linen	8,766
Kitchen Fuel	2,505
Laundry and Dry Cleaning	6,199
Licenses	3,130
Music and Entertainment	31,308
Operating Supplies	12,523
Other Operating Expenses	11,271
Uniforms	3,757
Total Other Expenses	70,160
Total Expenses	297,991
Departmental Income	$119,726

Comparative Income Statements

When measuring and evaluating the performance of a hotel, motel, club, or restaurant, a standard is needed. There are a number of possibilities. One is to use the prior year's results to measure against the current year. This approach reveals both favorable and unfavorable changes. Last year's performance may not necessarily be satisfactory, but comparing it with the current year can determine the direction of change. **Last year compared to current year**

Another standard used to measure performance is a budget. The budget is a forecast of the income statement. Variances from budget are analyzed to determine why the budget was not achieved. The organization can then take necessary steps to correct an unfavorable situation. **Current year to current budget**

A third means of measuring and evaluating performance is to compare the income statements of similar operations. For example, the operating results of similar restaurants can be compared. This compari- **Similar operations**

Exhibit 6

	Schedule B-3
Vacation Inn	
Telephone	
For the year ended December 31, 1981	
Revenue	
Local	$ 4,783
Long Distance	47,228
Service Charges	389
Less: Allowances	(372)
Total	52,028
Cost of Calls	
Local	3,587
Long Distance	35,421
Total	39,008
Rental of Equipment	7,497
Total Cost of Calls	46,505
Gross Profit (Loss)	5,523
Expenses	
Salaries and Wages	12,307
Employee Benefits	2,010
Total Payroll and Related Expenses	14,317
Other Expenses	6,816
Total Expenses	21,133
Department Income (Loss)	$(15,610)

Exhibit 7

	Schedule B-4
Vacation Inn	
Administrative and General Expenses	
For the year ended December 31, 1981	
Salaries and Wages	$ 96,997
Employee Benefits	13,478
Total Payroll and Related Expense	110,475
Other Expenses	
Commission on Credit Card Charges, Net	19,330
Date Processing Expense	8,400
Insurance — General	7.839
Miscellaneous	5,540
Postage and Telegrams	1,203
Printing and Stationery	465
Provision for Doubtful Accounts	5,432
Total Other Expenses	48,209
Total Administrative and General Expenses	$158,684

son reveals the areas in which one restaurant does a better job than another and identifies areas needing attention. These comparisons can be on an intra- or inter-company basis as well as against industry data published annually by several sources.* Exhibit 12 contains some

*Trends in the Hotel, Motel Business, Pannell Kerr Forster & Company, New York, NY, annually; U.S. Lodging Industry, Laventhol & Horwath, New York, NY, annually.

Exhibit 8

	Schedule B-5
Vacation Inn	
Marketing	
For the year ended December 31, 1981	
Sales	
Salaries and Wages	$22,420
Employee Benefits	4,580
Total Payroll and Related Expenses	27,000
Other Selling Expenses	6,421
Total Sales	33,421
Advertising	
Outdoor	4,500
Print	10,288
Total Marketing	$47,639

Exhibit 9

	Schedule B-6
Vacation Inn	
Property Operation, Maintenance, and Energy Costs	
For the year ended December 31, 1981	
Salaries and Wages	$ 27,790
Employee Benefits	3,862
Total Payroll and Related Expenses	31,652
Other Expenses	
Building	9,251
Electrical and Mechanical Equipment	16,243
Engineering Supplies	2,311
Furniture, Fixtures, Equipment & Decor	14,177
Grounds and Landscaping	4,414
Operating Supplies	2,749
Removal of Waste Matter	2,499
Total	51,644
Total Property Operation and Maintenance	83,296
Energy Costs	
Electric Current	19,012
Fuel	59,638
Water	7,770
Total Energy Costs	86,420
Total Property Operation, Maintenance, and Energy Costs	$169,716

statistics published by Pannell Kerr Forster & Company in their 1980 issue of *Trends in the Hotel Industry*.

When the businesses compared are substantially different in size, dollar comparisons are not too meaningful. To circumvent this problem, common size income statements can be developed. In a common size income statement each element is expressed as a percent of total revenue. Comparing the percentages eliminates the problem of significant differences in dollar amounts. An example of comparison of common size statements is given in Exhibit 13.

Common size statements in percents

Exhibit 10

	Schedule B-7
Fixed Charges and Income Taxes	
Vacation Inn	
For the year ended December 31, 1981	
Rent	
Real Estate	$117,225
Electronic Data Processing Equipment	18,000
Total Rent	135,225
Property Taxes	55,650
Insurance on Building and Contents	9,986
Total Rent, Property Tax, and Insurance	$200,861
Interest Expense	
Notes Payable	$ 52,148
Total Interest Expense	$ 52,148
Depreciation and Amortization	
Depreciation — Furniture, Fixtures, and Equipment	$ 85,272
Amortization — Leasehold Improvements	30,588
Total Depreciation and Amortization	$115,860
Federal and State Income Taxes	
Federal — Current	$ 43,307
State — Current	5,400
Total Federal and State Income Taxes	$ 48,707

Exhibit 11

Vacation Inn
Statement of Income
For the year ended December 31, 1981

				Current Period		
	Schedules	Net Revenues	Cost of Sales	Payroll and Related Expenses	Other Expense	Income (Loss)
Operating Departments						
Rooms	B-1	$1,041,200	$ ——	$185,334	$ 79,080	$776,786
Food and Beverage	B-2	626,165	208,448	218,532	79,459	119,726
Telephone	B-3	52,028	46,505	14,317	6,816	(15,610)
Total Operating Departments		1,719,393	254,953	418,183	165,355	880,902
Undistributed Operating Expenses						
Administrative and General Expenses	B-4			110,475	48,209	158,684
Marketing	B-5			27,000	20,639	47,639
Property, Operation, Maintenance and						
Energy Costs	B-6			31,652	138,064	169,716
Total Undistributed Operating Expenses				142,127	233,912	376,039
Total Income Before Fixed Charges		$1,719,393	$254,953	$560,310	$399,267	504,863
Rent, Property Taxes, and Insurance	B-7					200,861
Interest	B-7					52,148
Depreciation and Amortization	B-7					115,860
Income Before Income Taxes						135,994
Income Tax	B-7					48,707
Net income						$ 87,287

Exhibit 12

800 HOTELS AND MOTELS
Comparative Results of Operations—1980 vs. 1979
Percentage Distribution of Revenues and Expenses

	1980	1979
Revenues:		
Rooms	60.2%	59.2%
Food—Including Other Income	24.3	25.1
Beverages	9.0	9.4
Telephone	2.4	2.4
Other Operated Departments	1.9	1.8
Rentals and Other Income	2.2	2.1
Total Revenues	100.0%	100.0%
Departmental Costs and Expenses:		
Rooms	15.3%	15.1%
Food and Beverages	26.7	27.8
Telephone	3.1	3.2
Other Operated Departments	1.3	1.3
Total Costs and Expenses	46.4%	47.4%
Total Operated Departmental Income	53.6%	52.6%
Undistributed Operating Expenses:		
Administrative and General	7.8%	7.7%
Management Fees*	2.5	2.3
Marketing	3.6	3.6
Franchise Fees*	.5	.4
Guest Entertainment*	.1	.1
Property Operation and Maintenance	5.7	5.6
Energy Costs	4.7	4.2
Total Undistributed Expenses	24.9%	23.9%
Income Before Fixed Charges	28.7%	28.7%
Property Taxes and Insurance:		
Property Taxes and Other Municipal Charges	2.6%	2.8%
Insurance on Building and Contents	.5	.4
Total Property Taxes and Insurance	3.1%	3.2%
Income Before Other Fixed Charges**	25.6%	25.5%
Percentage of Occupancy	69.9%	72.8%
Average Daily Rate per Occupied Room	$45.55	$39.26
Average Daily Room Rate per Guest	$30.90	$26.43
Percentage of Double Occupancy	47.4%	48.5%
Average Size (Rooms)	263	261

	1980	1979
Rooms Department:		
Rooms Net Revenue	100.0%	100.0%
Departmental Expenses:		
Salaries and Wages Including Vacation	13.9%	14.0%
Employees' Meals	.4	.4
Payroll Taxes and Employee Benefits	3.0	3.0
Subtotal	17.3%	17.4%
Laundry and Dry Cleaning	1.5	1.8
China, Glassware, Silver and Linen	1.0	1.0
Commissions	1.5	1.5
Reservation Expenses	.7	.8
Contract Cleaning	.3	.3
All Other Expenses	3.0	2.7
Total Rooms Expenses	25.3%	25.5%
Rooms Departmental Income	74.7%	74.5%
Food and Beverage Department:		
Food Net Revenue	100.0%	100.0%
Cost of Food Consumed	37.0%	38.0%
Less: Cost of Employees' Meals	3.4	3.3
Net Cost of Food Sales	33.6%	34.7%
Food Gross Profit	66.4%	65.3%
Beverage Net Revenue	100.0%	100.0%
Cost of Beverage Sales	21.4	21.6
Beverage Gross Profit	78.6%	78.4%
Total Food and Beverage Revenue	100.0%	100.0%
Net Cost of Food and Beverage Sales	30.2	31.0
Gross Profit on Combined Sales	69.8%	69.0%
Public Room Rentals	1.8	1.8
Other Income	1.3	1.4
Gross Profit and Other Income	72.9%	72.2%
Departmental Expenses:		
Salaries and Wages Including Vacation	32.5%	31.8%
Employees' Meals	1.5	1.5
Payroll Taxes and Employee Benefits	7.2	7.1
Subtotal	41.2%	40.4%
Music and Entertainment	2.9	2.9
Laundry and Dry Cleaning	.9	.9
Kitchen Fuel	.3	.3
China, Glassware, Silver and Linen	1.9	1.8
Contract Cleaning	.4	.4
Licenses	.2	.2
All Other Expenses	5.0	5.0
Total Food and Beverage Expenses	52.8%	51.9%
Food and Beverage Departmental Income	20.1%	20.3%

*Averages based on total groups although not all establishments reported data.
**Income before deducting Depreciation, Rent, Interest, Amortization and Income Taxes.
NOTE: Payroll Taxes and Employee Benefits distributed to each department. See Figure No. 6 on Page 11 for Payroll Cost Data.

Figure No. 5

Exhibit 13

Common Size Income Statement For the year ended December 31, 1981		
	Percent of Total Revenue	
	Vacation Inn West	Vacation Inn East
Revenues		
Rooms	60.4%	57.8%
Food and Beverage	36.4	39.6
Telephone	3.2	2.6
Total	100.0	100.0
Costs and Expenses		
Rooms	15.4	16.1
Food and Beverage	29.4	32.0
Telephone	3.9	3.7
Administrative and General	9.2	9.7
Marketing	2.8	3.8
Property Operation, Maintenance, and Energy Costs	9.9	5.9
Rent, Property Taxes, and Insurance	11.8	7.8
Interest Expense	3.0	2.1
Depreciation and Amortization	6.7	10.7
Total	92.1	91.8
Income Before Income Taxes	7.9	8.2
Income Taxes	2.8	2.6
Net Income	5.1%	5.6%

Income Statement of Hilton Corporation

Hilton Corporation's income statement for 1979, 1980, and 1981 from its 1981 annual report to stockholders is shown in Exhibit 14. Notice that Hilton Corporation's income statement is less detailed than the income statement format suggested by the USASH. In addition to the dollar amounts for revenues through net income, earnings per share (EPS), "Net Income per Share," is also shown on the income statement provided to external users. EPS is determined by dividing the average number of shares of common stock outstanding into net income. An integral part of the income statement are the footnotes which were included in Exhibit 5 of Chapter 5.

Exhibit 14*

Hilton Hotels Corporation and Subsidiaries	*Consolidated Statements of Income* *(In thousands of dollars except share data)*			
Year Ended December 31,		**1981**	**1980**	**1979**
Revenue	Rooms	$218,952	216,153	198,021
	Food and beverage	161,411	155,010	150,471
	Casino	145,054	141,095	132,888
	Casino promotional allowances	(20,746)	(19,392)	(22,171)
	Management and franchise fees	34,586	30,229	24,857
	Interest and dividends	27,481	21,266	13,696
	Other	45,966	31,232	29,868
		612,704	575,593	527,630
Expenses	Rooms	63,557	59,523	55,497
	Food and beverage	118,330	112,581	107,462
	Casino	50,690	45,509	46,072
	Other operating expenses	112,777	102,606	95,083
	Property operations	51,003	44,971	40,503
	Lease rentals	6,591	5,923	4,876
	Property taxes	10,837	12,892	10,757
	Interest (net of $1,926, $2,625, and $97 capitalized)	10,955	8,572	12,086
	Depreciation	29,603	26,493	25,000
		454,343	419,070	397,336
Income from Operations		158,361	156,523	130,294
	Earnings from 22% to 50% owned companies	38,222	38,785	35,555
Income Before Sale of Properties		196,583	195,308	165,849
	Sale of properties	—	—	14,717
Income Before Income Taxes		196,583	195,308	180,566
	Federal and state income taxes	83,960	89,176	81,283
Net Income		$112,623	106,132	99,283
Net Income per Share		$4.22	4.00	3.76

See notes to financial statements

*Exhibit 14 is reproduced from the Hilton Corporation's *1981 Annual Report* with permission.

Discussion Questions

1. How do revenues and expenses affect the balance sheet of a business enterprise?
2. When a company uses the concept of responsibility accounting, how does it affect the development of the balance sheet?
3. Why is it desirable for a hotel or motel to use a uniform system of accounts?
4. What kinds of information found on the income statement are valuable for investors?
5. What are the characteristics of direct expenses and undistributed operating expenses?
6. Why are certain kinds of expenses called fixed?
7. What are the advantages of having the income statement data reported by operating department? What is the significance of departmental income?
8. What are the principal differences between an income statement prepared for internal use and one prepared for external distribution?
9. Against what standards are income statements measured? What does each standard measure?
10. What are common size income statements?

Problems

Problem 1

From the account balance given below for the Village Inn for the year ended December 31, 1981, prepare a Rooms Department statement.

	Debits	Credits
Allowances	$ 1,150	
China, Glassware, and Linen	5,375	
Commissions	1,340	
Employee Benefits	11,200	
Laundry and Dry Cleaning	9,850	
Operating Supplies	8,060	
Other Operating Expenses	5,375	
Reservation Expense	3,125	
Salary and Wages	68,500	
Room Sales		$448,900
Uniforms	895	

Problem 2

From the account balances given below for the Village Inn for the year ended December 31, 1981, prepare a Food and Beverage Department statement.

	Debits	Credits
Allowances	$ 285	
Beverage Sales		$ 79,090
China, Glassware, Silver, and Linen	3,770	
Cost of Beverage Sales	18,665	
Cost of Employee Meals	5,510	
Cost of Food Consumed	76,485	
Employee Benefits	15,610	
Food Sales		190,260
Kitchen Fuel	1,075	
Laundry and Dry Cleaning	2,665	
Licenses	1,345	
Music and Entertainment	13,460	
Operating Supplies	5,385	
Other Income		185
Other Operating Expenses	4,845	
Salary and Wages	78,350	
Uniforms	1,615	

Problem 3

From the account balances given below for the Village Inn for the year ended December 31, 1981, prepare a Telephone Department statement.

	Debits	Credits
Allowances	$ 160	
Cost of Local Calls	1,540	
Cost of Long Distance Calls	15,230	
Employee Benefits	865	
Equipment Charges	2,720	
Local Call Revenues		$ 2,055
Long Distance Call Revenues		20,310
Other Operating Expenses	75	
Printing and Stationery	135	
Rental of Equipment	3,225	
Salary and Wages	5,300	
Service Charges	165	

108 *Hospitality Accounting*

Problem 4

From the statements developed in Problems 1-3 and the data given below, prepare an income statement using the departmental format for the Village Inn for the year ended December 31, 1981.

	Debits Payroll	Other
Administrative and General Expenses	$47,500	$41,200
Property Operation, Maintenance, and Energy Costs	13,600	49,375
Rent, Property Taxes, and Insurance		86,370
Interest Expense		22,425
Depreciation and Amortization		49,820
Income Tax		20,945

Problem 5

Based on the information below, prepare an income statement for the manager of the Harolds Hotel. The manager wants to use it in part to determine how his department managers are performing. Prepare the income statement, using the same format as shown in Exhibit 11. Information is provided as follows:

Sales: Rooms	105,430
Food	52,400
Beverage	26,720
Depreciation	5,500
Rent expense	5,400
Insurance (Fire)	2,000
Interest expense	3,330
Property taxes	1,220
Food — Cost of Sales	36% of Food Sales
Beverage — Cost of Sales	25% of Beverage Sales
Repairs & Maintenance	1,980
Payroll, Fringe Benefits, and Payroll Taxes: Food	15,000
Beverage	10,000
Rooms	20,000
Advertising & Sales Promotion	3,400
Administrative & General	20,890
Loss on Sale of Equipment	10,400
Menus: Food	500
Beverage	200
Paper Supplies — Food	500
Paper Supplies — Beverage	200
Paper Supplies — Rooms	1,450
Utility Costs	18,500
Interest Income	4,000
Income tax rate	40% of pretax income

Chapter Seven

The Statement of Changes in Financial Position

Perspective

The last of the three major financial statements is the statement of changes in financial position. It shows the flow of funds in to and out of the business, specifically:

- the amount of working capital—current assets minus current liabilities—provided by operations
- changes in financial position for the accounting period
- financing and investing activities not affecting working capital

Five steps are needed to prepare the statement of changes in financial position as illustrated in the example of the Wayside Motel.

The information on the statement of changes in financial position is not directly available from the balance sheet or the income statement. As in the example, it reveals why working capital declined.

The Statement of Changes in Financial Position

Traditionally, the principal financial statements of lodging firms have been the income statement and the balance sheet. The balance sheet, as discussed in Chapter 5, shows the business's financial position at the end of an accounting period. The income statement, as discussed in Chapter 6, reflects the results of operations for an accounting period. These statements do not provide answers to user questions such as: How much working capital was provided by operations? How much was paid in dividends? How much was spent for equipment and furnishings? How much long-term debt was incurred?

An additional financial statement called the statement of changes in financial position is designed to answer these questions and more.

Flow of funds through business

This statement shows the flow of funds into and out of the business. Funds may be defined as simply cash, working capital (current assets less current liabilities), or it may mean all financial resources. The "all financial resources" approach is working capital plus all financing and investing activity not affecting working capital. Most lodging firms favor this broad approach, which is presented in detail in this chapter. However, a cash approach will also be presented briefly at the end of the chapter.

The major objectives of this statement are to:

- Show the amount of working capital provided by operations.
- Show the changes in financial position for the period.
- Show the financing and investing activities for the period that did not affect working capital.

Change in working capital

Working capital is the excess of current assets over current liabilities. Current assets include cash, marketable securities, notes receivable, accounts receivable, inventory, and prepaid expenses. They are resources that are used in revenue producing activities, acquiring fixed assets, and paying obligations. Current liabilities include notes payable, accounts payable, and accrued expenses. They represent obligations at the balance sheet date that must be paid in the coming twelve months. The change in working capital is measured in terms of the amount of working capital at the beginning of the period compared to the end.

Changes in the composition of the items making up working capital are not considered, only change in the amount of working capital. Accounting transactions that occur exclusively within the current asset and current liability accounts do not change the amount of working capital, only its makeup. For example, purchasing inventory on credit would result in an entry debiting inventory and crediting accounts payable. This entry would increase current assets and current liabilities by an equal amount but not affect working capital.

We do not have to examine each transaction in order to prepare a statement of changes in financial position. The accounting transactions that affect working capital involve both the current accounts (either assets or liabilities) and the noncurrent accounts (assets, long-term liabilities, and proprietorship). For example, the purchase of a delivery truck for cash would reduce a current asset account (cash) and increase a fixed asset account (trucks). This transaction would reduce working capital. By identifying the transactions that affect working capital, we can explain the changes in the financial position of the company.

Preparing the Statement of Changes in Financial Position

The income statement and balance sheet are the principal sources of information for preparing the statement of changes in financial position. In addition, details of transactions affecting noncurrent balance sheet accounts must be reviewed.

A five step approach is suggested for preparing the statement of changes in financial position:

1. Determine change in working capital for the period.
2. Determine how operations for the period have affected working capital.
3. Determine how changes in noncurrent balance sheet accounts have affected working capital.
4. Prepare the statement of changes in financial position.
5. Check the accuracy of the statement of changes in financial position.

Exhibits 1 and 2 contain the balance sheets and income statement for the Wayside Motel that illustrate these five steps.

The initial step in preparing the statement of changes in financial position is to determine the change in working capital for the accounting period. This is done by developing a schedule from the balance sheets showing each current asset and liability at the beginning and end of the accounting period. From this information, the change in each account and the net change in working capital can be calculated. Exhibit 3 gives the schedule for the working capital information for the Wayside Motel developed from the balance sheets.

Step 1

Calculate change in accounts and net change

The schedule shows that working capital has decreased significantly during the year, from $125,883 at the end of 1981 to $19,896 at the end of 1982. In the current asset accounts, marketable securities held at the beginning of the year have been sold. The current liability accounts show a new note payable and decline in the amount of accounts payable. So, current assets have decreased and current liabilities have increased. These two changes combine to show a decrease in working capital of $105,987.

Exhibit 1

	December 31, 1982	December 31, 1981	Increase (Decrease)
Wayside Motel			
Balance Sheets			
For December 31, 1981 and 1982			
Current Assets			
Cash	$ 39,278	$ 32,540	$ 6,738
Marketable Securities	—	100,000	(100,000)
Accounts Receivable	3,789	3,811	(22)
Supplies Inventory	11,936	10,833	1,103
Prepaid Insurance	4,667	4,318	349
Total Current Assets	59,670	151,502	(91,832)
Property and Equipment, At Cost			
Land	312,000	312,000	— 0 —
Building	1,827,817	1,572,805	255,012
Equipment and Furniture	241,470	213,843	27,627
Less Accumulated Depreciation	311,137	303,227	7,910
Total Assets	$2,129,820	$1,946,923	$ 182,897
Current Liabilities			
Notes Payable	$ 25,000	$ —	$ 25,000
Accounts Payable	6,821	18,776	(11,955)
Accrued Wages	7,953	6,843	1,110
Total Current Liabilities	39,774	25,619	14,155
Long-Term Liabilities			
Mortgage Payable	1,155,399	1,000,695	154,704
Shareholders' Equity			
Common Stock, No Par, Authorized 100,000 Shares, Issued 75,000 Shares	750,000	750,000	—0—
Retained Earnings	184,647	170,609	14,038
Total Liabilities and Shareholders' Equity	$2,129,820	$1,946,923	$ 182,897

Why working capital changes

The working capital schedule reflects the changes in composition and amount, but does not reveal why these changes took place. Working capital increases principally because of:

1. Profitable operations resulting in income for the period.
2. The sale of property or equipment.
3. Added investment by the owners of the business.
4. Borrowing funds repayable in future years.

The major causes of working capital decreases are:

1. Unprofitable operations resulting in a loss for the period.
2. Purchases of property and equipment.
3. Repayment of long-term debt.
4. Withdrawal of earnings (for example, payment of dividends).
5. Withdrawal of invested capital by the owners (for example, repurchase of capital stock that had been sold).

Exhibit 2

Wayside Motel Income Statement and Statement of Retained Earnings For the year ended December 31, 1982	
Revenues	
Rooms	$249,866
Food and Beverage	153,722
Telephone	13,936
Other Operating Income	1,006
Interest Income	785
Total	419,315
Costs and Expenses	
Rooms	65,037
Food and Beverage	124,161
Telephone	16,470
Administrative and General	50,677
Property Operation, Maintenance, and Energy Costs	54,478
Property Taxes and Insurance	11,462
Interest Expense	61,087
Depreciation	10,225
Total	393,597
Income Before Gain on Sale of Property	25,718
Gain on Sale of Property	3,000
Income Before Income Taxes	28,718
Income Tax	7,180
Net Income	21,538
Retained Earnings at Beginning of Year	170,609
Less: Dividends	7,500
Retained Earnings at End of Year	$184,647

Exhibit 3

Wayside Motel Working Capital Schedule Year ended December 31, 1982			
	December 31, 1982	December 31, 1981	Increase (Decrease)
Current Assets			
Cash	$39,278	$ 32,540	$ 6,738
Marketable Securities	—	100,000	(100,000)
Accounts Receivable	3,789	3,811	(22)
Supplies Inventory	11,936	10,833	1,103
Prepaid Insurance	4,667	4,318	349
Total	59,670	151,502	(91,832)
Current Liabilities			
Notes Payable	25,000	—	25,000
Accounts Payable	6,821	18,776	(11,955)
Accrued Wages	7,953	6,843	1,110
Total	39,774	25,619	14,155
Working Capital	$19,896	$125,883	$(105,987)

Identify nature of transactions

Step 2

Adjust for depreciation

Adjust for amortization and premiums or discounts on long-term debt

Adjust for sale of noncurrent assets

So to explain the changes in the financial position of a business enterprise, the nature of transactions affecting the amount of working capital must be identified.

The second step in preparing the statement is to determine how the income or loss for the period (operations) has affected working capital. The reported income or loss must be adjusted because the accrual method of accounting does not measure the actual change in funds. In the accrual method, expenses must be recognized in the accounting period or periods benefited rather than when the expenditure is made. So cost of equipment purchased in a single accounting period is depreciated over the period of time the firm benefits from its use.

Working capital is only affected in the period that the equipment was purchased. Since depreciation was deducted in determining net income on the income statement, depreciation must be added to income or subtracted from a loss in order to determine correctly the amount of working capital generated from operations.

Amortization of intangible assets and premium or discount on long-term debt require similar adjustments. An example of an intangible asset is the initial franchise fee. When the initial fee is paid, it reduces working capital without immediately affecting expense, so it is recorded as a deferred asset. When amortized as an expense over the life of the franchise agreement, it has no effect on working capital, and the amortization expense must be added to earnings for the period when measuring the effect of earnings on working capital.

The net income or loss from operations must also be adjusted by the gain or loss on the sale of property, equipment, and long-term investments (noncurrent assets). Gains (losses) from the sale of noncurrent assets are subtracted (added) from net income on the statement of changes in financial position. An example illustrates this process. A fixed asset with a net book value (cost less accumulated depreciation) of $5,000 is sold for $8,000 cash.

Questions	Answers
1. What gain or loss is recognized on the income statement?	Cash received ($8,000) less net book value ($5,000) equals gain ($3,000).
2. What current assets are provided by the transaction?	Cash of $8,000
3. How much does working capital increase because of the sale?	By the increase of current assets less the increase of current liabilities. Current assets (cash) increase by $8,000 while current liabilities are not affected. Therefore, working capital increases by $8,000.
4. How is net income on the statement of changes in financial position adjusted to reflect operations' effect on working capital?	The sale of the fixed asset is not part of operations as such, so the $3,000 gain must be subtracted from net income. If a loss from the sale of fixed assets had occurred, the loss would be added to net income.

Operations as a source of working capital would require the following adjustments for the Wayside Motel.

Net income	$21,538
Add back expenses not requiring	
working capital:	
Depreciation	10,225
Less gain on the sale of equipment	(3,000)
Total from operations	$28,763

The third step in preparing the statement of changes in financial position is to determine how changes in the noncurrent assets, noncurrent liabilities, and proprietorship accounts have affected working capital. The beginning and ending balance sheets are the initial source of information. Each noncurrent account is reviewed to determine if it has changed. From the Wayside Motel example, the following accounts have changed:

Step 3

Account	Balance 12/31/82	Balance 12/31/81	Increase (Decrease)
Building	$1,827,817	$1,572,805	$255,012
Equipment	241,470	213,843	27,627
Accumulated Depreciation	311,137	303,227	7,910
Mortgage Payable	1,155,399	1,000,695	154,704
Retained Earnings	184,647	170,609	14,038

Each of these changed accounts must be analyzed to determine which transactions affect working capital. This is accomplished by reviewing the account in the general ledger and, when necessary, the entry in the general journal.

Analyze changed noncurrent accounts as to effect on working capital

For the building account in our example, the general ledger shows the following:

Building	
1/1/82 Beginning balance	$1,572,805
5/31/82 Building addition	255,012
12/31/82 Ending balance	$1,827,817

The building account balance increased because an addition was added to the building. The $255,012 increase in the account represents a *use* of working capital.

The equipment account and the accumulated depreciation account show the following entries:

Equipment

1/1/82 Beginning balance	$213,843	3/12/82 Sale	$6,750
7/8/82 Purchases	34,377		
12/31/82 Ending balance	$241,470		

Accumulated Depreciation

3/12/82 Sale of equipment	$2,315	1/1/82 Beginning balance	$303,227
		12/31/82 Depreciation	10,225
		12/31/82 Ending balance	311,137

The equipment account transactions are both a source and use of working capital. The purchases of $34,377 represent a *use*, while the sale of an equipment item originally costing $6,750 is a *source* of working capital. The equipment general ledger account does not contain enough information to determine the effect of the sale on working capi-

Consult general journal tal. The general journal provides the needed information:

3/12/82	Cash		7435	
	Accumulated depreciation		2315	
	Equipment			6750
	Gain on the sale of equipment			3000

The proceeds of $7,435 from the sale represent a *source* of working capital. The gain of $3,000 is treated as a reduction in income when determining the amount of working capital provided from operations. The depreciation expense of $10,225 is an increase in working capital from operations.

The mortgage payable general ledger account shows the following entries:

Mortgage Payable

12/31/82 Mortgage payment	$50,000	1/1/82 Beginning balance	$1,000,695
		6/12/82 Increase in mortgage	204,704
		12/31/82 Ending balance	$1,205,399
			$1,155,399

The increase in the mortgage amount was related to financing of the building addition. It represents a *source* of working capital. The $50,000 payment represents a *use* of working capital.

The retained earnings account in the general ledger is:

Retained Earnings

6/30/82 Dividends declared	$7,500	1/1/82 Beginning balance	$170,609
		12/31/82 Earnings for year	21,538
		12/31/82 Ending balance	$184,647

The retained earnings account shows a *use* of funds for dividends declared. Earnings for the year are a *source* of working capital. However, as indicated earlier, they require adjustments to arrive at the actual amount of working capital provided by operations.

All of the changes in the noncurrent accounts of the Wayside Motel have now been analyzed and their effect on working capital determined. One common *source* of working capital not illustrated by this example is the sale of capital stock. Repurchase of capital stock is a *use* of working capital.

When transactions are only between noncurrent accounts, these changes do not affect working capital. For example, exchanging capital stock for equipment would not affect working capital since it does not involve a current account. The journal entry for this transaction is:

Equipment		10000	
Capital Stock			10000

Other transactions involving only noncurrent accounts include:

1. Exchange of preferred stock for common stock.

2. Exchanges — one equipment item for another.

3. Appropriation of retained earnings to a restricted retained earnings account.

4. Exchange of long-term debt for capital stock.

Although this type of transaction does not change working capital, in order to disclose all investing and financing activity of the business, this transaction is shown on the statement of changes in financial position. The item given up would be listed under sources of working capital and the item received under uses.

After all the noncurrent asset accounts have been reviewed, the fourth step is to prepare the statement. The format of this statement can vary, but it generally starts out with sources of working capital followed by uses. The bottom line shows the net increase or decrease in working capital. The statement prepared from the Wayside Motel

**Step 4
Preparing statement**

**Step 5
Check statement's
accuracy**

example is shown in Exhibit 4. Frequently, the working capital schedule, prepared in step 1, is shown at the bottom of this statement as additional information.

The fifth step in preparing the statement is to check its accuracy by comparing the statement's net decrease or increase in working capital with the amount on the schedule prepared in step 1, Exhibit 3. This provides reasonable assurances that all transactions changing working capital have been identified and accurately reported.

Exhibit 4

Wayside Motel Statement of Changes in Financial Position For the year ended December 31, 1982	
Sources of Working Capital	
Operations	
Net Income	$ 21,538
Add Expenses Not Requiring Working Capital	
Depreciation	10,225
Less Gain on the Sale of Equipment	3,000
Total from Operations	28,763
Mortgage Payable	204,704
Sale of Equipment	7,435
Total Sources of Working Capital	240,902
Uses of Working Capital	
Building Addition	255,012
Equipment Purchased	34,377
Dividends Declared	7,500
Mortgage Payment	50,000
Total Uses of Working Capital	346,889
Net Decrease in Working Capital	$(105,987)

Using the Statement of Changes in Financial Position

**What the statement
shows**

This statement provides information about the business enterprise not directly available from either the balance sheet or income statement. It shows that there was an addition made to the building and its cost as well as expenditures for related equipment. It also shows that the inflow from operations and additional borrowing did not completely offset the outflow for the addition, equipment, and mortgage payment. The statement reader understands why working capital declined.

The first portion of the statement reports the amount of working capital that has flowed into the organization from operations. The income or loss reported on the income statement has to be adjusted to determine the amount of working capital provided by operations.

The nonoperating sources and uses of working capital follow the inflow from operations, and these are not clearly indicated on the balance sheets. The change in a noncurrent account balance is the net of all account transactions. As in the Wayside Motel example, an account can have transactions that are both sources and uses of working capital.

Exhibit 5*

	Hilton Hotels Corporation and Subsidiaries	*Consolidated Statements of Changes in Financial Position* (In thousands of dollars)			

	Year Ended December 31,	1981	1980	1979
Source of Funds	Net income	$112,623	106,132	99,283
	Charges (credits) to operations not affecting working capital			
	Depreciation	29,603	26,493	25,000
	Deferred income taxes	6,862	4,465	3,594
	Gain on sale of properties	—	—	(14,717)
	Equity in earnings of 22% to 50% owned companies in excess of distributions	(7,661)	(4,998)	(6,955)
	Working capital provided by operations	141,427	132,092	106,205
	Proceeds on sale of properties	—	—	28,978
	Long-term debt financing	3,324	3,470	—
	Issuance of common stock upon conversion of debentures	302	2,124	23,327
	Payments and current maturities of notes receivable	2,597	557	740
	Proceeds from exercise of stock options	4,649	1,662	1,126
	Deferred income taxes — tax leasing transaction	11,048	—	—
	Other, net	3,029	6,009	4,420
		166,376	145,914	164,796
Use of Funds	Property and equipment additions			
	Hotel — casinos	80,947	18,101	19,421
	Hotels	40,479	29,310	18,684
	Property held for development	3,124	17,993	9,085
		124,550	65,404	47,190
	Payments and current maturities of long-term debt	4,264	6,337	25,222
	Conversion of debentures	305	2,147	23,592
	Cash dividends paid or payable	43,897	37,355	28,010
	Additional investments	16,351	1,387	2,353
		189,367	112,630	126,367
Increase (Decrease) in Working Capital		$(22,991)	33,284	38,429

Summary of Changes in Components of Working Capital

		1981	1980	1979
Increase (Decrease) in Current Assets	Cash and temporary investments	$ 53	12,000	31,110
	Accounts and notes receivable	4,338	4,838	(744)
	Inventories	162	(218)	197
	Other current assets	1,439	842	(18)
		5,992	17,462	30,545
Increase (Decrease) in Current Liabilities	Accounts and notes payable	24,414	8,795	(5,672)
	Current maturities of long-term debt	2,714	787	(3,577)
	Federal and state income taxes	1,855	(25,404)	1,365
		28,983	(15,822)	(7,884)
Increase (Decrease) in Working Capital		$(22,991)	33,284	38,429
Working Capital		$109,072	132,063	98,779

See notes to financial statements

*Exhibit 5 is reproduced from the Hilton Corporation's *1981 Annual Report* with permission.

By showing all the transactions affecting working capital, readers of this statement can understand all the factors changing the financial position of the business enterprise.

Statement of Changes in Financial Position of Hilton Corporation

Hilton Corporation's statement of changes in financial position from its 1981 annual report to stockholders is shown in Exhibit 5, which also includes a summary of changes in components of working capital. Note that the increase in working capital on the statement of changes in financial position equals that shown on the summary of changes in components of working capital. As with the balance sheet and income statement, the footnotes, as shown in Exhibit 6 of Chapter 5, are an integral part of these financial statements.

Statement of Cash Receipts and Payments

Many users of financial reports are more interested in the flow of funds defined as cash rather than as working capital or the all financial resources approach just presented. A major reason for this is that obligations are paid with cash, not working capital.

Changes in cash versus changes in working capital

The Financial Management Committee of the American Hotel & Motel Association has proposed a funds statement that shows the changes in cash. Exhibit 6 shows the format of this statement, the statement of cash receipts and payments. This statement differs from the statement of changes in financial position in that it shows changes in cash rather than changes in all financial resources. Further, this statement uses a direct approach of reporting operating activities by showing operating receipts and payments. In contrast, the statement of changes in financial position uses an indirect approach, in that it begins by listing net income then adjusting it by the items included in the income statement that do not affect working capital.

Exhibit 6*

Statement of Cash Receipts and Payments		
OPENING CASH BALANCE		**$201,580**
Operating Receipts		
Cash Sales	$ 97,830	
Collection of Charge Sales	379,250	
Other		
Total	$477,080	
Operating Payments		
Payroll	$133,210	
Payroll Taxes	8,057	
Payroll Deductions (Non-Tax)	76,152	
Utilities	46,571	
Insurance (Non-Property)	9,690	
Food and Beverage Inventories	27,215	
Operating Equipment Inventories	5,640	
Professional Fees	5,500	
Other Trade Payments	126,490	
Total	$438,525	
CASH FROM PROPERTY OPERATIONS	$ 38,555	
Other Operating Payments		
Property Taxes	$	
Property Insurance	6,025	
Lease Payments		
Interest Payments	15,200	
Management Fees	9,500	
Income Tax		
Total	30,725	
CASH FROM OPERATIONS	$ 7,830	
Non-Operating Cash Transactions		
Principal Payments	$ 5,560	
Proceeds from Outside Borrowing		
Proceeds from Sale of Assets		
Contributions/Advances from Owners		
Replacement Reserve Funding		
Capital Project Funding	5,281	
Dividends and Other Distributions		
Total	10,841	
NET INCREASE (DECREASE) IN CASH		**(3,011)**
CLOSING CASH BALANCE		**$198,569**

The above account titles are consistent with those set forth in the *Uniform System of Accounts for Hotels.*

*Geller, A. Neal and Heath, Loyd C., Solvency, Financial Statements, and the Importance of Cash-Flow Information, The Council H.R.A. Quarterly, November 1981. Reprinted with permission.

Discussion Questions

1. What additional information does the statement of changes in financial position provide that is not available from the balance sheet and income statement?

2. Why is the amount of working capital more important than the items making up working capital when explaining the changes in financial position?

3. What balance sheet accounts are considered current and noncurrent?

4. What balance sheet accounts are affected by (a) the sale of property or equipment no longer needed, and (b) the payment of dividends?

5. When using the accrual method, why does the reported income or loss require adjustments to correctly measure its effect on the financial position of the business enterprise?

6. What are the most commonly found adjustments to income or loss when measuring the effect of income or loss on changes in working capital?

7. Why do not all changes in noncurrent account balances affect the financial position of the business enterprise?

8. Why do the balance sheet account changes need to be analyzed in order to correctly prepare the statement of changes in financial position?

9. What transactions can change the retained earnings account?

10. List the steps in preparing the statement of changes in financial position?

Problems

Problem 1

The Overnight Motel purchased $20,000 in new equipment during the year ended December 31, 1981. The depreciation expense for the year amounted to $20,100. Net income was $26,300, and dividends declared and paid were $5,000. From the balance sheets given and the above information, prepare a statement of changes in financial position.

Overnight Motel Balance Sheets		
	December 31	
	1982	1981
Current Assets	$ 65,550	$ 48,380
Land	46,200	46,200
Building	374,550	374,550
Equipment	110,130	90,130
Less Accumulated Depreciation	(135,330)	(115,230)
Total Assets	$461,100	$444,030
Current Liabilities	$ 41,390	$ 45,620
Long-term Debt	152,610	152,610
Common Stock	200,000	200,000
Retained Earnings	67,100	45,800
Total Liabilities and Proprietorship	$461,100	$444,030

Problem 2

Prepare a statement of changes in financial position for the Village Hotel for the year ended December 31, 1982. The balance sheets and income statement are given below. During 1982, there were no sales of property, plant, or equipment.

Village Hotel Balance Sheets		
	December 31	
	1982	**1981**
Cash	$ 38,280	$ 48,510
Accounts Receivable — Net	69,060	58,760
Inventories	15,840	17,170
Prepaid Expense	1,920	2,150
Total Current Assets	125,100	126,590
Land	110,400	110,400
Building	629,100	629,100
Fixtures and Equipment	199,740	182,990
Less Accumulated Depreciation	(270,660)	(233,360)
Total Assets	$793,680	$815,720
Accounts Payable	$ 61,620	$ 58,790
Accrued Liabilities	12,780	14,300
Other Current Liabilities	22,640	18,790
Total Current Liabilities	97,040	91,880
Mortgage Payable	305,220	347,820
Common Stock	250,000	250,000
Retained Earnings	141,420	126,020
Total Liabilities and Proprietorship	$793,680	$815,720

Village Hotel Income Statement For the year ended December 31, 1982	
Revenues	
Rooms	$336,000
Food and Beverage	202,500
Telephone	17,800
Total	556,300
Costs and Expenses	
Rooms	85,700
Food and Beverages	163,500
Telephone	21,700
Administrative and General	51,200
Marketing	15,500
Property Operation, Maintenance, and Energy Costs	58,000
Rent, Property Taxes, and Insurance	65,600
Interest Expense	16,800
Depreciation	37,300
Total	515,300
Income Before Income Tax	41,000
Income Tax	15,600
Net Income	25,400
Retained Earnings Beginning of Year	126,020
Less Dividends	10,000
Retained Earnings End of Year	$141,420

Problem 3

Prepare a statement of changes in financial position from the financial statements for the Green River Motel given below. During the year, equipment was sold as follows:

Selling Price	$15,160
Cost	19,830
Accumulated Depreciation	12,300
Profit	7,630

Equipment was purchased during the year costing $30,000. Common stock amounting to $30,000 was also sold.

Green River Motel Balance Sheets		
	Year ended December 31 1982	1981
Cash	$ 35,090	$ 1,730
Accounts Receivable — Net	57,940	42,300
Inventories	14,520	6,560
Prepaid Expense	1,760	820
Total Current Assets	109,310	51,410
Land	84,700	84,700
Building	576,675	576,675
Fixtures and Equipment	183,095	172,925
Less Accumulated Depreciation	248,100	215,380
Franchise Cost	75,450	87,550
Total Assets	$781,130	$757,880
Accounts Payable	$ 56,485	$ 77,890
Accrued Liabilities	66,715	60,300
Other Current Liabilities	29,920	37,830
Current Portion of Long-term Debt	10,280	10,280
Total Current Liabilities	163,400	186,300
Long-term Debt	179,780	190,060
Capital Stock	275,000	250,000
Additional Paid-in Capital	30,000	25,000
Retained Earnings	132,950	106,520
Total Liabilities and Proprietorship	$781,130	$757,880

Green River Motel Income Statement and Statement of Retained Earnings Year ended December 31, 1982	
Revenues	
Rooms	$308,000
Food and Beverage	211,030
Telephone	13,870
Total	532,900
Costs and Expenses	
Rooms	82,060
Food and Beverage	156,670
Telephone	19,720
Other Operating Costs and Expenses	11,450
Administrative and General	40,240
Marketing	20,250
Guest Entertainment	11,400
Property Operation, Maintenance, and Energy Costs	28,440
Rent, Property Taxes, and Insurance	41,560
Interest Expense	11,190
Depreciation	45,020
Amortization of Franchise	12,100
Total	480,100
Income before gain on sale of property and income tax	52,800
Gain on sale of property	7,630
Income before income taxes	60,430
Income taxes	16,000
Net Income	44,430
Retained Earnings at Beginning of Year	106,520
Less Dividends Declared	18,000
Retained Earnings at End of Year	$132,950

Problem 4

The Mason Motel's comparative balance sheets at December 31 for 1981 and 1982 were:

	December 31 1981	December 31 1982
Current Assets		
Cash	$ 5,000	$ 10,000
Accounts Receivable (net of allowance)	25,000	30,000
Inventory	18,000	22,000
Fixed Assets		
Furniture and Fixtures	150,000	200,000
Buildings	500,000	500,000
Land	50,000	60,000
Less: Accumulated Depreciation on Fixed Assets	(100,000)	(150,000)
Total	$648,000	$672,000
Current Liabilities		
Accounts Payable	$ 10,000	$ 15,000
Accrued Expenses	5,000	10,000
Mortgage Payable (current portion)	15,000	15,000
Dividend Payable	5,000	—0—
Noncurrent Liabilities		
Mortgage Payable	300,000	285,000
Note from Stockholder	—0—	50,000
Equity		
Capital Stock	50,000	50,000
Paid-in Capital in Excess of Par	100,000	100,000
Retained Earnings	163,000	147,000
Total	$648,000	$672,000

Additional information is as follows:

1. The front office posting machine, which cost $8,000 and was depreciated by $4,000, was sold for $3,000.

2. No dividends were declared during the year.

3. The $50,000 note was received from Minnie Mason, the majority stockholder.

Required:

Prepare a statement of changes in financial position.

Chapter
Eight

Accounting for Expenses, Fixed Assets, and Inventory

Perspective

Three major business resources—expenses, fixed assets, and inventory—merit a chapter to themselves, but each requires a different accounting method.

The tools necessary for controlling operating expenses include purchase orders, disbursement vouchers, cash disbursements, and accounts payable journals.

Hotels and motels own property and equipment that generate revenue over several years—land, buildings, furniture, glassware, etc. Their value must be apportioned throughout their useful lives through the accounting concept of depreciation. Three methods of figuring depreciation—straight line, declining balance, and sum-of-the-years-digits—are explained and demonstrated.

Four methods of calculating the value of inventory and cost of goods sold are explained here:

- specific identification
- weighted average
- first-in, first-out
- last-in, first-out

Accounting for Expenses, Fixed Assets, and Inventory

This chapter discusses the accounting process for resources used in operations. These varied resources require diverse accounting methods to determine the amount of operating expense. Under the accrual method, expenses are recognized in the accounting period the organization benefits from their occurrence, regardless of when funds were expended. Some resources, such as property and equipment, benefit the organization over a long period of time. By recognizing depreciation, their costs are allocated to the periods benefited. Other resources, such as food and beverage inventories, are assets until they are consumed and become cost of goods sold. Many other goods and services are immediately recognized as operating expenses.

Several other topics covered in this chapter are related to accounting for operating expenses: internal controls over expenditures, alternative inventory valuation methods, calculation of cost of goods sold, and alternative methods for determining depreciation expense.

Accounting and Control Procedures for Operating Expenses

Purchase order — three part

The control techniques for general operating expenses include authorizing the expenditure and verifying that goods or services are received in the quantity and quality ordered before making payment. Authorization for expenditures can be recorded on a multicopy purchase order, describing the goods or services to be purchased, as shown in Exhibit 1. A useful purchase order form has three copies — one for the vendor, one retained by the person responsible for purchasing for the hotel, and one for the accounting department. Before an order can be placed, the individual responsible for the control of the expense must sign the purchase order.

Receiving procedures

The second step in controlling operating expenses is achieved through sound receiving procedures. Goods or services received are reviewed to determine their quantity, quality, and condition. They are counted, weighed, or measured, as well as inspected. A service performed is reviewed for approval by the person responsible for the expenditure. Normally, a receiving report giving information on the quantity of the items received is prepared. The receiving report may either be a separate document for each receipt or a form listing all the receipts for a period of time.

Exhibit 1

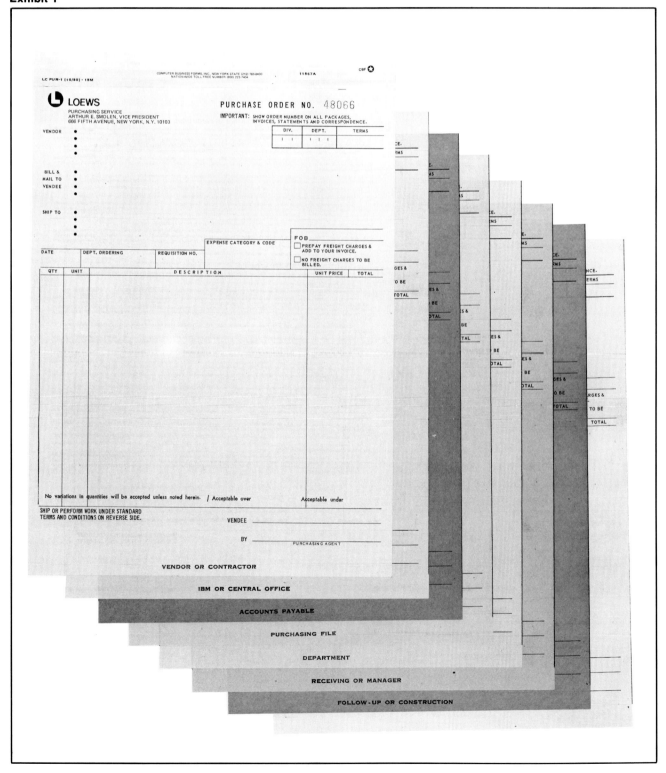

Verifying liability and recording transaction

The accounting department is responsible for verifying the liability and recording the transaction in the accounting records. The first step in this process is to compare the invoice received from the vendor with the purchase order and the receiving report. This step verifies authority, price, and quantities. Next the invoice is proved by checking the price extensions (multiplying the cost per unit by the number of units purchased) and down-footing (totaling downward) the amounts.

Determine cash discounts

Cash discounts are determined where applicable. A supplier may offer a cash discount to the hotel or motel to speed payment. Common sales terms invoicing discounts are "2/10, n/30", meaning a 2% discount of the invoice price may be taken if the invoice is paid within ten days of the invoice date. Alternatively, the invoice must be paid within thirty days. For example, three lounge chairs are purchased for a total of $600, with terms of 2/10, n/30. The invoice is dated April 1. If the invoice is paid by April 10, then $588 [600 − .02(600)] is remitted to the supplier.

When these steps are completed, the invoice is ready for payment, and the transaction can be entered in the accounting records. The timing of payment depends upon the terms of the sale; some invoices must be paid immediately, while others are payable once a month. The file of unpaid invoices at any point in time represents the hotel's accounts payable.

Prenumbered disbursement vouchers

Prenumbered disbursement vouchers are often used to record the liability and the authorization for its payment. After the supporting purchase orders, receiving reports, and invoices have been reviewed, one or more invoices for a single vendor are posted to the voucher, and payment is authorized. The use of vouchers establishes a procedure for recording and controlling the payment of liabilities. Furthermore, controlling disbursement vouchers through prenumbering insures that only properly authorized and correct payments are made. An example of this kind of voucher is shown in Exhibit 2.

Exhibit 2

Expense transactions as well as other cash disbursements are recorded in a special journal. This journal, called a cash disbursements and accounts payable journal, provides space for recording the cash disbursement (or liability incurred) and for charging the proper expense or other general ledger account. Entries in the journal for the payment of a liability are recorded in check number sequence. Even voided checks are listed to maintain a complete record of all checks. Since under the accrual method of accounting, all expenses incurred must be matched against all revenues earned during an accounting period, all unpaid expenses must be recognized in this journal at the end of the accounting period. Unpaid expenses are recorded by a debit to the proper expense account and a credit to accounts payable. When they are paid in the following accounting period, the journal entry is a debit to accounts payable and a credit to cash. Exhibit 3 is an example of a cash disbursement and accounts payable journal.

Cash disbursements and accounts payable journal

Exhibit 3

Cash Disbursements and Accounts Payable Journal

PAYEE	VOUCHER NUMBER	DATE	CHECK NUMBER	ACCOUNTS PAYABLE CREDIT	CASH DISBURSED CREDIT	CASH DISCOUNT CREDIT	ACCOUNTS PAYABLE DEBIT	COST OF GOODS SOLD FOOD DEBIT	COST OF GOODS SOLD BEVERAGE DEBIT	GENERAL LEDGER ACCOUNT	GENERAL LEDGER DEBIT

The documents supporting the accounts payable at the end of the accounting period are filed either alphabetically by vendor or by payment date. This file serves as a form of subsidiary ledger for accounts payable. The total amount due on the invoices equals the ending accounts payable balance entered in the journal and, subsequently, in the general ledger. For a more formalized form of subsidiary ledger a ledger account can be established for each vendor and liability and payment data entered.

Document file is subsidiary accounts payable ledger

In summary, operating expenses are controlled by comparing authorized purchase orders and receiving reports with the vendor's invoice before authorizing payment. Preparing disbursement vouchers for the liabilities furthers control. The accounting entry is recorded in a cash disbursements and accounts payable journal. At the end of the accounting period, the information in the journal is posted to the general ledger. This process is diagrammed in Exhibit 4.

Exhibit 4

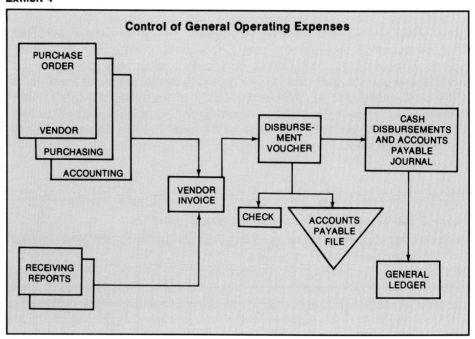

Inventory Valuation and the Cost of Goods Sold

Any hotel or motel activity that sells goods rather than services incurs an expense called cost of goods sold. For a restaurant, this is the cost of the food used in preparing the meals served. Other examples include the costs of the beverages used in preparing drinks, the gas sold in a service station, and the merchandise sold in a gift shop. In hotel or motel operations, food and beverage sales incur the largest cost of goods sold expenses.

For any accounting period, the cost of goods sold is the beginning inventory plus the purchases for the period less both the ending inventory and goods supplied to employees free of charge:

> Beginning Inventory + Purchases − Ending Inventory =
> Cost of Goods Consumed
>
> Cost of Goods Consumed − Free Goods to Employees =
> Cost of Goods Sold

Food is normally supplied free of charge to employees. The department in which the employee is working should be charged for the expense by debiting the department's employee benefits account and crediting cost of food sold.

Taking inventory   The inventory of stock on hand must be determined at the end of business on the last day of the accounting period. Inventory is taken by physically counting all the unused stock on hand and determining its dollar value. An accurate physical count and dollar value are essential in order to assign the cost of goods sold to the proper accounting period. For example, if, through error, some items are not counted and the physical inventory is understated, net profit will be understated for that period and overstated in the following period.

There are several methods for calculating the dollar value of the inventory on hand. Hotel and motel food and beverage inventories are usually valued by the specific identification method. In this method the amount actually paid for inventory items determines their values. Food and beverage items are marked with their costs when received. Tags are used for meats and other items without a suitable marking surface. Unmarked items must be looked up on the appropriate invoices to determine their costs. The costs are recorded at the same time as the physical count, and the dollar value is determined by extending the unit cost times the quantity on hand.

There are three other methods of calculating the dollar values of inventories: the weighted average method; the first-in, first-out (FIFO) method; and the last-in, first-out (LIFO) method. These methods may be suitable for use by hotels or motels for sales of goods other than food and beverages.

The weighted average method takes into consideration the cost of the units in the beginning inventory as well as the cost of the units purchased during the period. A separate calculation must be made for each item in the inventory. The total beginning inventory cost of the item plus the purchase costs of the same item, is divided by the total number of units of the item handled during the period. The figure thus obtained is the weighted average cost per unit, which is multiplied by the number of units on hand to determine the total dollar value of the ending inventory.

The first-in, first-out method assumes that the first units purchased were the first units sold, and that all sales are made in that sequence. Good inventory management dictates that the oldest stocks be sold first, and this method of valuing inventory follows this practice.

With the last-in, first-out method, although in reality the oldest stock still may be used first, for accounting purposes the sequence of assigning cost to the units sold is that the last units purchased are the first units sold. This method gains favor during inflationary periods. When last-in, first-out is used, the current costs are reflected in the cost of goods sold and are matched against revenues, which also increase as costs rise. So current higher costs are matched with current revenues.

The following simplified example illustrates the four inventory valuation methods and their effect on inventory values and cost of goods sold.

Calculating value of inventory

Specific identification

Weighted average

First-in, first-out

Last-in, first-out

		Units	Cost per Unit	Total Cost
Beginning Inventory		3	.50	$ 1.50
Purchases:	1/3	5	.62	3.10
	1/14	6	.60	3.60
	1/28	4	.65	2.60
		18		$10.80
Sales:	1/10	4		
	1/20	6		
	1/30	4		
		14		

Under the specific identification method, assuming that the oldest items were withdrawn for use first, the fourteen units sold have the following costs:

```
                3 @ $.50 = $1.50
                5 @  .62 =  3.10
                6 @  .60 =  3.60
                            ─────
                Total     $8.20 Cost of goods sold
```

The ending inventory has a value of four units at $.65 or $2.60.

In the weighted average method, the beginning inventory value of $1.50 is added to the purchases of $9.30. The total cost is $10.80 for the eighteen units handled, and the weighted average cost per unit is $.60. So the total cost of the fourteen units sold is $8.40 and the ending inventory of four units is valued at $2.40.

In the example under consideration, the first-in, first-out method produces the same values as the specific identification method. This is because the specific identification method assumes the oldest units were withdrawn first. If, by chance, this practice is not followed, and some later purchases are used first, the specific identification method results in a different value.

The last-in, first-out method results in the following costs for the fourteen units sold:

```
            4 units @ $.65 = $2.60
            6 units @  .60 =  3.60
            4 units @  .62 =  2.48
                             ─────
            Total           $8.68 Cost of goods sold
```

The ending inventory consists of one unit at $.62 and three at $.50, a total value of $2.12.

For each of the four valuation methods the results of this example are:

	Specific Identification	Weighted Average	First-in, First-out	Last-in, First-out
Cost of Goods Sold	$8.20	$8.40	$8.20	$8.68
Ending Inventory	2.60	2.40	2.60	2.12

Valuation method affects income

This example illustrates that the inventory valuation method selected does affect income. However, in most hotels, if an inventory method, once chosen, is followed consistently, then the effect of the inventory valuation method will be minor when viewing earnings over a period of time.

Control procedures

The control procedures for food and beverage purchases are similar to those used for other expenses. Purchase orders are used for wine and liquor and most other food items. They are generally not used for perishable food items purchased locally for immediate delivery. The receiving function is very important to control food and beverage costs. Goods are weighed or counted, and their quality and condition determined. Food and beverages in reserve stock must be kept in a locked area. For larger operations, a storekeeper may be employed, and requisitions used to withdraw items from stock.

Storekeeper and requisitions

Perpetual inventory records can improve control over beverage reserve stocks. For each kind of item carried in reserve stock, a record is kept of the quantity and cost. When purchases are placed in the reserve stock, they are added to the inventory, and withdrawals are deducted. Exhibit 5 is an example of a perpetual inventory card. At the end of each month a physical inventory is taken, the perpetual inventory records are verified and, when necessary, corrected. The perpetual inventory records also help in ordering beverages. To be managed properly, the reserve stocks should be kept at the lowest level, while still insuring that the item will not be out of stock before the next order is received.

Perpetual inventory

Exhibit 5

DATE	IN	OUT	TOTAL	DATE	IN	OUT	TOTAL	DATE	IN	OUT	TOTAL	DATE	IN	OUT	TOTAL

PERPETUAL INVENTORY CARD

MAXIMUM _____   MINIMUM _____

ITEM _____   SIZE _____   VENDOR 1 _____

BRAND _____   PROOF _____   VENDOR 2 _____   BAR PAR _____

When the documents supporting food and beverage purchases are reviewed for payment, vendor invoices are compared with receiving reports and purchase orders. When a purchase order has not been written, the quantity and prices on the invoice must be approved by the person responsible for food purchasing. The price extensions and footings (totals) on the invoice are verified as usual.

Food and beverage purchases are entered in the cash disbursement and accounts payable journal as payments are made to vendors. All food and beverage purchases received but still unpaid at the end of the month are entered in the journal at that time. The journal entry is a debit to purchases or cost of goods sold, and a credit to cash or accounts payable.

Journal entries

At the end of month, the total amounts debited to cost of goods sold are posted to the general ledger accounts. However, these amounts must be adjusted in order to arrive at the actual cost of goods sold for the month. Under the accounting method described above, all purchases have been debited to cost of goods sold; but since some items remain in stock, all the goods purchased have obviously not been sold. To accomplish this adjustment for remaining inventories, a physical inventory is taken and the dollar value calculated. Because both the beginning and ending inventories must be taken into consideration,

General ledger posting

Adjustment for remaining inventory

the cost of goods sold for any accounting period is determined as follows:

Add	Beginning Inventory Purchases
Equals	Goods Available for Sale
Less	Ending Inventory
Equals	Cost of Goods Consumed
Less	Free Goods to Employees
Equals	Cost of Goods Sold

Since the total amount debited to cost of goods sold and subsequently posted to the general ledger is actually the figure for goods available for sale, the correction needed, as seen in the calculation above, is the deduction of the ending inventory. Therefore, the ending inventory value is entered in the accounting records by a journal entry debiting inventories of merchandise and crediting cost of goods sold. So the journal entry is the actual cost of goods sold for the month. At the beginning of the next month, this entry is reversed to prepare the account for next month's calculation of cost of goods sold. In addition, the cost of goods provided to employees free of charge, such as food and beverage, is credited to costs of goods sold. Employee benefits for the departments in which the benefiting employees work is debited.

Accounting for Depreciation

Fixed assets

Fixed assets are the hotel's property and equipment that are used to generate revenues for periods longer than a year. In the Uniform System of Accounts, this class of assets includes land, building, permanent installations, furniture, fixtures, carpets, rugs, draperies, mechanical and electrical equipment, china, glassware, silver, linen, and uniforms. The fixed assets of a hotel or motel may constitute between 50% to 90% of its total assets, a considerably larger percentage than for most businesses. Not all hotels own all of these assets. Some hospitality firms, for example, lease their land, building, and equipment.

Depreciation

Under the accrual concept of matching expenses with revenues, a portion of the cost of a fixed asset must be recognized as an expense for each accounting period the asset is used in generating revenues. This is depreciation. The sole exception from the above list of long-lived assets is land, which is not regarded as subject to depreciation. Therefore, its purchase cost is recorded as the asset amount as long as the land is owned by the hotel or motel entity.

The amount of the annual depreciation expense of a fixed asset depends upon a number of factors:

1. The cost of the asset

2. Its estimated useful life

3. The estimated salvage value at the end of its useful life

4. The depreciation method to be used

Determining depreciation of fixed assets

The cost of a fixed asset is the total of the purchase price or construction cost, freight expense, and installation cost when applicable.

Its estimated useful life is the period of time that the asset is expected to be used in generating revenues. The salvage value is the estimated market value of the asset when it is retired from use. Some assets have value as used equipment, while others do not. The total cost of the asset less its salvage value is the portion of the cost subject to depreciation. The depreciation expense for any accounting period depends upon these factors and the method of calculating depreciation. The hotel and motel industry uses three principal depreciation methods: straight line method, declining balance method, and sum-of-the-years-digits method.

Straight line depreciation

The straight line method recognizes depreciation expense evenly through the asset's estimated life, assuming that the asset will provide benefits equally every year. Annual straight line depreciation is calculated in the following manner:

$$\frac{\text{Cost Less Salvage Value}}{\text{Estimated Life}} = \text{Annual Depreciation}$$

For example, an asset costing $10,000 with a salvage value of $2,000 and an estimated life of four years would have an annual depreciation of $2,000.

Declining balance depreciation

The declining balance method and the sum-of-the-years-digits method both assume that the asset depreciates to a greater extent in the earlier years. This assumption reflects market values for used equipment. The value of a piece of used equipment falls in the first few years by a greater amount than in each succeeding year.

The declining balance method is based on a percentage rate, in practice usually one and one-half or two times the straight line rate. In the straight line depreciation example, the four-year life produced a 25% depreciation rate. For the declining balance method, either 37.5% (one and one-half times the straight line rate) or 50% (double declining rate) is used. The first year's depreciation rate is applied to the total cost without regard to salvage values. Thereafter, the percentage rate is applied to the undepreciated balance at the beginning of the accounting period. Under this method, the asset is never fully depreciated, and its salvage value is the undepreciated balance at the end of its useful life. The annual depreciation is calculated as follows:

$$\text{Depreciation Rate} \times \text{Undepreciated Balance} = \text{Annual Depreciation}$$

Using the same example as with the straight line method and a double declining depreciation rate, depreciation of the asset would be computed in the following manner:

Year	Beginning of Year Undepreciated Balance	Depreciation	Accumulated Depreciation
1	$10,000	$5,000	$5,000
2	5,000	2,500	7,500
3	2,500	1,250	8,750
4	1,250	625	9,375

At the end of the fourth year, the undepreciated balance or salvage value is $625.

Sum-of-the-years-digits depreciation

The sum-of-the-years-digits method also provides for a larger depreciation expense in the early years. This method is based on a changing yearly depreciation rate and depends upon years of estimated useful life. First, depreciation rate is calculated in the following manner:

$$\frac{\text{Remaining Years of Life}}{\text{Sum-of-the-Years-Digits}} = \text{Applicable Yearly Depreciation Rate}$$

The sum of the digits designating each year of the asset's life is the sum-of-the-years-digits figure in the formula above. For a short life span, the sum-of-the-years-digits can be easily calculated, such as in our example $4+3+2+1=10$. But for longer life spans, a formula for determining sum-of-the-years-digits is $\frac{n(n+1)}{2}$ where n represents the estimated life of the asset. Therefore, for a fixed asset with a four-year life:

$$\text{Sum-of-the-years-digits} = \frac{n(n+1)}{2} = \frac{4(4+1)}{2} = \frac{20}{2} = 10$$

If n equals 20, the sum-of-the-years-digits is 210.

$$\frac{20(20+1)}{2} = \frac{20(21)}{2} = \frac{420}{2} = 210$$

The following table shows the results of the calculation for each year:

	Year	Remaining Years of Life at Beginning of Year	Depreciation Rate
	1	4	4/10
	2	3	3/10
	3	2	2/10
	4	1	1/10
Sum-of-the-Years-Digits	10		

Then the annual depreciation is calculated as follows: Applicable Yearly Depreciation Rate x Cost Less Salvage = Annual Depreciation. Using the earlier example of the $10,000 asset with a salvage value of $2,000, depreciation for the first year would be:

$$4/10 \times (\$10,000 - \$2,000) = \$3,200$$

Depreciation for the four years is calculated as:

Year	Rate	Depreciation for Year	Accumulated Depreciation
1	4/10	$3,200	$3,200
2	3/10	2,400	5,600
3	2/10	1,600	7,200
4	1/10	800	8,000

The undepreciated balance at the end of the fourth year is the $2,000 salvage value.

Exhibit 6 compares the depreciation expense using the three different methods, revealing that:

Three depreciation methods compared

1. The declining balance method results in greater depreciation expense in years 1 and 2 than the other methods.
2. The straight line method results in greater depreciation expense in years 3 and 4 than the other methods.
3. The declining balance method results in greater expense for the entire four years than the other methods.

Exhibit 6

Comparison of Depreciation Methods			
Year	Straight Line	Declining Balance	Sum-of-the-Years-Digits
1	$2,000	$5,000	$3,200
2	2,000	2,500	2,400
3	2,000	1,250	1,600
4	2,000	625	800
Total	$8,000	$9,375	$8,000

China, glassware, silver, linen, and uniforms present a special problem in determining depreciation expense for fixed assets. These items are continuously being replaced because of breakage and wear. As a result, this category of fixed assets would never be completely depreciated by any of the three depreciation methods above. An alternative method for china, glassware, silver, and linen items is to recognize the diminishing values by determining the fair value of the inventory of items at the end of the year. In using this method, all purchases are debited to the asset account. At the end of each year, a physical inventory is taken, and chipped or cracked china and glassware are excluded from the inventory. The fair value of the inventory is determined refering to the following schedule:

China, glassware, silver, linen, uniforms special methods of depreciation

Fair Value of China, Glassware, Silver, and Linen Expressed as a Percent of Cost				
At End of Year	China	Glassware	Silver	Linen
1	95	100	90	83 1/3
2	90	100	80	66 2/3
3	85	100	70	50
4	80	100	60	50
5 and Thereafter	75	100	50	50

The years in the table refer to the age of the restaurant, and the valuation applies to the average of all items in use regardless of age. It is assumed, however, that the equipment was new when the restaurant opened. The china, glassware, silver, and linen that are unused and still in reserve stock are valued at their cost. The difference between the calculated fair value and the asset value carried on the books is the china, glassware, silver, and linen expense for the year. The asset account is adjusted down to the computed value by the following journal entry:

	China, glassware, silver, and linen expense	XXX	
	China, glassware, silver, linen, and uniforms		XXX

Example of china depreciation method

Suppose the Erica Eatery had 120 soup bowls on hand at the beginning of the year, January 1, 1982. One hundred soup bowls were held in regular stock while the remaining twenty were retained in reserve stock. Each soup bowl in regular stock cost $.28, while each soup bowl in reserve stock cost $.30. During 1982, the Erica Eatery purchased forty soup bowls for $.32 each and placed them directly in reserve stock. Also during 1982, thirty bowls were transferred from reserve stock to regular stock to replace chipped and lost soup bowls. The physical inventory of soup bowls on December 31, 1982, showed one hundred soup bowls in regular stock and thirty soup bowls in reserve stock. Exhibit 7 reflects the flow of soup bowls during 1982. Exhibit 8 shows the calculation of soup bowl expense for 1982. The calculation assumes that 1982 is the Erica Eatery's third year of operations, and the flow of soup bowls is assumed to be on a FIFO basis.

Exhibit 7

Flow of Soup Bowls		
	Regular Stock	Reserve Stock
1/1/82 Inventory	100	20
Purchases	—	+40
Transfers	+30	−30
Chipped and Lost	−30	—
12/31/82 Inventory	100	30

Exhibit 8

Calculation of Soup Bowl Expense			
Step No.	Process	Calculations	Expense
1	Recognize expense for soup bowls on hand in regular stock at 1/1/82	100 (.28)(.05) =	$1.40
2	Recognize expense for soup bowls discarded due to chipping and soup bowls lost	30 (.28)(.85) =	7.14
3	Recognize expense for soup bowls transferred from reserve stock to regular stock during 1982	20 (.30)(.15) = 10 (.32)(.15) =	.90 .48
4	Sum of steps 1-3	Total	$9.92

The calculation of soup bowl expense may appear rather complex, but it consists of four fairly easy steps. First, the expense relating to soup bowls on hand in the regular stock at the beginning of the year is calculated by multiplying the number of soup bowls by the cost per soup bowl by the percentage to be expensed in 1982. The schedule for soup bowls (china) indicates 90% of cost at the end of the second year and 85% at the end of the third year. Since the Erica Eatery is in its third year of operation, the percentage to be expensed is 5% (90% − 85% = 5%). Second, soup bowls chipped and discarded or lost must be written-off by multiplying the number of bowls discarded and lost by their cost and then by 85%, the percentage for the end of the third year. Third, soup bowls transferred to the regular stock must be written-down to 85% as shown in the schedule of "Fair Value of China, Glassware, Silver, and Linen Expressed as a Percent of Cost." Therefore, the number of soup bowls transferred is multiplied by .15 (which is 1% − .85). For this step, note that twenty bowls cost $.30 each, and ten bowls cost $.32 each. Last, steps 1-3 are totaled.

Uniform depreciation

Uniforms generally have short economic lives. The amount of uniform expense charged each year depends on their estimated life spans. The asset account is increased by purchases of uniforms and reduced by the uniform expense.

Small lodging firms may use a different approach in accounting for china, glassware, silver, linen, and uniforms. Many small firms write-off the initial inventory of these items over a few years, but expense additional acquisitions of china, glassware, silver, linen, and uniforms when purchased.

Purchase of fixed assets

When purchasing fixed assets, the normal purchase order, receiving, and invoice procedures are followed. The purchase is entered in the cash disbursements and accounts payable journal when the payment is made or as an account payable at the end of the accounting period. The depreciation expense is journalized in the general journal.

Accounting for leasing fixed assets

In some instances, rather than purchase the equipment or building, the firm leases the item. The purpose of leasing is virtually the same as purchasing, which is "to have the item to use in its operation to provide services and thus generate revenues." Therefore, in many cases, there is no economic difference between purchasing or leasing an item. Historically, accountants have distinguished between purchases and leases that, in an economic sense, were the same. The Financial Accounting Standards Board (FASB), the accounting rule-making body in the private sector, has issued new rules requiring lessees to capitalize lease payments as fixed assets when the lease is essentially equivalent to a purchase. The FASB has established rules for determining whether or not a lease is equivalent to a purchase. This complex process is beyond the scope of this text. Several intermediate accounting textbooks contain fairly complete discussions of accounting for leases.

Discussion Questions

1. Explain how the following documents help control expenditures for operating expenses:
   a) Multi-copy purchase order
   b) Receiving report
   c) Disbursement voucher

2. How are the authority, price, and quantities for operating expenditures verified?

3. What elements make up the cost of goods sold for food sales?

4. In periods of rising prices, would the first-in, first-out or last-in, first-out inventory valuation method give the highest inventory valuation? Why?

5. What would happen to income for the period if some inventory items were not counted during the taking of inventory?

6. Why is it important that once an inventory valuation method is chosen, it be used consistently?

7. Describe how a perpetual inventory system works. What kinds of hotel or motel inventories might be kept on a perpetual inventory?

8. What cost elements make up the cost of a depreciable asset?

9. Might the declining balance or sum-of-the-years-digits depreciation methods come closer to measuring the yearly benefits received from an asset than the straight line method? Why?

10. What are the special problems involved in determining depreciation expense for china, glassware, silver, linen, and uniforms?

Problems

Problem 1

What is the cost of goods sold for the month of January, given the following information?

   a. Beginning inventory, $700

   b. Purchases during January, $17,432

   c. Ending inventory, $950

   d. Free food for food department employees during January, $300

Problem 2

The accounts used in the cash disbursement and accounts payable journal are listed below:

 a. Accounts Payable — credit
 b. Accounts Payable — debit
 c. Cash — credit
 d. Cash Discount — credit
 e. Cost of Goods Sold, Food — debit
 f. Cost of Goods Sold, Beverages — debit
 g. General Ledger — debit
 h. General ledger — credit

Required:

For each of the following transactions, indicate which accounts are debited and credited in the cash disbursements and accounts payable journal by indicating the letter of the account from the above list, along with the amount.

February 1. Payment is made for a food purchase of $4,300 within the time for an $86 cash discount.

 Account debited _____   Amount $ _____

 Account credited _____   Amount $ _____

 Account credited _____   Amount $ _____

February 2. Rent is paid for the month amounting to $1,000.

 Account debited _____   Amount $ _____

 Account credited _____   Amount $ _____

February 5. An invoice for $400 covering a purchase of guest supplies is paid. The invoice is dated February 1 and no discount is allowed.

 Account debited _____   Amount $ _____

 Account credited _____   Amount $ _____

February 28. At the end of the month, there is an unpaid invoice for a food purchase in the amount of $1,375. The items have been received and must be entered as an accounts payable.

 Account debited _____   Amount $ _____

 Account credited _____   Amount $ _____

Problem 3

The Relco Restaurant purchased a four-unit microwave oven for $1,880, subject to 6% sales tax and freight charges of $46. Installation costs including wiring were $112. The life of the new oven is estimated to be five years with no salvage value. Calculate the yearly depreciation expense for each of the five years, using each of the three depreciation methods discussed in the chapter — straight line, declining balance — 200%, and sum-of-the-years-digits methods.

Problem 4

At the end of the Eatery Restaurant's fiscal year, the data for china, glassware, silver, and accounts are:

	China	Glassware	Silver	Linen
Balance in Accounts before Adjustments	$13,505	$3,060	$6,650	$3,728
Cost of Reserve Stocks	1,012	315	—0—	—0—
Cost of Non-reserve Stocks in End of Year Inventory	7,900	1,506	6,130	3,400

The Eatery Restaurant is completing its third year of operation.

Required:
1. Calculate the fair value of the china, glassware, silver, and linen in inventory at the end of the year.
2. Determine the china, glassware, silver, and linen expense for the year.
3. Prepare a general journal entry to adjust the accounts.

Problem 5

The Casa Vana Inn purchased a front office posting machine for $5,000 on January 1, 1976. The machine was estimated to have a useful life of six years and a salvage value of $500. The sum-of-the-years-digits method of depreciation is used to calculate depreciation expense. On December 31, 1981, the front office machine was sold for $840.

Required:

1. Calculate the depreciation for the life of the posting machine.

2. Prepare a journal entry in general journal entry form to record the sale.

Chapter Nine

Accounting for Equities

Perspective

Liabilities—creditors claims—and proprietorship—owners' claims—are often referred to together as equities.

Accounting for equities breaks down into accounting for notes payable, accounts payable, unearned income, federal and state income taxes, long-term liabilities, mortgage payable, bonds payable and deferred income taxes.

Accounting for proprietorship—owners' equity—depends upon the form of the business: sole proprietorship, partnership, or corporation.

Corporations have additional accounting concerns since they incur significant organizational costs, must maintain stockholder equity accounts, and arrange for payment of cash dividends.

Accounting for Equities

The accounting equation for any business is assets equal liabilities plus proprietorship. Another way to state this relationship is assets equal claims to assets. Creditors and owners hold the claims to assets. These claims are often referred to as equities, so that the accounting equation is simplified to assets equals equities.

Liabilities and owners' claims

The two major classes of equities are liabilities and claims of owners. All claims to assets other than those of the owners are referred to as the liabilities or debts of the hospitality firm. Liabilities are amounts due to creditors, including suppliers of food and beverages, suppliers of labor (employees), suppliers of money (financial institutions), and the various governmental bodies that are owed taxes.

This chapter presents accounting for liabilities not previously discussed and owners' equity. Owners' equity is discussed from the viewpoint of the three basic types of ownership — sole proprietorships, partnerships, and corporations.

Current Liabilities

Current liabilities due in one year

A hotel or motel's obligations due within one year from a balance sheet date are commonly known as current liabilities. A firm's short-term financial strength is measured in part by comparing current assets to current liabilities. For firms in the hospitality industry, a 1 to 1 ratio of current assets to current liabilities is considered adequate. The current liabilities listed in the *Uniform System of Accounts for Small Hotels & Motels (USASH)* are:

1. Notes payable
2. Accounts payable
3. Current maturities of long-term debt
4. Unearned income
5. Federal and state income taxes
6. Accrued liabilities
7. Other current liabilities

Notes Payable

A promissory note is a written promise by the borrower to pay the lender a sum of money on demand or at a definite time. The borrower is referred to as the maker while the lender is referred to as the payee.

Exhibit 1 shows a promissory note. Notes may result from loans of money or from transactions with suppliers.

Exhibit 1   **Promissory Note**

Boston, Massachusetts _____19

On _____19_____, for value received,

THE SHERATON CORPORATION

hereby promises to pay to the order of _____

_____

at its _____ office

the sum of _____

_____ Dollars ($ _____).

with interest at _____% per annum, calculated on the basis of a 360 day year for the actual number of days elapsed, payable at maturity in Federal funds.

"This note is issued under, and is entitled to the benefits of, a certain credit agreement dated February 1, 1980 between the maker and

_____ "

THE SHERATON CORPORATION

Note Number _____ _____

Donald P. Summers
Vice President
Associate Treasurer

Generally, notes specify an annual interest rate. Interest is determined as follows:

Promissory notes specify interest and time

$$\text{principal} \times \text{interest rate} \times \text{time} = \text{interest}$$

Principal is the amount due, while time refers to the number of days from the making of the note until the payment of the note, divided by the number of days in a year. Frequently, 360 days are used in the denominator of the time element of the equation rather than the exact number of days in a year. The interest on a note dated January 1, 1982, for $1,000 at 12% interest due on April 1, would be calculated as follows:

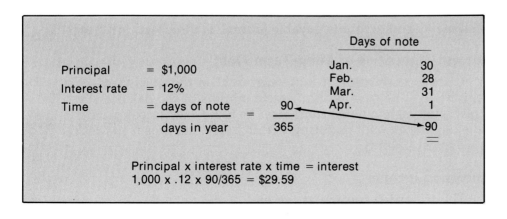

			Days of note	
Principal	= $1,000		Jan.	30
			Feb.	28
Interest rate	= 12%		Mar.	31
Time	= days of note	90	Apr.	1
	days in year	365		90

Principal x interest rate x time = interest
1,000 x .12 x 90/365 = $29.59

In determining the number of days of the note, generally the date the note was written is omitted, while the day the note is due is counted.

If 360 days is used as the denominator of the time element of the interest equation, the interest calculation is:

$$1,000 \times .12 \times 90/360 = \$30$$

Note the difference in interest is only $.41. However, on a $1,000,000 note, the difference would be $410.

Accounting entries for notes payable are illustrated below:

Activity	Accounting Entry
1. On February 1, the Joan Carol Club borrows $5,000 from the First Federal Bank of Armington for 80 days at an annual interest of 12%.	Cash 5000 Note Payable 5000
2. At the end of February the interest expense for the month is determined and recorded as follows: 5,000 x .12 x 27/360 = 45	Interest Expense 45 Interest Payable 45
3. At the end of March, the interest expense for the month is determined and recorded as follows: 5,000 x .12 x 31/360 = 51.67	Interest Expense 51 67 Interest Payable 51 67
4. On April 12, 1982, the note and interest expense are paid. Interest expense for April 1-12, 1982, is calculated as follows: 5,000 x .12 x 12/360 = 20	Interest Expense 20 Interest Payable 96 67 Notes Payable 5000 Cash 5116 67

The debit to interest payable is the sum of interest expense recorded at the end of February and March.

Accounts Payable

Accounts payable are described in the *USASH* as "amounts due creditors from whom provisions, stores, equipment or other purchases are made." These purchases are initially recorded on an accounts payable voucher, and then the vouchers are recorded in the cash disbursements and accounts payable journal as discussed in Chapter 8.

Current Maturities of Long-Term Debt

Current maturities — due within twelve months

Current maturities of long-term debt is the portion of long-term debt that will be paid within twelve months of the balance sheet date. If restricted cash, a noncurrent asset, is to be used to pay the debt, then generally the amount maturing within twelve months is not reclassified as a current liability.

Unearned Income

Eg, unearned rentals

The unearned income at the end of the year should be shown in the balance sheet as a current liability. An example of unearned income is unearned rentals. Assume the hotel rents space to an outside firm operating a gift shop at $300 per month. On January 1, the hotel receives $900 in rental for the months of January to March. The journal entry would be:

Cash			900	
Unearned rental income				900

On January 31, one third of the unearned rental income is recognized as earned by reclassifying the unearned rental income to rental income:

Unearned rental income			300	
Rental income				300

Thus, at the end of January, rental income on the income statement is $300, while unearned rental income, a current liability, is $600. At the end of February and March, $300 is reclassified as shown above. So at the end of March $900 of rental income is recognized for the year and the unearned rental income is reduced to $—0—.

Federal and State Income Taxes

Income taxes currently due to federal, state, and city governments are initially recorded in this account with a journal entry:

Income tax expense			XXX	
Accrued federal, state, and city income taxes				XXX

In certain situations a portion of the income tax expense is not due during the next twelve months and is recorded in a noncurrent liability account titled "deferred income taxes." The accounting for this occurrence will be discussed later in the chapter.

Accrued Liabilities

Expenses such as payroll and utilities are generally recorded when paid, unless there are amounts due at the end of the accounting period. Significant expenses not paid at the end of an accounting period should be accrued by recording adjusting entries in the general journal. For example, payroll for the last three days of an accounting period **Eg, payroll** may not be paid until the following period. However, an adjusting journal entry debiting the various payroll expense accounts and crediting accrued wages should be recorded as discussed in Chapter 12.

Other Current Liabilities

Other current liabilities per the *USASH* include credit balances in accounts receivable and advance deposits for room reservations. In addition, this caption of the balance sheet should include unclaimed wages, employee deposits for keys, badges, lockers, and any additional current liabilities not provided for elsewhere.

Long-Term Liabilities

Long-term liabilities are a hotel or motel's existing obligations that will be paid in accounting periods twelve months beyond the balance sheet date. Such obligations are notes payable, mortgages payable, and bonds payable. A long-term note payable is similar to the promissory note discussed previously, and accounting is similar to a short-term promissory note.

Mortgage Payable

A long-term note secured by a mortgage on property owned by the hotel or motel is referred to as mortgage notes payable, or often as simply mortgage payable. As an example of this form of financing, suppose Zebra Corporation acquires a restaurant for $1,000,000. Zebra Corporation uses $200,000 of its own cash and borrows $800,000 from the Ross National Bank. The note is for twenty-five years at 15% and is secured by a mortgage on the restaurant. Zebra Corporation owes a monthly payment of $10,246.70 to Ross National Bank. The journal entries to record the purchase and first monthly payment are:

Activity	Journal Entry		
Purchase of restaurant	Restaurant Building	1 000 000	
	Cash		200 000
	Mortgage		800 000
First payment	Mortgage Payable		246 70
	Interest Expense	10 000	
	Cash		10 246 70

The interest portion payment was calculated on the liability due at the beginning of the month as follows:

$$\text{principal} \times \text{interest rate} \times \text{time} = \text{interest expense}$$
$$800{,}000 \times .15 \times 1/12 = 10{,}000$$

The time element of 1/12 is for one month over the twelve months in a year. The difference between the payment and the interest portion of the payment is the amount the mortgage payable is reduced. Note the decrease in the mortgage payable is small initially, but slowly increases over the life of the mortgage note period, so that the $800,000 of principal is repaid after 25 years of monthly mortgage payments.

Bonds Payable

Corporations have historically issued bonds as one means of long-term financing. A bond is a written unconditional promise by the issuer of the bonds to pay the purchaser of the bonds the face value of the bond at the maturity date and interest at a rate specified on the face of the bond at specified dates. The accounting for bonds is fairly complex and is beyond the scope of this text.

Deferred Income Taxes

Deferred income taxes result from the tax effects of items reported in different accounting periods for financial and income tax purposes. Depreciation expense commonly results in deferred income taxes. For example, the Holly's Hotel uses the straight line method to depreciate its equipment for financial reporting purposes, but uses the double-declining balance method for tax purposes. The difference in income taxes based on the two methods is:

	Financial Reporting	Income Tax Reporting
Income before Depreciation and Income Taxes	$100,000	$100,000
Depreciation	10,000	15,000
Pretax Income	90,000	85,000
Income Tax Rate	.20	.20
Income Taxes	$ 18,000	$ 17,000

For financial reporting purposes, the income tax expense is $18,000, while only $17,000 is due the government in this period. The journal entry is as follows:

Income tax Expense		1 8 0 0 0	
Income Taxes Payable			1 7 0 0 0
Deferred Income Taxes			1 0 0 0

The income taxes payable of $17,000 is a current liability, while the deferred income taxes of $1,000 is a noncurrent liability.

Equity

Equity refers to the ownership of the hotel or motel. Owners have residual claims to assets. Accounting for the owners' equity is a function of the type of business organization — single proprietorship, partnership, or corporation. This section of the chapter describes each and presents the accounts for each. Advantages and drawbacks of each are beyond the scope of this text.

Organization determines accounting for owner's equity

Single Proprietorship

The single proprietorship is the simplest form of business and the owner is legally responsible for its operation. The results of the operation — profits and losses — belong to the single proprietor. Many small motels and restaurants are organized as single proprietorships.

Normally, two accounts are established for the proprietor. A capital account, for example, M. Casavana, Capital, is opened with the amount of the original investment. The capital account normally has a credit balance and is credited both for additional monies invested by the owner and for profitable operations. The capital account is debited as a result of unprofitable operations, and the drawing account is closed into the capital account at the end of each accounting period.

Capital and drawing accounts

The owner's withdrawals of money or other assets in anticipation of profits are recorded in the drawing account, for example, M. Casavana, Drawing.

The Casavana Inn's accounting for equity accounts of a single proprietorship is:

Activity	Journal Entries		
M. Casavana invests $25,000 in a ten-room motel called the Casavana Inn.	Cash M. Casavana Capital		25000 	 25000
During the first year, M. Casavana withdraws $1,000 for personal use.	M. Casavana, Drawing Cash		1000 	 1000
The Casavana Inn's first year operations are profitable, earning $5,000. (All revenue and expense accounts have been closed into the Income and Expense Summary Account.) The Income and Expense Summary Account is closed into M. Casavana, Capital, account.	Income and Expense Summary M. Casavana Capital		5000 	 5000
The M. Casavana, Drawing, account is closed into the M. Casavana, Capital, account at year end.	M. Casavana, Capital M. Casavana Drawing		1000 	 1000

Partnership

Contractual relationships

A partnership is an association of two or more individuals to carry on as joint owners a business operation to earn profit. A contractual relationship exists between the partners. The contract may be either oral or written. However, a written contract is desirable to avoid misunderstandings between partners. The agreement should include the ratio for sharing profits and losses, the investments, the withdrawals, and the rights and responsibilities of the partners.

Each partner has capital and drawing account

Two accounts are maintained for each partner — a capital account and a drawing account. The accounting for activities affecting these accounts is similar to the single proprietorship. The B & C Motel illustrates the process:

Activity	Journal Entries		

D. Bell and R. Chicklets invest $20,000 and $30,000 respectively in the B & C Motel as co-partners.	Cash
	    D. Bell, capital
	    R. Chicklets, capital
			50000
			
				20000
				30000

During the first year, D. Bell withdraws $3,000 for personal use, and R. Chicklets withdraws $5,000 for personal use.	D. Bell, Drawing
	R. Chicklets, Drawing
	   Cash
		3000
		5000
		        8000

The first year of operations is successful, earning $15,000 in profits. According to the partnership agreement, R. Chicklets is credited 60% of the profits while D. Bell is credited for 40% of the profits.	Income and Expense Summary
	   D. Bell, Capital
	   R. Chicklets, Capital
		15000
		      6000
		      9000

The drawing accounts are closed at the end of the year.	D. Bell, Capital
	R. Chicklets, Capital
	   D. Bell, Drawing
	   R. Chicklets, Drawing
		3000
		5000
		      3000
		      5000

Accounting for partnerships can be quite complex when a business has many partners, when partners join or withdraw from the partnership after the business has commenced, and when the partnership is dissolved. Accounting for these situations is beyond the scope of this text. The reader interested in studying these complex issues is encouraged to obtain more advanced accounting texts.

Corporation

A corporation is a distinct, separate legal entity whose life is not dependent upon its owners. A corporation is formed generally by the authority of state governments which issue a charter stating the powers and limitations of the particular corporation. Virtually all large hotel firms, such as Hilton, Marriott, Holiday Inn, Ramada Inn, and Hyatt, are corporations. Some hotel corporations are owned by other corporations. For example, Sheraton Corporation is owned by ITT. This form of organization is dominant not only for large hotel and restaurant chains but for all large-scale enterprises in the United States.

Distinct, separate legal entity

Organization Costs — In organizing a corporation, costs are incurred that benefit the corporation over its entire life. These organizational costs are capitalized and written-off to expense in future periods, generally three to five years. For example, Donald Smith spends $1,200 to organize the Smith Pizza Co. This amount is recorded as:

	Organizational costs	1200	
	Cash		1200

Amortization

The Smith Pizza Co. decides to amortize (write-off) the organizational costs over five years. The monthly adjusting entry to recognize the write-off is:

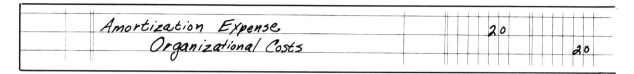

| Amortization Expense | 20 | |
| Organizational Costs | | 20 |

The monthly amount of $20 is determined by dividing the organizational costs of $1,200 by the number of months — sixty.

Stockholder Equity Accounts — Stockholders' equity consists of several accounts:

1. Common stock
2. Preferred stock
3. Paid-in capital in excess of par (stated) value
4. Retained earnings
5. Treasury stock

A corporation issues capital stock to its owners — stockholders — as evidence of their ownership in the corporation. Exhibit 2 shows a common share certificate of Loews Corporation. Different types of capital stock may be issued, each carrying with it different rights as specified on the stock certificate.

Common stock

The most common type of capital stock is called common stock. Stockholders who have common stock have the residual claim to assets after all claims of creditors and other stockholders have been satisfied.

Preferred stock

Capital stock with priority to assets and profits over common stockholders is called preferred stock. Dividends must be paid to preferred stockholders prior to paying common stockholders. However, there is no guarantee any dividends will be paid or the investment itself will be repaid.

A common feature of preferred stock is that it is cumulative. Dividends not paid for a year must be paid before common stockholders receive any dividends. For example, the McIntosh Food Corporation has $10,000 of 8% cumulative preferred stock outstanding in addition to common stock. In year 1, the corporation pays no dividend. However, in year 2, McIntosh Food Corporation wants to pay a dividend to common stockholders. But first it must pay the preferred stockholders $800 of dividends (10,000 x .08 = $800) for year 1 and $800 of dividends for year 2.

Par value

Often, capital stock is given a par value when the state authorizes it by granting the charter for the corporation. The par value is a nominal figure not necessarily related to the stock's market value or even what was paid for the stock. When the capital stock does not have a par value, generally the board of directors assigns a stated value to each share.

Capital stock may be sold at a price different than either its par or stated value. In most cases, stock is sold for more than par or stated value, and the excess, a premium, is recorded in an account called Paid in Capital in Excess of Par (or Stated if the stock has a stated value).

Exhibit 2

Common Share Certificate

When capital stock is sold for less than par or stated value, the difference is a discount and is recorded in an account called Discount on Stock. However, some states do not allow corporations chartered in their states to sell capital stock at a discount.

Retained earnings

A corporation's earnings are recorded in the retained earnings account. This account increases when a corporation is profitable and decreases when the corporation has losses, or when the board of directors of the corporation declares a dividend.

Treasury stock

Treasury stock is capital stock that the corporation has previously issued and later purchased to hold for possible reissuance.

The Blomstrom Hotel illustrates the accounting for capital stock transactions:

Activity	Journal Entries	Debit	Credit
1,000 shares of common stock, par value of $5, are sold to C. Walther for $6 per share.	Cash	6000	
	Common Stock		5000
	Paid in Capital in Excess of Par		1000
500 shares of preferred stock, stated value of $10, are sold to F. Martin for $7,000.	Cash	7000	
	Preferred Stock		5000
	Paid in Capital in Excess of Stated Value		2000
The Blomstrom Hotel reacquires 100 shares of common stock from C. Walther for $800.	Treasury Stock	800	
	Cash		800

Further accounting for capital stock, such as capital stock sold on a subscription basis and sale of treasury stock, are beyond the scope of this text. The reader interested in these topics should consult a more advanced text.

Cash Dividends — A corporation's distribution of profits to stockholders is called dividends. Dividends are *not* an expense of the corporation but a reduction of retained earnings.

Dividends paid by a corporation must first be declared by the corporation's board of directors. This declaration results in a legal liability to the corporation; therefore, a journal entry is recorded as follows:

	Debit	Credit
Retained Earnings	XXX	
Dividends Payable		XXX

Cash dividends are payable to stockholders as of a certain date called date of record, generally within one month after the declaration date. The payment date for the cash dividends generally follows by approximately two weeks. Therefore, the liability, dividends payable, recorded at the date of declaration is a current liability of the corporation.

Dividends payable is current liability

To illustrate the accounting for cash dividends, the Minor Motel is used:

Activity	Journal Entries		
The board of directors of the Minor Motel declare a cash dividend on April 1 of $5 per share to common stockholders of record on April 21. The cash dividends are to be paid on May 5; 1,000 shares of common stock are outstanding.			
April 1 — date of declaration	Retained Earnings Dividends Payable	5000	5000
April 21 — date of record	no entry		
May 5 — date of payment	Dividends Payable Cash	5000	5000

Statement of Retained Earnings — Financial statements issued by a hotel and motel corporation to outside users include an income statement, a balance sheet, a statement of changes in financial position, and a statement of retained earnings. The first three statements have been discussed at length previously. The statement of retained earnings is a statement to indicate the change in the retained earnings account during the year. Exhibit 3 illustrates a statement of retained earnings.

Exhibit 3

Edward Hotel Statement of Retained Earnings For the year ended December 31, 1982	
Retained earnings at January 1, 1982	$105,000
Add: Net income for 1982	45,000
Less: Dividends declared in 1982	30,000
Retained earnings at December 31, 1982	$120,000

If the Edward Hotel had operated at a loss in 1982, the net loss for 1982 would have been subtracted from the "retained earnings at January 1, 1982" on the statement.

Discussion Questions

1. Distinguish between current liabilities and long-term liabilities.
2. Is the entire amount of a mortgage payable considered a long-term debt? Why or why not?
3. What is the difference between federal and state income taxes payable and deferred income taxes?
4. How is interest calculated on a promissory note?
5. What are the two different types of capital stock discussed in this chapter, and how do they differ?
6. Why might a potential investor in preferred stock want the preferred stock to have the "cumulative" feature?
7. What is the difference between unissued capital stock and treasury stock?
8. What is the difference between par value and stated value in relation to capital stock?
9. What are the three important dates related to cash dividends? What entry, if any, records activity relating to dividends on each date?
10. What is the purpose of the statement of retained earnings?

Problems

Problem 1

The Erica Eatery issued a promissory note for $10,000 on January 1, 1982, for cash received. The annual interest rate is 15%, and the due date is October 31, 1982. The interest expense for the period January 1 to October 31, 1982, will be paid on October 31. For purposes of calculating interest, assume a year has 365 days.

Required:

1. What is the journal entry to record the note on January 1, 1982?
2. What is the adjusting entry on January 31, 1982, to record interest expense for January?
3. What is the entry to record the payment of the note and interest on October 31, 1982? (Assume interest expense had been accrued for each month prior to October 1, 1982.)

Problem 2

The Kouanda Motel Corporation has a balance in its retained earnings account of $18,000 on January 1, 1982. During 1982, its revenues were $400,000 and its expenses not including income taxes were $360,000. The income tax rate is 17%. During the year, cash dividends of $20,000 were declared. Also, $5,000 of dividends declared in 1981 were paid during 1982.

Required:

Prepare a statement of retained earnings for the Kouanda Motel Corporation for 1982.

Problem 3

Prepare journal entries in general journal form to record the following transactions for K & M Motel Enterprises.

a) Sold 4,000 shares of common stock to Kristy Marie for $80,000. The par value per share is $10.

b) Sold 3,000 shares of preferred stock to Monica Rae for $2,500. The stated value per share is $1.

c) Sold 1,000 shares of preferred stock to Barbara Marie for $1,200.

d) K & M Motel Enterprises purchased 500 shares of its common stock from Kristy Marie for $8,000.

e) The Board of Directors of K & M Motel Enterprises declared a dividend of $2 per share on common stock (3,500 shares outstanding) and $.10 per share on its preferred stock (3,000 shares outstanding).

Chapter Ten

Accounting in
the Front Office

Perspective

The front office is literally "up front"—located near the property's entrance where guests first arrive.

The front office records guest reservations, registrations, room rates and methods of settling accounts, while gathering information that becomes part of the accounting record for accounts receivable.

Several journals and ledgers are specific to the front office as are the source documents—vouchers.

Exact methods of recording transactions depend on the size of the operation and type of equipment available.

The chapter details accounting for the large amounts of cash handled in the front office and how to safeguard that cash. Suggested rules for accepting checks in payment of guest accounts can reduce the probability of bad checks.

Finally, the night auditor takes over the front office to complete the day's transactions and balance and check the accuracy of guests' accounts.

Accounting in the Front Office

Registration form information

The front office is the center of activities for both arranging accommodations and maintaining guests' accounts during their stay. It is called the front office because it is located near the entrance and is the point of contact between guests and management representatives.

When guests arrive at the front office, they are registered and the room rate and method of settling the account determined. In the process, information is obtained that becomes part of the accounting record. Since the information on the registration form is needed for several purposes, a multi-part form simplifies the recording of identical information. For instance, the guest's name, address, room number, and rate are needed for the guest folio record, which consists of a two (or more) part form called a ledger card and contains the guest statement and the accounting record for accounts receivable. Parts of this same information are needed for the room rack and telephone cards. Thus, a multi-part form produces both the folio record and the room rack and telephone cards. Exhibit 1 shows the various uses of a multi-part registration form.

During the guest's stay, front office personnel are responsible for entering on the folio record all charges for goods and services provided as well as payments received from the guest.

Organization of the Front Office

The front office is usually organized along functional lines. The degree of specialization depends upon the size of the hotel or motel. The manager, or innkeeper, is responsible for all front office activities.

Front office personnel

The major personnel for large hotels and motels include reservation clerks, room clerks, billing clerks, cashiers, and night auditors. In addition, some hotels and motels have personnel assigned exclusively to handle key, mail, and information services.

Reservation clerk

The reservation clerk makes reservations, as well as handles guest correspondence, maintains a file of advanced reservations, makes confirmations, and keeps a record of the availability of rooms — by type of

Exhibit 1

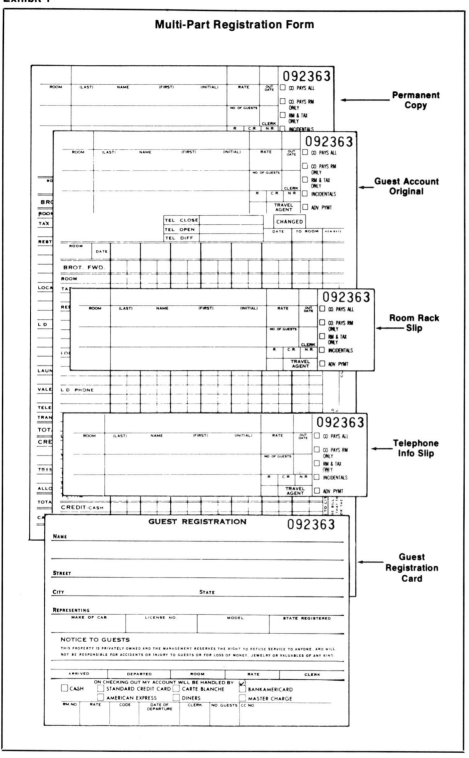

Multi-Part Registration Form

accommodation — on any future date. The reservation clerk may also process advance deposits received for reservations.

The room clerk for large hotels and motels is concerned with arri-   **Room clerk**
val and departure procedures. A guest registers upon arrival by filling out a registration card. The room clerk assigns a room and records the rental charge. Upon the guest's departure, the room clerk or a cashier

must determine that all recent charges have been posted to the guest's account. The bill is totaled and, depending on the method used to settle the account, the appropriate procedure is followed.

Guest services personnel

Guest services personnel provide mail, key, message, and information services. In large multistoried hotels and motels, these services may be offered on each floor rather than in a central location.

Billing clerk

The billing clerk is responsible for charging to guest accounts all vouchers representing food, beverage, room service, and merchandise purchases. A voucher is a record of transaction to be recorded on a guest's folio at the front desk. The billing clerk also posts credits for payments or allowances.

Cashier

The cashier handles all cash transactions in the front office. These transactions include cashing guests' checks, receiving payments, and making minor cash disbursements on behalf of guests. The cashier also is responsible for guest safe deposit boxes.

Night auditor

The night auditor works the late night shift. The night auditor posts any late charges or credits not posted by the billing clerk and enters the room rental charge in each guest account. The balance in each account is then calculated. The audit duties of the night auditor include determining that the day's postings to the accounts are accurate and in agreement with the supporting records. The organizational structure for a large facility would be:

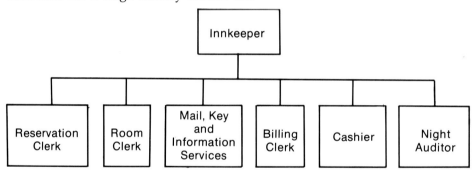

Smaller properties

Front office personnel of smaller properties have broader duties than the specialized job responsibilities described above. The room clerk may make reservations, provide all of the guest services, make postings to the guest accounts, and handle all cash receipts and disbursements in addition to the arrival and departure responsibilities. The night auditor, in addition to the regular duties, may function as the late night desk clerk.

Journals and Ledgers Used in the Front Office

Folio record enters accounting system

When front office personnel post transactions to the guest record, they are taking part in the accounting process. Information from the guest folio record becomes integrated into the hotel or motel accounting system. Charges that guests make to their folio accounts during their stays result from purchases of food, beverages, room service, laundry service, valet service, telephone use, and miscellaneous items. Credits to guest accounts result from cash payments, allowances, and transfers to another guest's account or the city ledger. In most properties, the front office seldom knows the precise time a guest will check out. Therefore, it is important that whoever is responsible for posting transactions post them as soon as possible after the information is received in the front office.

Vouchers

The voucher is the source document for posting a transaction to a guest account. It can be used exclusively to post to a guest account, or it may have a dual purpose, such as a food or beverage check has. Vouchers are prenumbered, used in numerical sequence, and carefully accounted for as a control measure. The information needed for posting to a guest account is the guest's name, room number, and the nature and amount of the item. The guest's signature on the voucher is additional verification of the transaction. Allowances representing adjustments, discounts, or the correction of errors frequently have to be made. The source document in these cases is an allowance or error voucher which must be properly authorized by the manager before it is posted to the guest's account.

Vouchers recorded on guest's folio

Guest Ledger

The guest folio accounts are filed by room number, and the file of accounts is known as the guest ledger. As vouchers are received, the folio card is pulled from the file, and the transaction is entered on the account. Exhibit 2 shows samples of assorted vouchers.

Allowance or error voucher

Exhibit 2 **Assorted Vouchers**

NAME Goldman DATE 9/21 1979 ROOM OR ACCT No 108

Posted

Folio Number

	TIME	CHARGES		
HOUR OF CALL	1:00 A.M. (P.M.)	TOLL	2	66
DISCONNECTED		TAX		
CONNECTED		SERVICE		
MINUTES	7	TOTAL	2	66

SP

LAUNDRY

NAME Vinton DATE 9/21 1979 ROOM OR ACCT. NO. 102

Posted

Folio Number

EXPLANATION		
Shirts	2	25
	2	25

SIGNED BY Lloyd Vinton

Approved R.S.

DATE 9/21 1979

NAME Zimmerman ROOM OR ACCT NO 107

Posted

Folio Number

EXPLANATION		
COD Package	14	95

Roy Zimmerman SIGNATURE

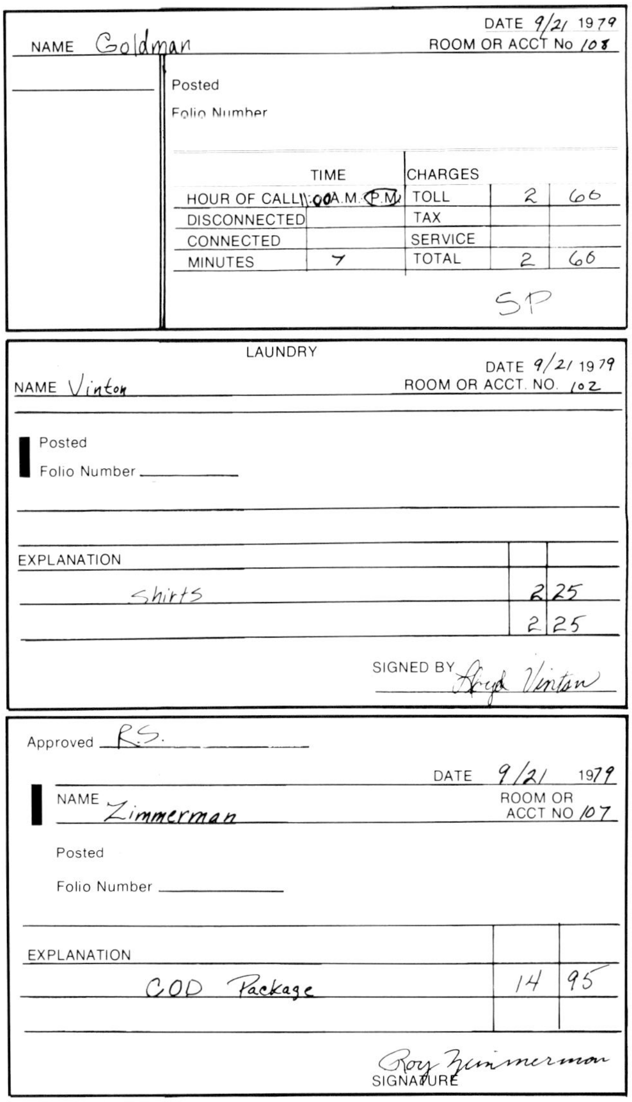

Methods of Recording Transactions

Manual, mechanical, computer

The nature of the journals and ledgers used in the front office depends on the equipment available for recording transactions. There are three possibilities. Transactions can be handwritten as part of a manual system. For small hotels or motels, a manual system can be both efficient and economical. When a facility has seventy-five rooms or more, a mechanical system using key-driven machines becomes economical. This machine records transactions on guest accounts and at the same time accumulates data in registers. Register totals are used to make accounting entries as well as to verify the accuracy of guest accounts. The third possibility is an electronic computer for recording transactions. In the past only large operations used computers as part of an integrated accounting system. However, now some hotels and motels of less than 200 rooms are using computers in their front office operations.

Manually recording transactions

In a manual system charges and payments are handwritten on the guest ledger record. Cash transactions require a second accounting record, called the front office cash receipts and disbursements journal, shown in Exhibit 3. This journal provides columns to record each element of the cash transaction as well as to identify the guest and room number. When cash is received, it results in a debit to the cash in a bank account and a credit to either the guest's account or to an account in the city ledger. Cash disbursements are recorded by a credit to cash in the bank and a debit to the appropriate account in the guest or city ledger (explained in detail later). Transactions recorded in the journal must be posted to the guest or city ledger account. At the end of each

Exhibit 3   **Front Office Cash Receipts and Disbursements Journal**

DATE	ROOM NUMBER	NAME	CASH RECEIPTS				CASH DISBURSEMENTS			DETAIL
			DEBITS		CREDITS		DEBITS		CREDIT	
			Cash in bank	Other	Guest	City	Guest	City	Cash in bank	

work shift, the journal can be subtotaled, and the amount of cash recorded therein compared with the amount received during the period.

Protecting Cash

Cash is the most vulnerable asset. In order to insure that cash is protected, policies, procedures, and responsibility for handling cash must be established. Front office employees have three requirements in handling cash. First, they need sufficient funds to make change. Next, they must be able to record each transaction involving cash. Finally, employees must record the amount of cash they receive during their work shifts.

Employees' bank

To meet the first requirement, employees are supplied with a fixed sum of money called a bank. The bank is kept supplied with currency and coins suitable for making change. Employees provided with a bank are required to sign a statement acknowledging the amount of the bank and its purpose. The employee must have a safe place to keep the bank when off duty. A bank report detailing the type of currency and coins making up the bank is prepared at the end of the work shift. For control purposes, banks are verified periodically by surprise count.

A report of the amount of cash received and disbursed by each employee is prepared at the end of the work shift. One method is to use a deposit report envelope of the type shown in Exhibit 4. It both reports on the cash received and holds the cash until the report is verified and a bank deposit slip prepared. The deposit report envelope lists in detail the amount and nature of the cash and checks received.

Exhibit 4 **Cashier's Receipts Envelope Report**

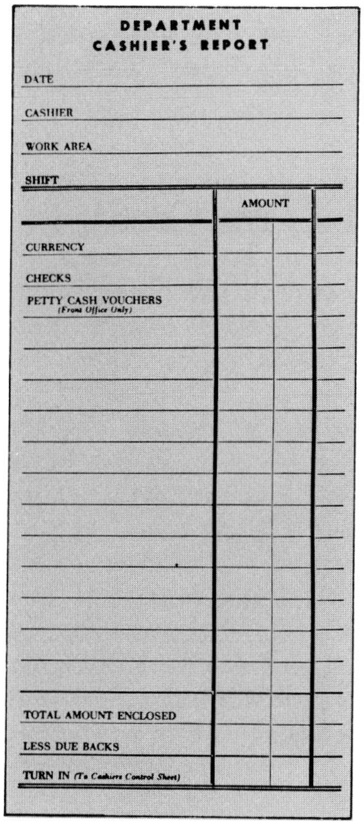

DEPARTMENT
CASHIER'S REPORT

DATE
CASHIER
WORK AREA
SHIFT

	AMOUNT
CURRENCY	
CHECKS	
PETTY CASH VOUCHERS (Front Office Only)	
TOTAL AMOUNT ENCLOSED	
LESS DUE BACKS	
TURN IN (To Cashiers Control Sheet)	

After it is prepared, it is placed in a locked slot-box safe. A witnessed record of all deposit report envelopes placed in or removed from the safe gives further control. Cash receipts should be deposited in a local bank at least daily by the individual responsible for this function.

Rules for Accepting Checks

Management should establish rules for accepting checks in payment of guest accounts. For example:

1. Checks greater than a prescribed amount should be authorized by the manager.
2. Checks made payable to cash, bearer, or self must be endorsed by the manager.
3. No check made payable to a company will be cashed unless authorized by the manager.
4. Third party checks are not acceptable except when presented by a well-known guest who has established credit with the hotel or motel.
5. Checks of which part of the amount is to apply on a guest's account with the balance returned in cash should have the following receipt form rubber-stamped on the back:

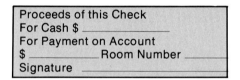

> Proceeds of this Check
> For Cash $ _____
> For Payment on Account
> $ _____ Room Number _____
> Signature _____

This type of receipt prevents the check from being used later as evidence that the full amount of the check was applied against the account balance.

6. When a check is received, the employee should immediately endorse the check with a "for deposit only" rubber stamp.

Extending Short-Term Credit to Guests

Credit transactions

City ledger

During the guest's stay at the hotel or motel, short-term credit is extended by allowing the guest to charge items to his or her account. Under a variety of circumstances, credit may also be extended to individuals not currently staying in the hotel. For example, a departing guest may want to be billed at a home or company address. An individual or group having a function at the hotel may wish to be billed later. Local businesses and individuals who use the hotel facilities on a continuing basis may want to be billed monthly for charges incurred. A guest may use a national credit card or a travel agent coupon to settle the account, and then the hotel must bill those organizations for the amount due. These kinds of credit transactions are kept in an accounts receivable ledger known as the city ledger and are separate from the accounts of guests currently staying at the hotel. The city ledger is an alphabetical file of accounts resulting from the type of transactions described above. Billings are made at periodic intervals, depending upon the nature of the account.

Front office personnel are involved in many transactions that result in extending credit for a city ledger account. They may also be responsible for posting such transactions to the city ledger.

With key-driven machines, any type of transaction can be posted to the guest ledger account by inserting the ledger card and depressing the appropriate keys. A cash receipts and disbursements journal is not necessary when using a key-driven machine since registers within the machine accumulate the data needed for accounting entries.

Key-driven machines

Purpose of the Night Audit

The night auditor's job, in the simplest terms, is to complete the posting of transactions and to balance and determine the accuracy of the guest accounts. The night auditor posts the room rental charges and other late charges at the end of the day. After all transactions have been posted and the ending balance in each account calculated, the night auditor develops information reports and tests the accuracy of the guest ledger account balances. The auditor's objective is to maintain effective control over the revenues generated by guest credit transactions. In many hotels and motels, this function is expanded to include revenue producing cash transactions as well.

Auditor maintains control over revenues from guest credit

The night auditor assumes control over the front office posting and cashier activities when one business day ends and another begins in order to insure a proper cutoff. The cutoff time for many hotels and motels is 2:00 A.M., but it varies, depending upon the closing hours of food and beverage operations.

Verifying the accuracy of guest account balances begins with preparing a report summarizing the day's postings of transactions by type. The total for each kind of transaction can then be cross-checked with the amounts on control reports or vouchers relating to the same transactions as prepared by other employees. Any discrepancy between the amount posted to the guest ledger accounts and the amount reported by the control media must be investigated, and the error must be corrected. The ending balance in the guest ledger can be verified by adding the day's total debits to the guest accounts to the beginning balance in the ledger and subtracting the total of the day's credit transactions.

Verifying guest accounts

The manner in which the night auditor conducts the audit depends on two major factors. The first is the degree of verification necessary. The verification process may range from checking each posted item against its source document to verification based only on total control amounts. The auditor is governed in this matter by how frequently out-of-balance conditions are discovered. A skilled front office staff will make few mistakes, and the night auditor will be able to use total control amounts to verify the accuracy of the account balances. With a less skilled staff, accounts will require a much greater degree of verification.

Degree of verification varies

The second factor influencing the audit procedures is the front office equipment: manual, handwritten system, key-driven posting machine, or computer.

Night Audit Steps

The exact steps to complete the night audit depend on the system and equipment in use in the front office. A key-driven machine or computer reduces the amount of work required. The following must be accomplished regardless of the system and equipment:

1. Enter any unposted vouchers to the guest ledger accounts.
2. Verify the vouchers posted to the guest accounts during the business day.
3. Post the daily room rental charge and applicable room tax to the guest ledger accounts.
4. Review the guest accounts closed out during the business day.
5. Prepare a report summarizing the guest account transactions for the day.
6. Verify the summarization report.
7. Correct guest ledger account errors.

Manual Night Audit Method

With a manual system the front office staff, by hand, posts vouchers as they occur to the guest folio accounts. The night auditor posts any voucher not posted by the day staff. The night auditor also posts the daily room rental charge and any applicable tax to the guest folio accounts.

Vouchers examined

As part of the audit process, the night auditor examines the vouchers, the source documents for all but the room charge and tax postings. All vouchers must be accounted for to be certain that all the proper charges have been made to guest accounts. To aid in this, vouchers are prenumbered and the numerical sequence is checked, often against numerical order check-off sheets. The night auditor should then review the vouchers to see that they are properly filled out and mathematically accurate. When necessary, vouchers should be compared with the postings to each guest account. Finally, vouchers are totaled by department for later comparison with audit reports.

Daily room charge entered

The night auditor enters the daily room charge on each guest folio account, using rate information noted when the guest registered. On a multipart form, providing a registration card, a guest folio, and a room rack card, the rate was entered on the three records with one writing. With separate registration cards and guest folio cards, rate information on both records should be compared. The numerical sequence of the guest folio accounts must be examined to be certain the accounts receivable balance includes all guest accounts. Again, a numerical check-off sheet helps to account for the sequence of cards.

Review folios of departed guests

The guest folio accounts for guests who have checked out during the day are kept in a separate file. The night auditor reviews these accounts to determine that payment was received and that the debits posted to the account equal the credits. When the hotel has granted an account credit or when a national credit card was used in settling the account, the auditor reviews the transfer to the city ledger.

Calculate account's ending balance

The room charge posting is the last posting for the day. Following this, the ending balance in each account can be calculated. However, in some manual systems the account balance is not determined until the guest checks out.

Daily transcript

The next audit step is preparation of the daily transcript report, an example of which is shown in Exhibit 5. This report puts information posted to the guest ledger accounts during the past day in a convenient form for verifying its accuracy. The report lists, for each account, beginning balance, debits by department (room, restaurant, beverage,

Exhibit 5   **Daily Transcript Report**

Room Number	Previous Balance	DEBITS						CREDITS			Ending Balance
		Room	Room Tax	Restaurant	Beverage	Phone	Misc.	Cash Payment	Allowances	Transfer to City Ledger	

Exhibit 6   **Daily Room Report**

Daily Room Report

Date _____ 19 _____

ROOM NUMBER	NUMBER GUESTS	RATE	TAX	FOLIO	ROOM NUMBER	NUMBER GUESTS	RATE	TAX	FOLIO	ROOM NUMBER	NUMBER GUESTS	RATE	TAX	FOLIO
101					160					219				
102					161					220				
103					162					221				
104					163					222				
105					164					223				
106					165					224				
107					166					225				
108					167					226				

Total Rooms Sales _____   No. of Guests _____   Total Rooms Occupied _____
Tax _____   Average per Room _____   Complimentary Room _____
% Occupancy _____   Average per Guest _____

Signature of Night Auditor

etc.), credits to the accounts (payments, allowances, etc.), and ending account balance. In order to have the complete posting information, the data for guests who checked out during the past day, banquet and meeting room accounts, and advanced deposits are also posted. Each column is then totaled, and the report is cross-footed (added across) to determine if the report is mathematically accurate. The column totals for each kind of activity are compared with the respective departmental control reports or the adding machine tape totals of vouchers.

The room revenue total is compared with two control reports. The **Total room revenue** first is the room revenue report, as shown in Exhibit 6. This report is **control** prepared by the evening desk clerk at the shift's end. The night auditor enters late arrivals on the report. The source of information for the room revenue report is on the room rack. For each occupied room, a card is inserted in the room rack, listing the guest's name, the number of occupants, and the room rate.

The room revenue report, usually prepared by an employee other than the night auditor and from a different information source, is an excellent method of verifying the room charges posted by the night auditor.

Housekeeper's report

A second report, also essential to controlling room revenue accounting, is the housekeeper's report, which the housekeeper prepares from the maids' reports. The list of rooms shown as occupied on the housekeeper's report is compared with the room revenue report to verify that all revenues are being recorded. An occupied room not found on the room revenue report is called a sleeper. The housekeeper's report is also used to identify skippers or potential skippers, those who leave without paying their bills. Exhibit 7 shows an example of a housekeeper's report.

Exhibit 7   **Housekeeper's Report**

Housekeeper's Report

Date _____ , 19 _____   A.M. / P.M.

ROOM NUMBER	STATUS	ROOM NUMBER	STATUS	ROOM NUMBER	STATUS	ROOM NUMBER	STATUS
101		148		195		242	
102		149		196		243	
103		150		197		244	
104		151		198		245	
105		152		199		246	
106		153		200		247	
107		154		201		248	
108		155		202		249	
109		156		203		250	
110		157		204		251	

Remarks:

_____
Housekeeper's Signature

Legend: ✓   - Occupied
OOO - Out-of-Order
  -   - Vacant
B   - Slept Out (Baggage Still in Room)
X   - Occupied—No Baggage
C.O. - Slept In but Checked Out Early A.M.
E.A. - Early Arrival

Verifying restaurant and beverage charges

Restaurant and beverage charges to the guest accounts appearing on the transcript report are verified in two ways. An adding machine tape total of the restaurant and beverage checks posted to the accounts is compared with the totals shown on the transcript report. This step determines that the correct amounts have been posted. To be certain that all beverage and restaurant transactions charged by guests have reached the front office for posting, the transcript totals are compared with information generated when the sale was recorded in the department. This may be either a cash register audit tape that reports the total of all charges to room accounts, or, if an audit tape is not available, a cashier's report covering the day's transactions.

Verifying miscellaneous charges

The total telephone, valet, and other miscellaneous charges to guest accounts are also verified by comparing the adding machine tape totals of the vouchers with the transcript amounts and, when possible, with independently prepared departmental control reports.

Cash receipts and disbursements control

In a manual system, guest cash payments received and guest cash disbursements are recorded in a front office cash receipts and disbursements journal. The transcript report total for these items is verified by comparing it with the cash receipts and disbursements recorded in the journal.

Guest accounts and city ledger accounts must often be corrected for overcharges and errors by means of allowance vouchers. The total of these allowances for the day is verified by comparing the transcript amount with an adding machine tape of the allowance vouchers. Further verification is possible if an allowance journal is used to journalize this kind of transaction. A review of the allowance vouchers should be made to determine that they have been approved by the person responsible for authorizing allowances.

Verifying total allowances

When a transcript total is out of balance with control information, the night auditor must locate and correct the error. This usually involves comparing the source documents with the ledger postings. When all transcript totals have been verified and/or differences reconciled, the night auditor has completed the review of the guest ledger and ascertained that all charges incurred and credits received during the day have been properly recorded in the guest accounts.

Night Audit Procedures Using Key-Driven Machines

When transactions are posted to guest accounts on a key-driven front office machine, the transaction totals needed in the verification process are accumulated in registers within the machine. For example, when posting a restaurant check charged by a guest to his account, the amount will be added to the food sales register at the same time. At the end of the day, the machine can print out the grand total of food sales posted to guest accounts. Only the number of registers in the machine limits the kinds of transactions that can be recorded.

Machine registers accumulate transaction totals

In a key-driven system, as in a manual system, the night auditor posts the room rental charges to the guest accounts, but uses the front office machine. At the same time, a trial balance of guest ledger balances is accumulated in a machine register. After this step, the totals in all registers are printed out on a report to be used in the verification process.

Night Audit Procedures for a Computerized System

The computer's ability to accumulate data in any format desired and output the information quickly greatly aids night audit procedures. A properly designed computerized system will also eliminate some human errors of a manual or key-driven posting machine system, such as incorrectly picking up the previous balance, posting to the wrong account, and losing guest folios.

The computer does many of the tasks the night auditor typically performs. By activating a program, the computer adds the room rate to each guest account based on information stored within the system. The computer updates each account balance whenever a transaction is posted to an account. The night audit program outputs a report on all the day's transactions by room number and type of transaction. The audit report is similar in detail to the transcript report of a manual system. The output also includes a report of cash and related account

Computer performs many night audit tasks

Manual verification

payment transactions. An audit report can be obtained at the end of each shift and/or at the end of the day.

The computer posts the room rate and prepares the equivalent of the transcript or machine balance reports of other systems. The verification process is somewhat simplified, but is still largely a manual process. Even with all the computer's automatic features, it is still possible to post the wrong amount to a guest account. Therefore, there must still be independently prepared control media and supporting vouchers to compare with the audit report. When there are discrepancies between the controls and the audit report, the individual vouchers are compared with the audit report detail to locate the error. When the error is corrected, the final audit report is run.

Miscellaneous Duties of the Night Auditor

Verifying city ledger

When the accounting office maintains the city ledger, the night auditor must verify that all transfers from the guest ledger are properly recorded. Some hotels and motels have the front office handle all city ledger transactions, making it necessary for the night auditor to include all these transactions in the review. If a manual or key-driven system is used, the procedures used for the guest ledger are extended to city ledger transactions as well.

In a manual system, it is unnecessary to list each city ledger account on the transcript. The balance from the previous day is listed together with the transactions affecting the city ledger accounts for that day. The columns are totaled, and the ending balance is determined. This total is reconciled by comparing it with a tape of the city ledger account balances. If a key-driven machine is used, city ledger accounts are posted via the machine. The city ledger accounts are included in the trial balance and verified by the daily report or the machine balance report.

The night auditor may be assigned several control duties not directly related to audit of the guest ledger. The night auditor may be responsible for clearing and setting all cash registers, maintaining the supply of register audit tape, and verifying the numerical sequence of folios, vouchers, and food and beverage checks. The night auditor usually completes the room revenue report and enters sales, income, accounts receivable data, and room statistics on the daily report of operations.

Reports for accounting department

The final duty of the night auditor is to assemble reports that are forwarded to the accounting department. For a manual system, they include:

1. The daily transcript

2. The cash report

3. All paid guest accounts

4. All departmental charge and credit vouchers, accompanied by an adding machine tape for each

5. The city ledger transfer report and the guest ledger accounts being transferred

6. The departmental cash register tapes (when they are the auditor's responsibility)

7. The daily report of operations completed according to the auditor's responsibility

8. The room revenue and housekeeper's reports.

For a key-driven system, the machine balance report or daily report and the audit tape replace the transcript report. All other reports are the same.

When all information is verified, all totals are proved, and all required reports are compiled, the night auditor has discharged the basic duties.

Discussion Questions

1. Why is it desirable to have guest accounts receivable records maintained by the personnel working in the front office of a motel or hotel?

2. There are three possible means of recording guest accounts receivable records. What are they, and when is it appropriate to use each one?

3. Explain the nature of the accounting transactions entered in the front office cash receipts and disbursements journal.

4. What control methods are used in connection with the cash receipts handled by front office personnel?

5. What is the nature of the accounts receivable transactions maintained in the city ledger? In what ways are they handled differently from guest folio accounts?

6. In what ways do key-driven machines shorten the time required by the front office personnel to maintain guest ledger accounts?

7. What is the function of the night auditor and why must these procedures be done each business day?

8. What procedures in a manual system are followed to be certain that the room rental charged each guest is correct?

9. What are the principal advantages of a key-driven front office machine over a manual system in performing the night audit procedures?

10. What are some factors that cause an out-of-balance condition revealed by the night audit?

Problems

Problem 1

Part A. Page 3 of the daily transcript report for Vacation Inn is given below. Post the information given below for the remaining two rooms (309 and 310) to the transcript and calculate the column totals. The daily transcript report should be cross-footed to be certain it is in balance. The ledger cards for rooms 309 and 310 show the following information:

	309	*310*
Previous balance	$ —0—	$ —0—
Room rental	22.00	24.00
Tax	.36	.42
Restaurant	—0—	4.85
Beverage	3.00	—0—
Balance	$25.36	$29.27

Part B. The following information is from Vacation Inn's control reports.

Room revenues	$2,468.00
Restaurant	745.35
Beverages	144.25
Phone	14.30
Miscellaneous	89.75
Cash payments	2,060.00

Required:

1. What kind of control media might be available for each of the above items?

2. Outline what procedures should be followed to locate the error when items from the daily transcript report do not agree with the control media.

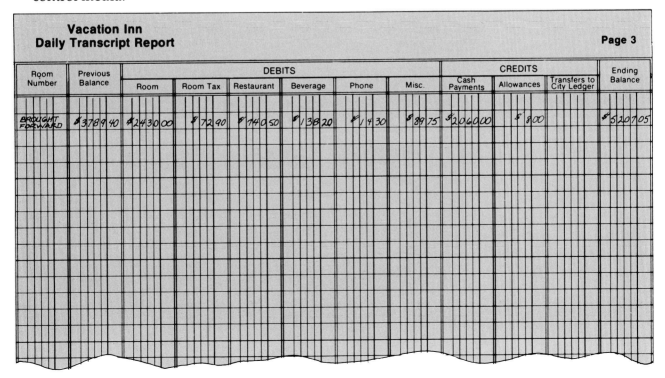

Room Number	Previous Balance	DEBITS						CREDITS			Ending Balance
		Room	Room Tax	Restaurant	Beverage	Phone	Misc.	Cash Payments	Allowances	Transfers to City Ledger	
BROUGHT FORWARD	$3,789.40	$2,430.00	$72.90	$140.50	$138.20	$14.30	$89.75	$2,060.00	$8.00		$5,207.05

Vacation Inn
Daily Transcript Report   Page 3

Problem 2

Enter the following transactions in a front office cash receipts and disbursements journal. Exhibit 3 shows an example of this journal.

a. Received a check for $137.62 as payment from the Nars Company in settlement of their account. The Nars Company's receivable record is kept in the city ledger.

b. Cash amounting to $28.50 was disbursed to purchase two theater tickets that Mr. and Mrs. Jones staying in room 1014 had asked the hotel to pay for when delivered.

c. Tim Early, staying in room 1209, checked out and paid his $38.42 bill by cash.

d. Jane Smith paid $32.73 for her stay at the hotel when she registered in room 906.

e. When a wedding cake arrived from the Village Bakery, cash was disbursed amounting to $148. It was for the Lundgren wedding reception scheduled for this evening. The account for the reception is maintained in the city ledger.

f. Joe Petersen paid $100 on his account. He is currently staying in room 707.

Problem 3

Erica Smith checks into the University Inn, a 300 room hotel. She is assigned room 424 at a rate of $45 per day. Over the four day period of June 15-18, she incurs the following charges:

June 15 —	dinner	$15.95
	telephone	3.50
June 16 —	breakfast	$ 6.20
	laundry	4.50
	telephone	2.40
	bar	5.50
June 17 —	breakfast	$ 5.80
	telephone	8.40
June 18 —	lunch	$ 6.50
	dinner	25.50
	telephone	14.50
	laundry	8.20

Prior to her arrival, the University Inn had received a $100 deposit from her company. The $100 was originally recorded in the city ledger and is transferred to her folio upon arrival. In addition, on June 17 she paid another $50 on her account. Ms. Smith checked out on June 19 and settled her account with a check for the balance. One June 16, the night auditor discovers that she was overcharged $1 on laundry, and an allowance voucher for $1 is prepared and the amount is posted to her account.

The hotel is required to charge a 4% room tax in addition to the daily rate of $45.

Required:

Properly complete the folio provided on the following page for Erica Smith's activities. Compute the balance due for each day and carry the balance forward for the next day.

| ROOM | 424 | | | | | No. | | | | | |

NAME Erica Smith

UNIVERSITY INN

	CHANGED		
	DATE	TO ROOM	NEW RATE

| DATE OF ARRIVAL | | | RATE | | PER | | CLERK | | | |

DATES												
Balance Forward												
ROOMS												
TAX												
RESTAURANT												
LONG DISTANCE												
LAUNDRY												
BEVERAGE												
MISC. (DETAIL)												
CREDITS	CASH											
	Allowances											
	Transfers											
TOTAL CREDITS												
BALANCE DUE												

ALL BILLS PAYABLE UPON PRESENTATION

Problem 4

The following are reports and forms used at the front desk.

a. allowance vouchers
b. guest folios
c. daily report
d. room revenue report
e. front office cash receipts and disbursements journal

Required:

Determine the appropriate report(s) or form(s) which each of the following transactions will affect.

1. On September 20, 1981, $76.25 was received through the mail in full payment of Mr. Gordon's account.

2. An advance deposit was received from Mrs. Jones on September 21, 1981 for $64.

3. Mr. Clark was overcharged in error for his dinner by $5. The dinner was charged to his room.

4. Jim Fox, a guest at the hotel, paid $50 cash toward his account.

5. Cash amounting to $25 was paid out for flowers ordered by Janice Kraw, a guest.

6. Collections of $131.40, $84.62 and $35.76 were received from AMEX, Master Charge, and VISA, respectively.

7. The night auditor recorded daily totals and statistics and determined period to date totals from this report.

8. The night auditor posted room charges and sales tax for the night of September 21, 1981.

Chapter Eleven

Accounting for Sales

Perspective

Hotel and motel sales revenues come from guest and meeting room rentals, restaurants, lounges, telephone, valet service, laundry, and miscellaneous activities. These transactions are not recorded separately in the accounting records but accumulated for a day or even longer, then entered.

So there must be an efficient, accurate system for recording sales and handling cash received and accounts receivable related to sales revenue. Two possible methods of recording sales are special journals and the daily report of operations.

Other elements of accounting for sales and controlling food and beverage sales involve voucher systems, cash register controls, cashier responsibilities, accounting for cash, recording of credit sales, and accumulating data by meal or day.

The chapter illustrates a summary sales journal, allowance vouchers and allowance journal, and finally the preparation of the daily report of operations.

Accounting for Sales

Sales revenue sources

Control for sales is vital

Journalizing sales

Sales cash receipts and accounts receivable

Accounts receivable — two levels of reporting

Knowledge of front office functions, including the night auditor, helps in understanding how hotel revenue transactions are recorded. Now, a more detailed study of hotel and motel accounting methods is in order.

Sales revenues are derived from guest and meeting room rentals, restaurants, lounges, telephone, valet service, laundry, and other miscellaneous activities. The uniform and repetitive nature of sales transactions makes it desirable to accumulate sales for either a business day or a longer period before entering them in the accounting records. Since transactions are not recorded separately, control methods for sales and the resulting cash receipts or accounts receivable are very important. They are designed to insure that all sales are acknowledged in the accounting records and that all cash receipts and accounts receivable related to sales revenues are properly handled.

There are several different ways to journalize sales. They can be recorded by a daily entry in a sales journal or a monthly entry in the general journal. With the latter method, sales are recorded on an internal management report generally called the daily report of operations. At the end of the month, the month-to-date sales figure is entered in the general journal.

Recording cash receipts and accounts receivable elements of the sales transactions has similar options. Cash receipts can be recorded on a front office machine or in a front office cash receipts and disbursements journal. In both cases the information is also entered on the daily report of operations. When the special journal is not used, a monthly general journal entry is made using the daily report as the basis for the entry. The alternative methods of recording sales transactions are shown in Exhibit 1.

Accounts receivable involves two levels of reporting. A detailed record of charges and payments by guest or customer is required. In addition, the total amount of accounts receivable due the hospitality service firm must be recorded. The guest ledger and city ledger, called subsidiary ledgers, contain detailed postings by account. The general ledger contains the accounts receivable control account (or accounts).

Exhibit 1   **Alternative Methods of Recording Sales Transactions**

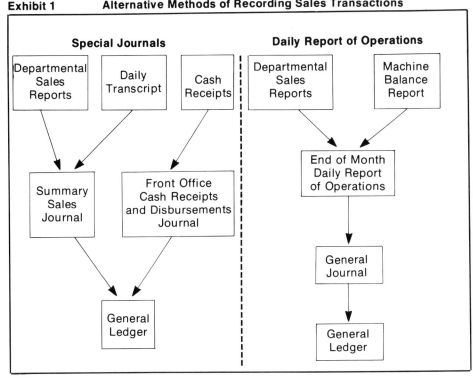

The accumulated totals of all accounts receivable charges and payments posted to the subsidiary ledgers are also posted to the control account. The frequency of updating the control account balances depends on the accounting system and equipment in use.

In accounting for sales revenues, as with all transactions, the first step is analysis to determine the debit and credit elements. The trans-action must be journalized and posted to the general ledger during the accounting period. How these steps are accomplished, however, depends upon the kind of sales transaction, the accounting system, and the supporting control methods.

Determine debit and credit elements

The night auditor records guest room sales while posting the room rental charge to the guest ledger account. They are summarized on a daily transcript or a machine balance report. After verifying the sales with the room revenue report, the night auditor records room sales in a special journal or by a general journal entry.

Sales of Food and Beverage

Food and beverages are sold repetitively in a uniform and routine manner. Rather than record each transaction as it occurs, sales are ac-cumulated for a specified time period before making an entry. Several control measures assure that all food and beverage sales are accurately accounted for.

The control system starts with the voucher used to record the sale. The guest check, as it is called, is prenumbered. The supply of guest checks is kept under the control of management and, as required, a numerical sequence of checks is assigned to each server. The check may be a single slip of paper on which to record the customer's order and the appropriate charges comprising the sale. An alternative is a two-part guest check; the server surrenders one copy in order to obtain food from the kitchen. This helps to insure the proper charges for food dispensed. Assigning a sequence of checks to each server and account-

Control starts with voucher

Exhibit 2   Guest Check and Restaurant and Beverage Sales Controls

HUNDRED				CONSECUTIVE NUMBER RECORD				SERIES	
00	50	00	50	00	50	00	50	00	50
1	51	1	51	1	51	1	51	1	51
2	52	2	52	2	52	2	52	2	52
3	53	3	53	3	53	3	53	3	53
4	54	4	54	4	54	4	54	4	54
5	55	5	55	5	55	5	55	5	55
6	56	6	56	6	56	6	56	6	56
7	57	7	57	7	57	7	57	7	57
8	58	8	58	8	58	8	58	8	58
9	59	9	59	9	59	9	59	9	59
10	60	10	60	10	60	10	60	10	60
11	61	11	61	11	61	11	61	11	61
12	62	12	62	12	62	12	62	12	62
13	63	13	63	13	63	13	63	13	63
14	64	14	64	14	64	14	64	14	64
15	65	15	65	15	65	15	65	15	65
16	66	16	66	16	66	16	66	16	66
17	67	17	67	17	67	17	67	17	67
18	68	18	68	18	68	18	68	18	68
19	69	19	69	19	69	19	69	19	69
20	70	20	70	20	70	20	70	20	70
21	71	21	71	21	71	21	71	21	71
22	72	22	72	22	72	22	72	22	72

Cashier's Record of Checks Distributed to Waiters

Opening and Closing No. of Checks and Waiter's Signature

_____Cashier   _____19___

Waiter No.	Check No.	No. Served	Waiter's Signature	Waiter No.	Check No.	No. Served	Waiter's Signature

ALBERT PICK
HOTELS · MOTOR INNS

DATE	NO SERVED	SERVER	TABLE NO — ROOM

FOOD TOTAL
BEVERAGE
TOTAL
TAX
GRAND TOTAL

SERVER   DATE

Register records sale

ing for all the checks issued achieves control over each sale. Exhibit 2 shows an example of a guest check and its related control documents.

Another important part of the control process is having one person make the sale and a second person receive payment. Control is enhanced when a cashier uses a cash register to receive payment. Both cash and charge food and beverage sales are recorded on the register. The cashier inserts the guest check in the cash register, and through operating the keys, rings each element of the sale separately. A restaurant or lounge sale may include food, beverage, miscellaneous items such as cigarettes, and sales tax. A charge sale may also include a tip. The cash registers used by food and beverage operations can accumulate amounts for each of these elements, according to whether the sale was cash or charge. At the end of the meal period, the total amount of each sales element and totals for cash and charge sales can be determined. When the cashier depresses the appropriate key, the register prints the amounts on a tape within the register. Exhibit 3 diagrams the operating panel of the type of cash register used. Bars and lounges use similar registers to accumulate information pertinent to their operations while recording sales.

In addition to the proper operation of the cash register, cashiers are responsible for safeguarding all cash and checks received during their work periods. Strict control is maintained over cash receipts for two reasons. First, a large portion of food and beverage sales are cash transactions; and second, cash receipts are the most vulnerable of assets. The cashier is supplied with a bank to provide funds for making change. Identical control procedures as for the front office are used for all cashiers having banks. Each cashier is responsible for the cash and checks received in payment of guest checks. All cash and checks must be accounted for at the end of the work shift.

Cashier responsible for cash and checks received

Exhibit 3

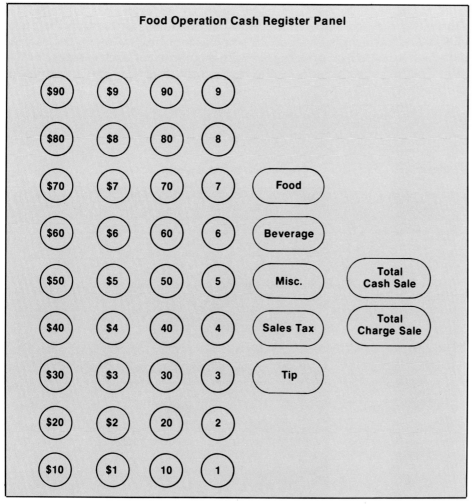

Receipts equal cash sales minus charge tips

Night audit verifies cash receipts

Credit sales

Sales data by meal and day

First, charge tips are paid to the server out of register funds. Control over these disbursements is aided by a charge tip report or voucher signed by the recipient. The cashier then separates the bank fund from cash receipts and prepares a bank report. Finally, the cashier prepares a receipts envelope that lists the detailed amounts of currency, coins, and checks received during that shift. The cash and checks in the report envelope should equal the amount of cash sales less charge tips paid to the servers. The register produces totals for both these figures. Any amounts over or short are reported on the form. The cashier deposits the receipts in a locked slot-box safe. Each deposit placed in the safe and each receipts envelope removed is recorded. The cash receipts are verified as part of the audit procedures comparing guest checks, cash register readings, and the cashier's report.

Finally, the cashier is responsible for handling food and beverage sales that are charged. A guest may request that the check be included on the room account, or may use either a national credit card account or a hotel or motel charge account. When the guest wants to have the room account charged for the amount of the check, he or she will be required to sign the check and record the room number. When a credit card is used, the appropriate credit card voucher form must be prepared for the card user's signature. Exhibit 4 is a credit card voucher form. The American Express form contains three parts — one for the business, the guest, and American Express.

For information on operations, management requires sales data by meal period. For accounting purposes, sales transactions are accumulated for at least a day before the sales are entered in a journal. The sales entry may be made from a number of sources, including the guest checks and cash register tapes. In some accounting systems, the cashier lists each guest check on a report with a column for each element of the sale. Totaling the columns of the report produces the sales information for the entry.

Exhibit 4 **Credit Card Voucher Form**

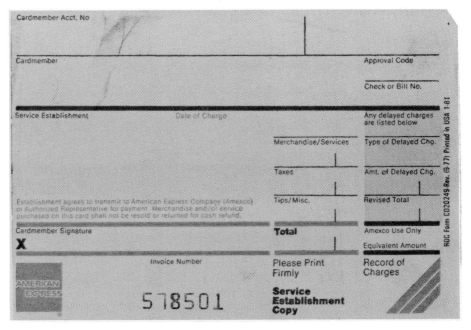

The entry for recording the food and beverage sales in general journal format is given below:

Cash			x x x					
Accounts Receivable			x x x					
Food Sales							x x x	
Sales Taxes Payable							x x x	

The entry recognizes the cash received, the portion of the sales that was charged, the total sales revenue, and the sales tax liability. Similar information is entered in a summary sales journal.

Telephone, Valet, Laundry, and Sundry Sales

Hotels and motels provide their guests with a number of conveniences such as telephone, valet, and laundry service. Fees for these services are usually charged to the guests' room accounts. A voucher is prepared from which both sales revenue accounting and the receivable entry on the guest account can be made. Sales revenues are usually accumulated for a period of time before they are journalized. The receivables, on the other hand, must be recorded as soon as feasible because the guest may wish to check out at any time.

Telephone sales are a good example of the procedure for recording this kind of sale. Long distance call charges, including a service charge, are recorded on a prenumbered voucher. The voucher is used to post the charges to the guest accounts. Each long distance call voucher is listed on a summary sales report form called a telephone traffic report. This report serves a two-fold purpose. It accumulates the sales prior to recording the journal entry, and it serves as an auditing procedure by providing a checklist to insure that all telephone charges have been posted to the guest accounts. Hotels and motels may or may not charge for local telephone calls. When a charge is made, a voucher system similar to the one for long distance calls is used. Some hotels and motels have an automatic metering system to record the number of local calls made from a room. This system becomes the basis for posting the charges to the guest accounts. Exhibit 5 shows examples of a

Eg, telephone sales

Exhibit 5   **Telephone Voucher and Traffic Report**

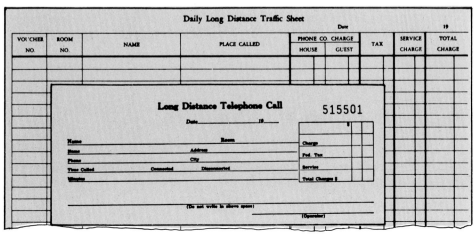

telephone voucher and a traffic report. The sales revenues from valet, laundry, and other sundry sales are recorded in the same manner, using vouchers to document the sale.

Summary Sales Journal

All sales, whether cash or charge, are either accumulated on a sales report and journalized once a month or entered daily in a summary sales journal. The latter method helps in posting to the ledger by providing a column heading for each debit and credit account affected by a sales transaction. In addition to sales revenues accounts, sales transactions affect sales taxes payable and either cash in the bank or accounts receivable, depending upon the type of sale. The sales are entered daily in the appropriate column by type of sale. At the end of the month, the columns are totaled and posted to the general ledger. An example of a summary sales journal used by hotels and motels is shown in Exhibit 6.

Exhibit 6   **Summary Sales Journal**

Summary Sales Journal
Month of _____ 198 __

DATE	DEBITS			CREDITS							TOTAL SALES
	CASH IN BANK	ACCOUNTS RECEIVABLE GUEST	CITY	ROOM SALES	FOOD SALES	BEVERAGE SALES	TELEPHONE SALES	VALET AND LAUNDRY	MISC. SALES	TAXES PAYABLE AND ACCRUED	

Allowances

When guest accounts and city ledger accounts must be corrected for overcharges and errors, an allowance voucher, shown in Exhibit 7, should be prepared and approved by management prior to posting to the guest's folio. The journal entry to record allowances may be based on the month's accumulation of allowances and made in the general journal, or in a special allowance journal, shown in Exhibit 8. An allowance is treated as a reduction of sales revenues and accounts receivable.

The Daily Report of Operations

Contents of daily report of operations.

The daily report of operations, containing the financial and statistical results of operations, is prepared as a source of information for management. Typically the report includes:

1. Sales revenue information by source

2. Accounts receivable information

Exhibit 7

Allowance Voucher

ALLOWANCE   114632

DATE _____ 19 _____

NAME _____ ROOM OR ACCT. NO. _____

DATE	SYMBOL	AMOUNT

DO NOT WRITE IN ABOVE SPACE

EXPLANATION _____

AC-87 (4/78)   SIGNED BY _____

Exhibit 8   Allowance Journal

Allowance Journal
Month of _____ 198 ___

VOUCHER NUMBER	DATE	NAME	ROOM NUMBER	DEBITS							CREDITS		
				ROOM	FOOD	BEVERAGE	TELEPHONE	VALET AND LAUNDRY	MISC. SALES	TAX PAYABLE & ACCRUED	CASH IN BANK	ACCOUNTS RECEIVABLE	
												GUEST	CITY

3. Bank deposit figures
4. Bank balance information
5. Room, food, and beverage statistical information
6. Food and beverage purchase information
7. Manhour and payroll cost statistics

The report gives information for the day and, where applicable, the to-date totals for the month, and the last year period to-date. Exhibit 9 is an example of a typical daily report of operations.

Exhibit 9

Daily Report of Operations

SHERATON WASHINGTON HOTEL

DAILY REPORT—REVENUE JOURNAL

FRS No. 303

DATE _____ 19 ____

ACCOUNT (CREDITS)	ACCT. NO.	TODAY	ALLOW TODAY	NET TODAY	NET TO DATE THIS MONTH	POST	FORECAST TO DATE THIS MONTH	LAST YEAR TO DATE THIS MONTH
ROOMS—Transient—Reg								
Transient—Group								
Permanent								
Extra Earnings								
Airlines								
TOTAL ROOMS REVENUE								
FOOD—Courtyard Cafe								
Room Service								
Americus								
20th Century								
L'Express								
Early Light								
Quickie Breakfast								
Snack								
Pool								
Sub-Total-Rests								
Banquet								
Hospitality								
Misc. S & W								
Misc. Income								
TOTAL FOOD REVENUE								
BEVERAGE—Courtyard Cafe								
Room Service								
Americus								
20th Century								
L'Express								
Early Light								
Lobby Bar								
Cash Bar								
Pool								
Sub-Total-Outlet								
Banquet								
Misc. S & W								
Misc. Income								
Hospitality								
TOTAL BEV. REVENUE								
MINOR OPERATED DEPT.								
TELEPHONE—Local								
L/Distance								
L/D Comm.								
TOTAL TELEPHONE								
GUEST LAUNDRY								
GUEST VALET								
POOL								
CONVENTION SERVICES								
MISC.								
TOTAL MINOR REVENUE								
R & OTHER INCOME REV.								
TOTAL REVENUE								

Date

ROOM STATISTICS	Acct. No.	NUMBER OF ROOMS					% OF OCCUPANCY/AVERAGE RATE						
		Today	Month to Date				Today	Month to Date				
		Today	Actual	Fcst.	L. Year		Today	Actual	Fcst.	L. Year		
NO. ROOMS IN HOTEL (At EOM)												
NO. ROOMS IN HOTEL (Month)												
ROOMS HOUSE USE												
TOTAL AVAILABLE ROOMS												
ROOMS VACANT												
ROOMS OUT OF ORDER												
TOTAL OCCUPIED OVERALL												
TRANSIENT—REGULAR—OCC'Y.												
—GROUP—OCC'Y.												
TOTAL TRANSIENT—OCC'Y.												
TOTAL—COMP.—OCC'Y.												
TOTAL PERMANENT OCC'Y.												
NUMBER OF GUEST												
AVERAGE RATE OVERALL												
AVERAGE RATE REGULAR												
AVERAGE RATE GROUP												
AVERAGE RATE TRANSIENT												
AVERAGE RATE PERMANENT												
TOTAL UNITS SOLD												
TRANS. UNIT OCC'Y												
TRANS. UNIT DOUBLE OCC'Y												

FOOD STATISTICS		BREAKFAST	LUNCH		DINNER		TOTAL		LAST YEAR	
		FCST	ACT	FCST	ACT	FCST	ACT	FCST	ACT	AV. CK.	TOTAL AV. CK.
COURTYARD CAFE	Today										
	To Date										
ROOM SERVICE	Today										
	To Date										
AMERICUS	Today										
	To Date										
20TH CENTURY	Today										
	To Date										
L'EXPRESS	Today										
	To Date										
QUICKIE BREAKFAST	Today										
	To Date										
BANQUET REG.	Today										
	To Date										
HOSPITALITY	Today										
	To Date										

Prepared by _____

Date _____

Right section table (ACCOUNT (CREDITS)):

ACCOUNT (CREDITS)		ACCT. NO.	TODAY	ALLOW TODAY	NET TODAY	NET TODAY THIS MONTH	POST
ACCTS. PAY.:	Room Sales Tax						
	F & B Tax						
	Occ. Tax						
	5% Tax						
	Union Tip						
	Cash Tip						
	Clearing						
	Adv. Dep.-Applied						
	Adv. Dep.-Pymt Folio						
	Adv. Dep.-Gen. Cashier						
ROOMS:	Misc.						
FOOD:	Cost Emp. Meals						
	Cost of Sales						
	Misc.						
BEVERAGE:	Cost of Sales						
	Misc.						
A & G:	Over/Short						
	Postage						
	Loss & Damage						
	Misc.						
R. & O. Inc.:	Space Rental						
	Vending Machines						
	Misc.						
	Commissions						
CONV. SERV.:	P.R. Rent						
	P.R. Sund.						
	Exh. Rent						
	Exh. Sund.						
	Misc.						
DEFERRED:	Perm.						
	L. Dist. Comm.						
	R. & O. Inc.						
	Conv. Serv.						
TOTAL CREDITS							B

Left upper section (BALANCE FROM PREVIOUS DAY):

BALANCE FROM PREVIOUS DAY	GUEST LEDGER	CITY LEDGER	POST
Paid Outs			
Guest Ledger Charges			
Cash Folio & Paid Check			
Guest Rec. Transfers			
Allowances			
Inter Hotel Transfers			
Guest Rec. Transfers			
Payment Folio			
Inter Hotel Transfers			
TOTAL TODAY			
WRITE OFFS			
BALANCE TO DATE			

Left middle section (ACCOUNT (DEBITS)):

ACCOUNT (DEBITS)	ACCT. NO.	TODAY	NET TODAY	NET TODAY THIS MONTH	POST
CASH: Demand Deposit					
Lock Box					
A/R: Guest Ledger					
City Ledger					
TOTAL DEBITS					C

Left lower section (ACCOUNT (CREDITS)):

ACCOUNT (CREDITS)	ACCT. NO.	TODAY	ALLOW TODAY	NET TODAY	NET TODAY THIS MONTH	POST
CASH: Exchange Check						
ACCTS. REC.: G.H.I.						
Branch						
RES. FOR B.D.:						
SPECIAL DEPOSITS: Advance To Officers						
ACCTS. PAY.: S - MED						
S - GL						
S - LTD						
Slush Fund						
Check Room						
TSC						
Doggetts						

TOTAL A + B = C

**Parts of daily report
can double as
accounting record**

The daily report of operations gives accounting data primarily in the areas of sales revenues, cash in the bank, and accounts receivable balances. It is prepared after the revenues and receivable balances have been verified. Consequently, portions of the report may be regarded as the accounting record. The information shown for sales revenues on the report may substitute for a sales journal. At the end of the month, the sales may be posted to the general ledger directly from the daily report of operations. The accounts receivable balances shown in the report are the same information as found in the general ledger control account for accounts receivable, thus providing one more check of accuracy. The accounts receivable balance, however, is calculated by subtracting the credits in the front office cash receipts and disbursements journal from the total debits to accounts receivable in the summary sales journal. Therefore, the decision to use the daily report of operations in place of the sales journal depends in part on the type of equipment available to keep track of sales transactions. Some posting machines can record all sales and cash transactions, eliminating the need for the special journals. With proper control maintained, using the information in the daily report of operations can save much accounting time.

Discussion Questions

1. What characteristics of sales transactions make it desirable to accumulate them rather than record them individually in the accounting records?

2. What are the alternatives for accumulating sales transactions?

3. How are vouchers controlled when used as part of the sales transaction process?

4. In what types of sales is the use of vouchers appropriate?

5. How are the accounts receivable and cash aspects of sales transactions recorded in the accounting records?

6. What are the advantages of using a sales journal to record sales rather than the general journal?

7. What control measures insure that all food and beverage sales are properly and accurately recorded?

8. What kinds of information are found in the daily report of operations? How can this report be incorporated into the accounting system?

9. Explain what is meant by a subsidiary accounts receivable ledger?

10. What kinds of sales transactions are kept in the city ledger? How are these sales different from those kept in a guest folio ledger account?

Problems

Problem 1

Vacation Inn uses a summary sales journal for recording sales and a front office cash receipts and disbursements journal to record guest transactions involving cash receipts and disbursements.

Required:

Part A. Enter the following transactions of January 1 in the journals provided on the next page.

1. Paid $18 for two theater tickets at the request of John Jones, in room 407, charging this amount to his account in the guest ledger.

2. The room sales, obtained from the night auditor's transcript report, totaled $542.

3. Food sales, obtained from an adding machine total of guest checks, showed the following information:

Cash sales	$315
Amount charged to guest accounts	235
Amount charged to national credit cards (city ledger)	57
Sales tax	31

4. Telephone sales, supported by vouchers and reported in total in the telephone traffic report, amounted to $35. Telephone sales are classified as miscellaneous sales and charged to guest accounts.

5. The following guests checked out of the Inn, having paid their bills:

Room Number	Amount
315	$34.75
207	53.32
214	25.00
106	17.50
110	24.75

Part B. Total the columns in both journals and enter the totals by account from the journals in the following T-accounts. The T-accounts are used to represent ledger accounts with debits entered on the left side and credits on the right. After the amounts have been entered, add all the posted amounts to determine the account balance. As a check of the accuracy of your work, verify that the total of accounts with debit balances equals the total of accounts with credit balances.

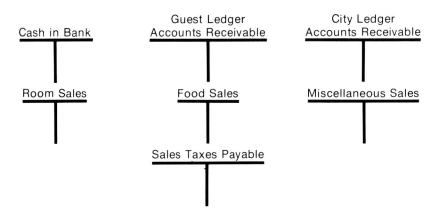

Vacation Inn Sales Journal

	DEBITS			CREDITS			
Date	Cash in Bank	Accounts Receivable Guest	Accounts Receivable City	Room Sales	Food Sales	Misc. Sales	Sales Tax Payable

Vacation Inn
Front Office Cash Receipts and Cash Disbursements Journal

Room Number	CASH RECEIPTS				CASH DISBURSEMENTS			
	DEBITS		CREDITS		DEBITS		CREDITS	
	Cash in Bank	Other	ACCOUNTS RECEIVABLE GUEST	CITY	ACCOUNTS RECEIVABLE GUEST	CITY	Cash in Bank	

Problem 2

At the end of the business day for the Eatery Restaurant, the cash register tape totals showed the following amounts:

Food	$718.60
Beverage	103.75
Miscellaneous Sales	38.30
Sales Tax	43.03
Tips	9.75
Cash Sales Total	677.74
Charge Sales Total	235.69

Required

1. Explain how the tips are handled.
2. Prepare a journal entry in general journal form to record this activity.

Problem 3

The University Inn's daily report for April 15, 1982, is as follows:

Daily Report University Inn Date: 4/15/82	Today	Period To-Date	Last Year To-Date
Revenue			
Room	$2,250.00	$242,523.00	$230,425.00
Tax	90.00	9,701.00	9,217.00
Restaurant	1,141.20	115,842.26	108,842.26
Phone Long Distance	68.00	7,026.50	6,814.56
Laundry	75.00	16,172.19	15,946.74
Total	3,624.20	391,264.95	371,245.56
Room Status			
Singles Sold	44	4,830	4,982
Doubles Sold	31	3,255	3,300
Total Sold	75	8,085	8,282
Total Available	100	10,500	10,500
Percent	75.00	77.00	78.88
Revenue/Room Sold	48.32	48.39	44.83
Food Operations			
Sales	1,141.20	115,842.26	108,842.26
Cost	404.21	40,660.63	38,606.35
Percent	35.21	35.10	35.47
Accounts Receivable			
Guests	15,621.70		14,986.24
Direct Bill	33,796.09		31,843.19
Credit Card	4,942.21		4,637.84
Total	54,360.00		51,467.27

Below is sales, cost of sales, and accounts receivable information for April 16, 1981 and 1982.

	April 16	
	1981	1982
Revenue		
Room	$ 2,186.00	$ 2,300.00
Tax	87.44	92.00
Restaurant	1,002.26	1,274.91
Phone Long Distance	62.50	75.95
Laundry	157.85	149.15
Room Status		
Singles Sold	45	44
Doubles Sold	32	32
Cost of Sales		
Food	390.14	429.87
Accounts Receivable		
Guests	15,421.36	16,422.81
Direct Bill	32,007.85	33,697.43
Credit Card	4,926.47	4,894.21

Required:

Prepare the daily report for the University Inn for April 16, 1982.

Daily Report University Inn

Date: 4/16/82

	Today	Period To-date	Last Year To-date
Revenue			
Room			
Tax			
Restaurant			
Phone Long Distance			
Laundry			
Total			
Room Status			
Singles Sold			
Doubles Sold			
Total Sold			
Total Available			
Percent			
Revenue/Room Sold			
Food Operations			
Sales			
Cost			
Percent			
Accounts Receivable			
Guests			
Direct Bill			
Credit Card			
Total			

Chapter Twelve

Payroll Accounting

Perspective

And last comes payroll—certainly not the least for the hospitality firm, where labor is a high percentage of cost.

Accounting documents needed to prepare payroll include the employee master file and work record. Government reporting requirements must be observed. Payroll is most commonly kept in a separate payroll journal and subsequently entered in a general ledger. Management needs payroll cost information by department or function, plus payroll and related expenses must appear separately on the income statement.

The chapter illustrates payroll calculation for both salaried and hourly employees, accompanied by an explanation of gross pay, deductions, withholdings, and net pay. The chapter then reviews accounting and reporting of tips, along with minimum wage legislation and its effect on hospitality industry firms.

Payroll Accounting

Payroll costs, which include salaries and wages, fringe benefits, and payroll taxes, are by far the largest expense of a hotel or motel, as shown in Exhibit 1. Efforts to control this expense and to manage the work force start with the careful selection of employees. An employment application form, providing information on a prospective employee's personal, work, education, medical, and military background helps in this task. References are also checked when making employment decisions. Once the employee is hired, a number of control methods promote employee efficiency, see that he or she is paid the proper wage, and hold payroll costs to a minimum.

Payroll controls

Procedures are adopted to insure that employees are paid for the proper number of hours. Time clocks record the hours the employee works. Hiring an employee, changing wage rates, paying overtime, and terminating employment are all recorded on a system of forms requiring authorized signatures. Overall, the level of employment is controlled by preparing work schedules to budget the work force requirements for the period immediately ahead, taking into consideration the anticipated occupancy rate and other events. One of the major objectives of a work schedule is to allow each employee to obtain maximum regular time while limiting the necessity for overtime, since overtime pay is more costly than regular time pay.

Payroll Accounting Requirements

Calculating each employee's pay and developing the accounting records and related government reports are recurring work of the accounting department. For control purposes, these duties should be separate from hiring, timekeeping, and payroll distribution.

Employee master file

In order to prepare the payroll and related reports, the accounting department requires a master information file on each employee and the employee's work record for each pay period. The master file should contain as a minimum the following information:

Exhibit 1

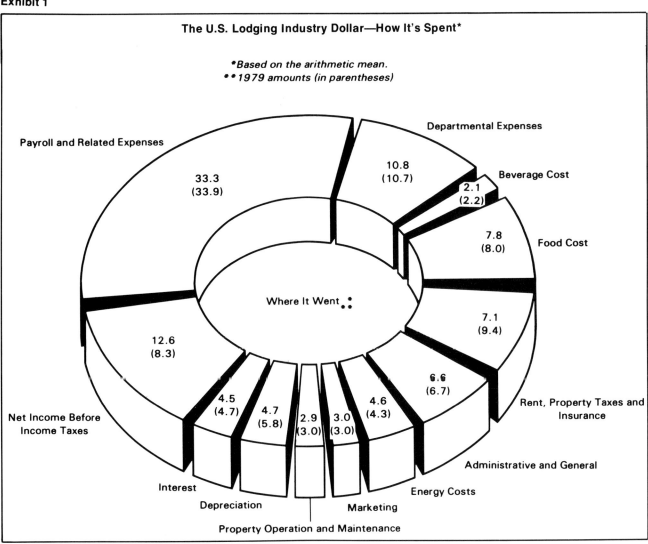

The U.S. Lodging Industry Dollar—How It's Spent*

Based on the arithmetic mean.
** *1979 amounts (in parentheses)*

Departmental Expenses
10.8 (10.7)

Beverage Cost
2.1 (2.2)

Payroll and Related Expenses
33.3 (33.9)

Food Cost
7.8 (8.0)

Where It Went **

Rent, Property Taxes and Insurance
7.1 (9.4)

Net Income Before Income Taxes
12.6 (8.3)

6.6 (6.7)

Administrative and General

4.5 (4.7)

4.7 (5.8)

2.9 (3.0)

3.0 (3.0)

4.6 (4.3)

Energy Costs

Interest

Depreciation

Property Operation and Maintenance

Marketing

1. Name
2. Address
3. Social Security Number
4. W4 (Withholding Allowance Certificate)
5. Wage rate
6. Deduction information

The employee's work record provides the number of hours worked during the pay period (for hourly wage personnel) and includes data on paid absences, vacations, and other exceptions.

Employee work record

With the master file and work record information on hand, the accounting department can calculate the employee's pay, make the appropriate accounting entries, and collect the information needed for government and other reports. After the employee's pay is calculated

*U.S. Lodging Industry 1981, Laventhol & Horwath, Certified Public Accountants, Philadelphia, PA, 1981, p. 29.

Payroll journal

(in the manner to be discussed here), a check or cash envelope and an earnings statement are prepared. This statement lists the gross wages and details deductions and amounts withheld to arrive at the net pay. The accounting entry for payroll may be made in either the cash disbursements and accounts payable journal, a special payroll journal, or the general journal. Of the three, a payroll journal is most common. Subsequently, of course, the journal information is entered in the general ledger. Also for each employee a detailed record called an individual earnings record must be kept by calendar year. This indicates the gross wages earned and the amounts withheld and deducted. Furthermore, the individual earnings record should be designed with the government reporting requirements in mind.

Government reporting requirements

Governmental reporting requirements are substantial. The amounts withheld for federal, state, and city income taxes must be forwarded to the proper agency and periodically reported. Similar requirements must be followed for the Federal Insurance Contribution Act tax and unemployment taxes. One further payroll accounting requirement is the preparation of reports for internal purposes. Management needs payroll cost information by department or function.

Payroll expenses in income statement

In accordance with the Uniform System of Accounts for Small Hotels and Motels (USASH), payroll and related expenses are shown separately from other department expenses in the income statement, whether the department is a profit center or a cost center. Exhibit 11 in Chapter 6 shows the income statement prescribed by the USASH. The accounting department's inputs and outputs in the payroll preparation process are shown in Exhibit 2.

Exhibit 2   Payroll Accounting Requirements

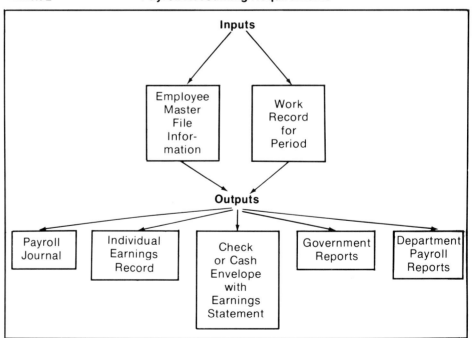

Calculation of the Payroll Amounts

The individual employee's net pay is determined by the hours worked, the straight-time and overtime wage rates, and the amounts to be withheld and deducted.

A hotel or motel normally uses several time periods in calculating wages depending upon job classification. Many hourly employees are paid weekly or bi-weekly. Management personnel are usually paid a straight salary semi-monthly or once a month. The hourly employees record hours worked by a time clock or a sign-in sheet. Exhibit 3 is an example of a time clock card. The time clock records on the card the times at which the employee checks in or out of the work area. The number of hours employees work during the pay period must be calculated from the time card information. Department heads are asked to review and approve time cards before they are used to calculate the number of hours worked. Frequently department heads keep an independent record of their own to verify the time card information.

Salaried employees

Hourly employees time card

Gross wages for hourly personnel are determined by multiplying the number of hours worked by regular and overtime rates. The initial wage rate or salary is established when the employee is hired. Any change in rate must be made on a change of rate form and properly authorized by the responsible individual. When an hourly employee works more than the standard number of hours in any week, he or she is paid an overtime rate. Unauthorized overtime can be controlled by requiring department heads to fill out an overtime authorization. This form accompanies the time cards when they are submitted to the accounting department at the end of the pay period. Examples of the change in rate form and the overtime form are shown in Exhibit 4.

Overtime control

Exhibit 3

Exhibit 4

Time Clock Card

PAY PERIOD ENDING .... 19 ___						

No.

NAME _____

REG. TIME HRS. _____ RATE _____ AMT. _____

OVERTIME HRS. _____ " _____ " _____

W.T. _____ CITY T. _____ TOTAL EARNINGS _____

F.I.C.A. _____ BONDS _____

INS. _____ OTHER _____

HOSP. _____ TOTAL DEDUCTIONS _____

STATE T. _____ AMOUNT DUE _____

	MORNING IN	NOON OUT	NOON IN	NIGHT OUT	EXTRA IN	EXTRA OUT
16						
1-17						
2-18						
3-19						
4-20						
5-21						
6-22						
7-23						
8-24						
9-25						
10-26						
11-27						
12-28						
13-29						
14-30						
15-31						

Balance due shown above is correct and receipt is acknowledged

_____
Signature

Change in Rate of Pay and Overtime Forms

AUTHORIZATION FOR
CHANGE IN RATE OF PAY

Employee _____

Position _____

Present Rate of Pay _____

New Rate of Pay _____

Effective Date _____

Approval _____   _____
            Dept. Head   Innkeeper

Date _____ 19 ___

EXTRA TIME AUTHORIZATION

DEPARTMENT

Bar	☐	Food Service	☐	Employee _____
Kitchen	☐	Housekeeping	☐	Extra Time Hours _____
Front Office	☐	R & M	☐	Requested by _____
				Approved by _____
_____				Reason _____
Other ☐				_____

Subtractions from wages

Deductions and withholding amounts are ordinarily subtracted to arrive at the net pay. Withholding amounts are for income and social security taxes. Deductions are usually voluntary and depend on the types of benefits and plans available from the employer. The following list of the kinds of subtractions made from the wages of employees in the hotel and motel industry is fairly complete.

Taxes

Federal, state, and city withholding amounts for income taxes
Federal Insurance Contribution Act tax (Social Security tax)
State unemployment compensation tax (selected states)

Other

Savings bonds
Medical insurance
Life insurance
Retirement contribution
Charitable contribution
Capital stock purchase plan
Savings plan, credit union
Charge for meals
Payroll advance
Garnishment of wages
Union dues

Calculating federal withholding

Usually federal income tax is the largest amount withheld from an employee's wages. The amount withheld depends on a number of factors, including marital status, number of personal exemptions claimed, wage level, length of the pay period, low income allowance, and percentage standard deduction. The amount withheld is normally sufficient to cover an employee's tax liability on his wages if he claims the standard deduction. Employees with large itemized income tax deductions can arrange to have smaller amounts withheld. Exemption information is obtained from the Employee's Withholding Allowance Certificate, Form W4, shown in Exhibit 5. There are two methods of determining withholding taxes. The first method is through tables supplied by the Internal Revenue Service. Separate tables are available for different pay periods and marital statuses. In the other method, the amount of the wage subject to a percentage rate is determined by use of tables. Both methods result in approximately the same withholding amounts. State and city income taxes have similar withholding requirements, and tables are generally available to determine the amount to be withheld.

FICA deduction

The Federal Insurance Contribution Act (FICA) tax (better known as the Social Security tax) is based on a fixed percentage of each employee's wages up to a specified level of earnings. For example, in 1982 earnings up to the $29,700 level were subject to a 6.70% rate. Under legislation existing in 1982, the level of wages covered from 1982 on will automatically be tied to the cost of living index. The percentage rates will increase as follows.

1982 to 1984	6.70%
1985	7.05
1986 to 1989	7.15
1990 and after	7.65

Exhibit 5

Form **W-4** (Rev. January 1982)	Department of the Treasury—Internal Revenue Service **Employee's Withholding Allowance Certificate**	OMB No. 1545-0010 Expires 4-30-83
1 Type or print your full name		2 Your social security number

Home address (number and street or rural route)

City or town, State, and ZIP code

3 Marital Status
- ☐ Single ☐ Married
- ☐ Married, but withhold at higher Single rate

Note: If married, but legally separated, or spouse is a nonresident alien, check the Single box.

4 Total number of allowances you are claiming (from line F of the worksheet on page 2) . . . .

5 Additional amount, if any, you want deducted from each pay . . . . $

6 I claim exemption from withholding because (see instructions and check boxes below that apply):
a ☐ Last year I did not owe any Federal income tax and had a right to a full refund of **ALL** income tax withheld, **AND**
b ☐ This year I do not expect to owe any Federal income tax and expect to have a right to a full refund of **ALL** income tax withheld. If both a and b apply, enter "EXEMPT" here . . . . ▶
c If you entered "EXEMPT" on line 6b, are you a full-time student? . . . . ☐ Yes ☐ No

Under the penalties of perjury, I certify that I am entitled to the number of withholding allowances claimed on this certificate, or if claiming exemption from withholding, that I am entitled to claim the exempt status.

Employee's signature ▶   Date ▶   , 19

7 Employer's name and address (including ZIP code) (FOR EMPLOYER'S USE ONLY)   8 Office code   9 Employer identification number

Because of the earnings level cutoff of the FICA tax, accounting staff must be careful that the deduction stops when earnings exceed the amount taxable.

Tip income

Employees with tip income of $20 or more a month must report such income to their employer by the 10th day of the month after the tips are received, since tip income is subject to withholding for both federal income tax and FICA tax. Employers may use Form 4070, shown in Exhibit 6, to report tips. Alternatively, a simple written statement will suffice. Tip income is included with the employee's wages in determining the amounts of these taxes and is reflected in the amount withheld from wages paid. Some hotels and motels require a few em-

Exhibit 6

Form **4070** (Rev. March 1975) Department of the Treasury Internal Revenue Service	**Employee's Report of Tips to Employer**	**Social Security Number**
Employee's name and address		Tips received directly from customers . $
Employer's name and address		Tips received on charge receipts . . $
Month or shorter period in which tips were received		
from , 19 , to , 19		Total tips . $
Signature		Date

Meals and lodging

ployees to live on the premises. In other cases, employees are furnished meals because of the nature of their work. When this is done at the convenience of the employer, the value of the meals or lodging is not considered wages subject to income tax, FICA tax, or other payroll taxes.

Deductions from wages other than for taxes are generally fixed amounts determined from the information in the master file for each employee. All the amounts withheld and deducted represent amounts due to others by the hotel and motel and are recorded as liabilities in the accounting records.

Payroll Calculation Methods

Determining an employee's wages and deductions requires several calculations and references to tables and files. After the payroll is calculated, the accounting records and government reports must be prepared. The time available to perform these functions is always limited. Various kinds of equipment and methods can be used to help meet payroll requirements.

Manual payroll — less than fifty employees

With less than fifty employees, the payroll and accounting and government reports can be prepared by hand. The only equipment required is an adding machine or calculator. The second level of equipment is a writing board or pegboard, so that several payroll records can be written at the same time. There is a great deal of duplication of information in the payroll journal, the employee's earnings record, and his earnings statement. The writing board positions these records one on top of the other where the information is duplicated, so by using carbon paper, the data is written only once. This method is used when the number of employees ranges from twenty-five to two hundred. All of the calculations must be made on an adding machine or a calculator.

Writing board — twenty-five to two hundred employees

Over two hundred — machines required

When the work force is over 200 persons, the computational and record-keeping tasks are of such magnitude that the use of mechanical equipment becomes practical. Payroll or bookkeeping machines are primarily of value in preparing the payroll record, although there are payroll machines that can make calculations.

Computer payroll

The electronic computer, with its ability to make computations and store and accumulate data, is a very good device for computing the payroll amounts, preparing the checks, and printing out all payroll reports. When a hotel or motel has a computer installation, payroll is one possible application. The random access storage file stores the master information file on each employee. Each employee's time may be entered in the employee's file as frequently as every day if management wants daily payroll cost information. The output of the computerized payroll system, besides informational reports, includes the payroll journal, the paycheck and earnings statement, and government reports.

Outside computer payroll

Most hotels and motels can use a computerized payroll system because service bureaus and banks offer the use of their computers for payroll preparation. The hotel's accounting department prepares the data on employees hours and information to update the master file. The service bureau or bank takes this information and does the rest of the payroll work. Because the computer time required to prepare the payroll is very short, and because a variety of businesses can use the same computer payroll program, a service bureau or bank can offer this service at a competitive cost.

The Accounting Records for Payroll

The accounting elements of a payroll transaction include payroll expense, cash disbursements, and the liability for amounts withheld and deductions made. But the accounting records extend beyond journalizing and posting the payroll transaction to general ledger accounts. Individual employee data needed for the earnings statement and government reports must be recorded. Several alternatives are available for journalizing these transactions.

When payment is made by check, it is customary to have an accounting record for each disbursement. This can be accomplished by the use of a payroll journal, shown in Exhibit 7. It provides a means of recording each check and accumulating in their respective columns payroll expense, liabilities for amounts deducted, and net disbursement (cash account credit). Entries for all employees in each department are made together in the payroll journal so that departmental payroll costs can be calculated easily. At the end of the accounting period, the payroll journal columns are totaled and posted to the general ledger.

Payroll journal

Exhibit 7   **Payroll Journal**

An alternative to a payroll journal is a payroll summary report, containing the same information as the payroll journal. At the end of the accounting period, the payroll summary report is totaled, and a general journal entry covering the payroll for the period is prepared. With only a few employees, a third alternative is to record payroll transactions in the cash disbursements and accounts payable journal.

Payroll summary report

An individual employee's earnings record is kept in order to provide the information necessary for government reports. The earnings record should be designed to accumulate information in the same form as needed in the reports. For federal government reporting, the employee's earnings record should provide the following:

Federal government reporting

Federal Insurance Contribution Act
The year-to-date accumulated earnings including tips and the value of meals and lodging provided (in order to determine when the taxable earnings level has been reached)
Annually the amount of FICA tax withheld
Federal Income Tax
Annually the amount of federal income tax withheld
Federal Unemployment Tax Act (FUTA)
The year-to-date accumulated earnings (to determine when the taxable earnings level has been reached)

State and city reporting

State and city reporting requirements are in addition to the federal requirement. Generally they are limited to the amounts withheld for state and city income taxes. Exhibit 8 shows the column headings for an employee's earnings record.

Exhibit 8   **Employee's Earnings Record**

NAME: ADDRESS: SOCIAL SECURITY NUMBER:	**Employee's Earnings Record**												
Pay Period Ending	EARNINGS				Wages for WH	Meals & Lodging	Wages for F.I.C.A.	DEDUCTIONS					NET PAY
	Regular	Overtime	Gross	Tips				F.I.C.A.	Fed. Income WH	St. Income WH	Ret. Cont.	Health Ins.	

Payroll adjusting entry

Reversing entry

Since the pay period is usually one or two weeks in length, the end would not normally fall on the last day of the accounting period. In order to recognize the total payroll expense for this period, an adjusting entry must be made. The payroll costs from the end of the last pay period to the end of the accounting period have to be determined. These costs can be built up from the available information. Or, if the first payroll of the next period is recorded before the adjusting entry has to be made, the payroll expense can be apportioned between the two accounting periods on the basis of the number of pay period days that fall in each. The adjusting entry is made in the general journal by a debit to the various departmental salaries and wages and a credit to accrued expense. At the beginning of the next accounting period, this entry is reversed. (An entry to reverse an adjusting entry is referred to as a reversing entry.) An example will illustrate this process. Assume the adjusting entry was as follows:

	Labor - Rooms Dept.		400	
	Labor - Food Dept.		300	
	Labor - Administration		100	
	Wages Payable			800

The reversing entry, recorded in the general journal the first day of the following accounting period, would be as follows:

	Wages Payable		800	
	Labor - Rooms Dept.			400
	Labor - Food Dept.			300
	Labor - Administration			100

This reversing entry offsets the labor expense for the first pay period in the present accounting period against the labor expense of the previous period, paid during the present period.

Government Reporting Requirements

Reporting for state and city governments is primarily for income tax withholding and for state unemployment compensation tax. It would be impossible to cover all the different state and local reporting requirements in this book. Typically, state and city income taxes are assessed as a percent of income, and tables are available to determine the amount to be withheld. State unemployment compensation taxes are related to the FUTA and are another payroll cost.

The federal reporting requirements apply to all employers and require frequent reporting throughout the calendar year. Payroll withholding amounts for federal income and FICA taxes must be deposited with a Federal Reserve Bank or a designated commercial bank at various time intervals. The frequency of these intervals depends upon the amount of the employer's liability. In addition to the employee FICA assessment, the hotel or motel is assessed an amount equal to the employee's FICA tax (excluding FICA tax on tips), and the employer's portion must be included with the deposit. The schedule of deposit requirements is shown in Exhibit 9. For each calendar quarter, Form 941 (Exhibit 10) must be filed.

Exhibit 9   Deposit Requirements for Federal Income and FICA Taxes

TAX LIABILITY	DEPOSIT REQUIREMENT
Under $300 per quarter	Paid with quarterly return
Under $500 per month But more than $300 per quarter	If the accumulated liability exceeds $500 by the end of the second month of the quarter, a deposit must be made by the 15th of the third month and the balance paid with the return.
Over $500 per month but under $3,000	For the first two months of the quarter the deposit must be made by the 15th of the following month. The third month deposit must be made by the last day of the following month.
Over $3,000 per month	If the cumulative liability exceeds $3,000 by the 3rd, 7th, 11th, 15th, 19th, 22nd, 25th or last day of the month, a deposit must be made within 3 banking days.

This form reports the following information:

1. Total wages, tips subject to withholding, and other compensations

2. Total FICA wages paid

3. Total taxable tips

4. Total income tax withheld

5. Total FICA tax withheld

6. A record of the federal tax deposits

With the Form 941 for the fourth quarter, a Form W2 must be filed for each person employed during the year. As many as four copies of

218 *Hospitality Accounting*

Exhibit 10

Form **941**
(Rev. January 1982)
Department of the Treasury
Internal Revenue Service

Employer's Quarterly Federal Tax Return

▶ For Paperwork Reduction Act Notice, see page 2.

OMB No. 1545–0029
Expires 10–31–82

T	
FF	
FD	
FP	
I	
T	

Your name, address, employer identification number, and calendar quarter of return. (If not correct, please change.)

Name
Trade
Address

If address is different from prior return, check here ▶

Record of Federal Tax Liability and Deposits

If you are a first-time 3-banking-day depositor (see Specific Instructions on page 4) check here . . . . ▶ ☐

If you are not liable for returns in the future, write "FINAL" . . . . . ▶
Date final wages paid . . ▶

	a. Date wages paid	b. Tax liability	c. Date of deposit	d. Amount deposited
	Day	Overpayment from previous quarter . . ▶		
First month of quarter	1st–3rd A			
	4th–7th B			
	8th–11th C			
	12th–15th D			
	16th–19th E			
	20th–22nd F			
	23rd–25th G			
	26th–last H			
I	Total . . ▶			
Second month of quarter	1st–3rd I			
	4th–7th J			
	8th–11th K			
	12th–15th L			
	16th–19th M			
	20th–22nd N			
	23rd–25th O			
	26th–last P			
II	Total . . ▶			
Third month of quarter	1st–3rd Q			
	4th–7th R			
	8th–11th S			
	12th–15th T			
	16th–19th U			
	20th–22nd V			
	23rd–25th W			
	26th–last X			
III	Total . . ▶			
IV	Total for quarter (add lines I, II, and III) . .		Column b total must equal line 13	
V	Final deposit made for quarter. (Enter 0 if included in line IV.)			

1 Number of employees (except household) employed in the pay period that includes March 12th (complete first quarter only) . . ▶

2 Total wages and tips subject to withholding, plus other compensation

3 Total income tax withheld from wages, tips, annuities, sick pay, gambling, etc .

4 Adjustment of withheld income tax for preceding quarters of calendar year . . .

5 Adjusted total of income tax withheld . . . . . .

6 Taxable FICA wages paid:
$
times 13.4% equals tax .

7 a Taxable tips reported:
$
times 6.7% equals tax .
b Tips deemed to be wages (see instructions):
$
times 6.7% equals tax .

8 Total FICA taxes (add lines 6, 7a, and 7b) . . . . .

9 Adjustment of FICA taxes (see instructions) . . . .

10 Adjusted total of FICA taxes .

11 Total taxes (add lines 5 and 10) . . . .

12 Advance earned income credit (EIC) payments, if any . .

13 Net taxes (subtract line 12 from line 11) . . . . .

14 Total deposits for quarter. Add lines IV and V, column d, and enter here. . . . . ▶

15 Undeposited taxes due (subtract line 14 from line 13). Enter here and pay to Internal Revenue Service . ▶
16 If line 14 is more than line 13, enter overpayment here ▶ $ and check if to be: ☐ Applied to next return, or ☐ Refunded.

Under penalties of perjury, I declare that I have examined this return, including accompanying schedules and statements, and to the best of my knowledge and belief it is true, correct, and complete.

Signature ▶   Title ▶   Date ▶

Please file this form with your Internal Revenue Service Center (see instructions on "Where to File").   Form **941** (Rev. 1–82)

Form W2 go to the employee to be included with his income tax returns. Form W2 contains the following payroll information:

1. Federal income tax withheld

2. Amount of wages, tips, and other compensations earned

3. FICA employee tax withheld

4. Total FICA wages

5. Uncollected FICA employee tax on tips

6. State and local income tax information

Form W3 also is filed annually with the W2 forms for each employee and functions as a transmittal form for these income and tax statements.

The FUTA taxes the employer to provide funds for unemployment compensation payments. Like the FICA tax, FUTA is assessed on wages paid up to a specified level at a fixed percentage. In 1982, the first $6,000 in wages were covered, and the rate was 3.4%. States also impose unemployment taxes. The federal government gives the employer partial credit for payments to the states. Payments for FUTA are made quarterly, and Form 940, containing the calculation of the federal tax, is filed annually by January 31 of the following year. The same record used to accumulate calendar year wages for FICA tax can be used to determine the FUTA tax liability.

Unemployment compensation tax

The employer's payroll tax expense is debited to the payroll taxes and employee benefits account and credited to either cash in bank or taxes payable. When the adjusting entry is made to recognize a partial payroll at the end of the accounting period, the payroll tax expense should also be included in the adjustment.

Payroll Bank Account

Most hotels and motels that pay their payroll by check establish a separate bank account for payroll. After the paychecks are prepared and the total disbursement is known, funds are transferred from the regular bank account to the payroll account. The separate account for payroll offers better control, since only sufficient funds to cover the current payroll are deposited. Furthermore, a separate bank statement is obtained that can be reconciled item by item with the payroll expenditures recorded in the payroll journal. The use of distinctive checks also helps to prevent fraud.

Separate payroll account for control

Minimum Wage Legislation

In 1938, the federal government enacted minimum wage legislation. The minimum wage, which started at $.25 per hour in 1938, was $3.35 as of January 1, 1982. Many states have also passed minimum wage legislation.

The major provisions of the federal minimum wage law are:

1. Coverage: hotels and motels with annual sales of at least $362,000

2. Rate: $3.35 per hour

3. Tip credit: 40%

4. Overtime: overtime must be paid at a minimum of time and one-half for hours in excess of 40 hours per week

Tip credit provision

The tip credit provision presently allows an employer to take a credit of up to 40% of the minimum wage which is $1.34 ($3.35 x .4 = $1.34). This tip credit is allowed so long as the tipped employee receives tips at least equal to the tip credit.

To illustrate the applicability of the minimum wage law, assume that Joanne Schmidt, a server at the Blue Star Cafe, worked 45 hours during the week. She is a tipped employee and received $65 in tips for the week. The Blue Star Cafe has annual sales of approximately $400,000 and must pay minimum wages. Joanne's hourly wage rate is $2.01, the minimum wage of $3.35 minus the tip credit of $1.34. Her gross pay is calculated as follows:

Regular hours		40
Overtime hours	5	
× overtime factor	× 1.5	7.5
		47.5
Minimum wage rate		× 3.35
		159.13
Less: Tip credit (45 hours. @ 1.34)		60.30
Gross Payable		$98.83

Note that her tips of $65 exceeded the required tips so that her employer could take the maximum tip credit. Further, she was paid time and one-half for five overtime hours. FICA will be withheld from her pay on $98.83 plus the declared tips of $65. Her employer is required to pay FICA taxes only on $159.13. The difference of $4.70 is the excess of declared tips over the tip credit. The law requires FICA from the excess to be withheld only from employee's earnings and not matched by employers.

State minimum wage legislation

Many states have also passed minimum wage legislation. In some cases, the state law is more stringent than the federal law. For example, the maximum allowable tip credit for Michigan hotels and motels is 25%, and further, any Michigan hospitality firm serving liquor is subject to the state minimum wage legislation. However, for a more complete discussion of the minimum wage legislation the reader is encouraged to research the law for the state or states of interest.

Discussion Questions

1. What kinds of information must be included in the employee master file and the work records for the period?
2. What are the dangers when the same person has the responsibility for payroll accounting and also keeps the time records and distributes the payroll?
3. What information should appear on the employee's earning statement?
4. Why must the accounting system for payroll provide for detailed information by employee?
5. What are the equipment options for payroll and what are the circumstances that would result in their use?
6. What employee information must be maintained in order to determine the amount of (a) FICA tax, (b) Federal Income Tax, and (c) FUTA tax?
7. What alternative accounting records can be used for maintaining payroll?
8. Why must certain payroll records be maintained on a calendar year basis? What happens if the business enterprise has a different fiscal year?
9. What federal payroll taxes are a cost of doing business for the employer?
10. How should payroll costs be reported for internal use?

Problems

Problem 1

Jack Jones is an employee of the Red Cedar Inn working in the front office. From his employee master file, the following information is obtained:

    a) Wage rate, $6.75 an hour

    b) Married, claiming three personal exemptions

    c) Deduction for health insurance — $11.40 biweekly

The work record for the period ended April 21st shows that Jones worked 86 hours. An extra time authorization form showed approval for six hours. Employees of the Red Cedar Inn are paid bi-weekly and receive time and one-half for overtime. The FICA rate for the year is 6.65% on the first $29,700 in earnings. Jack Jones' year-to-date earnings are $5,620.

Required:

1. Calculate Jones' gross earnings, federal income tax withholding (table on facing page), FICA tax withholding, deduction for health insurance, and his net pay. There is no state income tax.

2. The unemployment compensation tax rate is .7% for the federal portion (FUTA) and 3% for the state's portion. The first $6,000 in earnings are covered. Calculate the federal and state unemployment tax expense and employer's FICA tax expense for Jack Jones for this payroll period.

3. Based on the problem above, fill in the amounts for the following general journal entry:

Salary and Wages	$_____	
Federal Retirement (FICA)	_____	
Federal Unemployment (FUTA)	_____	
State Unemployment	_____	
Cash in Bank		$_____
Accrued Liabilities		_____

MARRIED Persons—BIWEEKLY Payroll Period
(For Wages Paid After September 1981 and Before July 1982)

And the wages are—		And the number of withholding allowances claimed is—										
At least	But less than	0	1	2	3	4	5	6	7	8	9	10
		The amount of income tax to be withheld shall be—										
$700	$720	$112.30	$102.70	$93.10	$83.50	$75.70	$68.00	$60.30	$52.60	$45.60	$39.40	$33.30
720	740	117.30	107.70	98.10	88.50	79.70	72.00	64.30	56.60	48.90	42.60	36.50
740	760	122.30	112.70	103.10	93.50	83.80	76.00	68.30	60.60	52.90	45.80	39.70
760	780	127.30	117.70	108.10	98.50	88.80	80.00	72.30	64.60	56.90	49.20	42.90
780	800	132.30	122.70	113.10	103.50	93.80	84.20	76.30	68.60	60.90	53.20	46.10
800	820	137.30	127.70	118.10	108.50	98.80	89.20	80.30	72.60	64.90	57.20	49.50
820	840	142.30	132.70	123.10	113.50	103.80	94.20	84.60	76.60	68.90	61.20	53.50
840	860	147.30	137.70	128.10	118.50	108.80	99.20	89.60	80.60	72.90	65.20	57.50
860	880	152.30	142.70	133.10	123.50	113.80	104.20	94.60	85.00	76.90	69.20	61.50
880	900	157.30	147.70	138.10	128.50	118.80	109.20	99.60	90.00	80.90	73.20	65.50
900	920	163.30	152.70	143.10	133.50	123.80	114.20	104.60	95.00	85.40	77.20	69.50
920	940	169.50	157.70	148.10	138.50	128.80	119.20	109.60	100.00	90.40	81.20	73.50
940	960	175.70	163.70	153.10	143.50	133.80	124.20	114.60	105.00	95.40	85.80	77.50
960	980	181.90	169.90	158.10	148.50	138.80	129.20	119.60	110.00	100.40	90.80	81.50
980	1,000	188.10	176.10	164.20	153.50	143.80	134.20	124.60	115.00	105.40	95.80	86.20
1,000	1,020	194.30	182.30	170.40	158.50	148.80	139.20	129.60	120.00	110.40	100.80	91.20
1,020	1,040	200.50	188.50	176.60	164.70	153.80	144.20	134.60	125.00	115.40	105.80	96.20
1,040	1,060	206.70	194.70	182.80	170.90	159.00	149.20	139.60	130.00	120.40	110.80	101.20
1,060	1,080	212.90	200.90	189.00	177.10	165.20	154.20	144.60	135.00	125.40	115.80	106.20
1,080	1,100	219.10	207.10	195.20	183.30	171.40	159.40	149.60	140.00	130.40	120.80	111.20

Problem 2

For the annual wage amounts listed below, calculate the employee FICA withholding amount, federal unemployment tax (FUTA), and state unemployment tax. The FICA tax is based on a rate of 6.7% on the first $32,000 in income, and unemployment tax is based on the first $6,000 of earnings. The federal unemployment tax rate is .7%, and the state unemployment tax rate is 3%.

a) $35,000

b) $12,000

c) $ 5,000

Problem 3

Ms. Kristina Marie, server at the Monica Motel's restaurant, worked 44 hours for the week of June 1-7. The Monica Motel has annual sales of $750,000. During the week Kristina received $100 in tips. Her wage rate is minimum wage less the 40% tax credit allowed by the minimum wage law.

Required:

Part A.

1. Calculate her gross pay from the motel.
2. Calculate the amount of FICA to be withheld from her pay. (Assume the rate is 6.7%, and that she is below the maximum amount.)
3. Calculate the amount of FICA the Monica Motel will be required to contribute based on Kristina's gross pay and tips.

Part B. Assume Kristina's total tips are $50 for the week. Recalculate the three items in Part A.

Problem 4

Ms. Chris Rowreys is a waitress at the Good Food Cafe. She worked 40 hours for the week of May 11-17 and 46 hours for the week of May 18-24. During the first week she received $70 in tips, and the second week she received $100. Her wage rate is minimum wage less a 40% tip credit and she is paid once a week. Her year-to-date earnings are $5,880.

Required:

From the above information, calculate the following for each week's wages:

1. Chris Lowrey's gross pay
2. Amount of FICA to be withheld from her paycheck at a 6.7% rate (assume that she has not exceeded the limit).
3. Amount of FICA to be paid by the Good Food Cafe
4. FUTA and state unemployment tax. The federal and state unemployment rates are .7% and 3% respectively and are based on the first $6,000 of earnings.

Glossary

ACCELERATED DEPRECIATION—methods of depreciation that result in higher depreciation charges in the first year and gradually decline over the life of fixed assets.

ACCOUNT—record containing information regarding a particular type of business transaction.

ACCOUNTING—process of identifying, measuring, and communicating economic information (see accrual and cash basis)

ACCOUNTING CYCLE—sequence of principal accounting procedures of a fiscal period: analyzing transactions, journal entry, posting to ledger, trial balance, adjustments, preparation of posting to ledger, trial balance, adjustments, preparation of periodic financial statements, account closing, post-closing trial balance

ACCOUNTING EQUATION—the accounting equation (referred to also as the fundamental accounting equation) is assets = liabilities + proprietorship

ACCOUNTING PRINCIPLES—the basis for accounting methods and procedures. Various principles include cost, consistency, and matching.

ACCOUNTING SYSTEM—subsystem of the information system providing financial reporting for external purposes

ACCOUNTS PAYABLE—liabilities incurred for merchandise, equipment, or other goods and services connected with the operation of the property that have been purchased on account

ACCOUNTS RECEIVABLE—obligations owed to the organization from sales made on credit

ACCRUAL BASIS ACCOUNTING—system of reporting revenues and expenses in the period in which they are considered to have been earned or incurred, regardless of the actual time of collection or payment

ACCRUED EXPENSE ACCOUNT—account of expenses that have been incurred but have not yet been paid

ACCUMULATED DEPRECIATION—a contra-asset account used for accumulating depreciation charges for various fixed assets

ADJUSTING ENTRIES—entries required at the end of an accounting period to record internal transactions

AGING REPORT—report in which accounts receivable are listed by the length of time the account has been outstanding

ALLOWANCE JOURNAL—accounting record that serves to reduce or reverse a sale when an allowance is given

AMORTIZATION—the process of writing-off an intangible asset against revenue over its life

ASSET—resource available for use by the business, i.e., anything owned by the business that has monetary value

AUDITING—the process of verifying accounting records and financial reports prepared from accounting records

BAD DEBTS—an expense incurred due to failure to collect accounts receivable

BALANCE SHEET—statement of the financial position of the hotel or motel at a given date, giving the account balances for assets, liabilities, and ownership equity

BANK—fixed sum of money provided to an employee who handles cash

BANK STATEMENT—record of transactions and account balance, prepared by the bank, to be compared with cash balance as shown in accounting records

BEGINNING INVENTORY—goods available for sale on the first day of the accounting period

BILLING CLERK—person responsible for charging to guests all vouchers representing food, beverages, room service, and merchandise purchases

BOOKKEEPING—the recording, summarizing, and classifying parts of accounting

BOOK VALUE—the difference between the cost of a fixed asset and the related accumulated depreciation. This is also referred to as net book value.

BUSINESS TRANSACTION—an event or condition that must be recorded.

CAPITAL STOCK—shares of ownership of a corporation

CASH BASIS ACCOUNTING—reporting of revenues and expenses at the time they are collected or paid

CASH DISBURSEMENTS AND ACCOUNTS PAYABLE JOURNAL—accounting record of expense transactions and other cash disbursements

CASH RECEIPTS AND DISBURSEMENTS JOURNAL—accounting record of each element of a cash transaction; includes guest identification and room number

CASHIER—person responsible for handling all cash transactions made in the front office

CERTIFIED PUBLIC ACCOUNTANTS (CPA)—public accountants who have been licensed to engage in public practice

CHART OF ACCOUNTS—listing of general ledger accounts by type of account including account number and account title

CITY LEDGER—subsidiary ledger listing accounts receivable of guests who have checked out—also all other receivables

CLEARING ACCOUNT—account used to temporarily store information as part of an accounting procedure

CLOCK CARDS—cards used in a time clock to record time spent on the job by employees

CLOSING ENTRIES—journal entries prepared at the end of the period (normally yearly) to close the temporary proprietorship accounts into the permanent proprietorship accounts

COMMON STOCK—capital stock of a corporation that generally allows its holders to have voting rights

CONTRA-ASSET ACCOUNT—accumulated depreciation account that reduces the fixed asset to an amount called the net book value

CORPORATION—a form of business organization that provides a separate legal entity apart from its owners

COST CENTER—any segment of the company whose expenses can be accumulated into meaningful classifications of data to provide information for management

COST OF GOODS SOLD—expense incurred in procuring the goods (rather than the services) that are to be resold in the operation of business

CREDIT—decrease in an asset or increase in a liability or capital—entered on the right side of an account; such amounts are said to be credited to the account

CURRENT ASSETS—resources of cash and items that will be converted to cash or used in generating income within a year through normal business operations

CURRENT LIABILITIES—obligations that are due within a year

DEBIT—increase in an asset or decrease in a liability or capital—entered on the left side of an account; such amounts are said to be debited or charged to the account

DECLINING BALANCE DEPRECIATION METHOD—method of distributing depreciation expense based on a declining percentage rate, providing for a larger depreciation expense in the early years

DEDUCTIONS FROM INCOME—also referred to as undistributed operating income per the *Uniform System of Accounts for Small Hotels and Motels*. It consists of three general overhead expenses of administration and general, marketing, and property operation, maintenance and energy costs.

DEFERRED EXPENSE—postponement of the recognition of an expense already paid

DEPRECIATION—portion of the cost of a fixed asset recognized as an expense for each accounting period the asset will be used in generating revenues (Methods: see Sum-of-the-years'-digits, Declining balance, Straight line)

DISBURSEMENT VOUCHER—form used as a means of recording the liability and authorization for payment

DIVIDENDS—a distribution of earnings to owners of a corporation's stock

DOUBLE ENTRY SYSTEM—system of recording any business transaction equally to debits and credits

DOUBTFUL ACCOUNTS—accounts receivable that may not be collected

DRAWING ACCOUNT—an account in which withdrawals of cash by the owner of a business organized as a sole proprietorship are recorded

ELECTRONIC DATA PROCESSING—equipment in an information processing system that operates electronically

EMPLOYEE'S EARNINGS RECORD—a record for each employee to record gross pay, taxes withheld, deductions, and net pay

ENDING INVENTORY—goods available for sale on the last day of the accounting period.

EXPENSE—cost incurred in providing the goods and services offered

FEDERAL INCOME TAX—the income taxes calculated on the firm's taxable income according to the federal tax laws

FEDERAL INCOME TAX WITHHELD—taxes withheld from employees' gross pay that must be paid to the federal government

FINANCIAL ACCOUNTING STANDARDS BOARD—the private sector group that promulgates accounting standards

FINANCIAL EXPENSE—expense associated with owning or renting the property, interest expense, and income taxes

FINANCIAL POSITION—the position of a firm at the end of the accounting period as shown by the balance sheet

FINANCIAL STATEMENT—formal medium for communicating accounting information, e.g., balance sheet, income statement, statement of retained earnings

FIRST-IN, FIRST-OUT (FIFO) METHOD OF INVENTORY VALUATION—costs charged against revenue in the order in which they were incurred

FIXED ASSETS—long-lived assets of a firm that are tangible e.g., land, equipment, buildings

FOOTING—totaling of columns

FRONT OFFICE—point of contact between guests and representatives of management-location where accommodations are arranged and guests' accounts are maintained during their stay

GENERAL JOURNAL—record of all accounting transactions

GENERAL LEDGER—principal ledger containing all of the balance sheet and income statement accounts

GUEST FOLIO—form containing current guests' statements

GUEST LEDGER—subsidiary ledger listing accounts receivable of current guests

GUEST SERVICES PERSONNEL—employees who provide mail, key,message, and information services for guests

HEAT, LIGHT, AND POWER—in the past utility costs of a firm were referred to as heat, light, and power

HOUSE PROFIT—amount left after the common operating expenses have been deducted from revenue—used to cover the fixed capital expenses and provide a net profit

INCOME AND EXPENSE SUMMARY—a temporary account into which revenue and expense accounts are closed at the end of the accounting period.

INCOME STATEMENT—report on the profitability of operations, including revenues earned and expenses incurred in generating the revenues for the period of time covered by the statement

INFORMATION SYSTEM—all the activities involved in obtaining the information necessary to operate a hotel or motel smoothly and efficiently

INTEREST EXPENSE—the charge for borrowing money. It is calculated by multiplying the principal times the interest rate times the fraction or more of a year the money is borrowed.

INTERIM STATEMENT—statement prepared in the periods between annual reports

INVENTORY—food, beverages, and supplies (See Beginning inventory and Ending inventory)

INVENTORY VALUATION—(See Weighted average, First-in, first-out, Last-in, first-out)

INVOICE—statement containing the names and addresses of both the buyer and the seller, the date of the transaction, the terms, the methods of shipment, quantities, descriptions, and prices of the goods

JOURNAL—accounting record of business transactions (See Allowance journal, Cash disbursements and accounts payable journal, Cash receipts and disbursements journal, General journal, Payroll journal, Sales journal, and Special journal)

JOURNALIZE—to record a transaction in a journal

LAST-IN, FIRST-OUT (LIFO) METHOD OF INVENTORY VALUATION—most recent costs incurred charged against revenue

LEDGER—group of related accounts that comprise a complete unit (See General ledger, Subsidiary ledger, Guest ledger, and City ledger)

LIABILITIES—obligations of a business—largely indebtedness related to the expenses incurred in the process of generating income (See Current and Long-term liabilities)

LONG-LIVED OR LONG-TERM ASSETS (FIXED ASSETS)—investments or resources of the hotel or motel that will be used to generate income for periods longer than a year

LONG-TERM LIABILITIES—obligations that will not be due for a comparatively long time (usually more than a year)

MATCHING PRINCIPLE—the concept that requires recording expenses in the same period as the revenues to which they relate

MORTGAGE—security on a loan that gives the creditor a lien on property owned by a debtor

NET INCOME—the bottom line on an income statement when revenues exceed expenses

NET LOSS—the bottom line on an income statement when expenses exceed revenues

NET WORTH—the claims of the owners to assets of a firm. Also, assets less liabilities equal net worth.

NIGHT AUDITOR—person responsible for posting late charges or credits to guests' accounts; also for checking accounts to see whether or not the day's postings are accurate and in agreement with supporting records

NOTES PAYABLE—a written promise by a borrower to pay money to a lender on demand or at a definite time

OPERATING EXPENSE—cost incurred in providing the goods and services offered by hotels and motels

ORGANIZATIONAL COSTS—the costs to incorporate a business

OWNERSHIP EQUITY—financial interest of the owners of a business—assets minus liabilities

PAID-IN CAPITAL—the capital acquired from stockholders of the corporation

PARTNERSHIP—a form of business organization involving two or more owners that is not incorporated

PAYROLL JOURNAL—journal providing a means to record checks, total payroll expense, liabilities for amounts deducted, and the net disbursement

PAYROLL SUMMARY REPORT—form that can be used in place of a payroll journal to record payroll expense, liabilities for amounts deducted, and net wage and salary disbursements

PERPETUAL INVENTORY RECORD—record of inventory kept up-to-date by entering all additions to and subtractions from stock.

PHYSICAL INVENTORY—detailed listing of the merchandise on hand at a specific time

POST—transfer data entry in the journal to the appropriate account

PREPAID EXPENSES—expenditures made for expense items prior to the period the expense is incurred

PURCHASE ORDER—order for materials sent by the purchasing department

RECEIVING REPORT—report on items received, prepared at time of delivery

REQUISITION—written order to withdraw items from stock

RESERVATION CLERK—person responsible for making reservations

RETAINED EARNINGS—an account for recording undistributed earnings of a corporation

REVENUES—amounts charged to customers in exchange for goods and services

REVERSING ENTRY—entry that is the exact reverse of the adjusting entry to which it relates

ROOM CLERK—person concerned with the arrival and departure procedures

ROOM RACK—visual file—a rack containing slots numbered to correspond to the room numbers of a hotel or motel

SALES JOURNAL—journal used for posting all sales transactions

SALVAGE VALUE—estimated market value of an asset at the time it is to be retired from use

SOLE PROPRIETORSHIP—an unincorporated business organized by one person

SPECIAL JOURNAL—journal used to accelerate the recording of specific kinds of accounting transactions

STATEMENT OF CHANGES IN FINANCIAL POSITION—a basic financial statement that shows sources and uses of funds for an accounting period

STATEMENT OF RETAINED EARNINGS—periodic report of transactions affecting the accumulated earnings of the hotel or motel that have not been distributed to stockholders as dividends

STOCKHOLDERS' EQUITY—the difference between assets and liabilities of a corporation

STRAIGHT LINE DEPRECIATION METHOD—method of distributing depreciation expense evenly throughout the estimated life of the asset

SUBSIDIARY LEDGER—special ledger that provides more detailed information about an account; controlled by the general ledger—used when there are several accounts with a common characteristic

SUM-OF-THE-YEARS'-DIGITS DEPRECIATION METHOD—method of distributing depreciation expense, with a more rapid depreciation in early years, by estimating the number of years of useful life, adding the digits, and then dividing the sum by the number of years remaining to determine the depreciation rate for the current year

TELEPHONE INFORMATION CARD—record of information regarding incoming telephone calls

TRANSACTION ANALYSIS—process of analyzing a transaction into the appropriate accounts; entering debits and credits equally in the accounting record

TREASURY STOCK—capital stock of a corporation that the corporation has repurchased for future issuance

TRIAL BALANCE—listing and totaling of all the general ledger accounts on a worksheet

VOUCHER—document used for posting a transaction to a guest account

WEIGHTED AVERAGE METHOD OF INVENTORY VALUATION—total cost of a particular commodity available for sale divided by the total number of units of that commodity, resulting in the unit cost to be charged against revenue earned by sale of that commodity

WORKING CAPITAL—current assets minus current liabilities

WORKSHEET—working paper used as a preliminary to the preparation of financial statements

The Educational Institute Board of Trustees

Anthony G. Marshall, CHA, Dean
School of Hospitality Management
Florida International University
Tamiami Campus
Miami, Florida

Harold J. Serpe, CHA
President
Midway Hospitality Corporation
Brookfield, Wisconsin

Porter P. Parris, CHA
Hospitality Industry Consultant
Houston, Texas

Peter E. Van Kleek, CHA
Director—Hospitality
 and Development
Johnson & Wales College
Providence, Rhode Island

Anthony M. Rey, CHA
Senior Vice President,
 Community Relations
Resorts International, Inc.
Atlantic City, New Jersey

Robert V. Walker, CHA
Chairman of the Board
The Kahler Corporation
Rochester, Minnesota

Kenneth Scripsma
Coordinator, Hotel Management
 Program
Orange Coast College
Costa Mesa, California

Ferdinard Wieland, CHA
General Manager
Hotel du Pont
Wilmington, Delaware

Index